JUDICIAL POLICY MAKING
THE POLITICAL ROLE OF THE COURTS
Revised Edition

GLENDON SCHUBERT
University of Hawaii

with an introduction by
Martin M. Shapiro

SCOTT, FORESMAN AMERICAN GOVERNMENT SERIES
Joseph C. Palamountain, Jr., Editor

SCOTT, FORESMAN AND COMPANY
Glenview, Illinois Brighton, England

For

Kathy

Library of Congress Catalog Number: 73–82373
ISBN: 0–673–07914–7

Copyright © 1974, 1965 Scott, Foresman and Company,
Glenview, Illinois 60025.
Philippines Copyright 1974 Scott, Foresman and Company.
All Rights Reserved.
Printed in the United States of America.

Regional offices of Scott, Foresman and Company are
located in Dallas, Texas; Glenview, Illinois; Oakland,
New Jersey; Palo Alto, California; Tucker, Georgia;
and Brighton, England.

FOREWORD

The American system of government strikes a balance between unity and diversity. There is a unity to our system, but it is a unity which tolerates—indeed, requires for its vigor and viability—a broad diversity of institutions, processes, and participants. By organizing the analysis of the sprawling complexity of the American system into smaller, coherent, but interlocking units, the Scott, Foresman American Government Series attempts to reflect this pluralistic balance.

This approach, we believe, has several important advantages over the usual one-volume presentation of analytical and descriptive material. By giving the reader more manageable units, and by introducing him to the underlying and unifying strands of those units, it puts him in a better position to comprehend both the whole and its components. It should enable him to avoid the not-uncommon circumstance of viewing the American system as a morass of interminable and unconnected facts and descriptions.

This approach certainly permits us to tap the expertise and experience of distinguished scholars in the fields of their special competence. Each writes about his specialties, and none is forced to deal with subjects remote from his ken or heart for the sake of "completeness." The unity of the series rests on the interlocking of the various volumes and, in the general emphasis on policy and policy-making, on the method of analysis as opposed to simple description. It does not rest on a unity of approach. The authors vary in their values, their accents, and the questions they ask. To have attempted to impose unity in these matters would have been to water down the series, for the diversity of approach reflects the diversity of the system, its participants, and its commentators. But the final value of this series and its ultimate balance between unity and diversity rest, of course, in the use to which it is put by the reader.

Glendon Schubert's volume forcefully illustrates the desirability of asking experts to write about their fields of special competence for the beginning student. He imparts to the reader the heady joy of new discoveries and the power of new analytical tools in an area often regarded as thoroughly explored and well understood. Casting a cool but sensitive eye on institutions and processes often obscured by myth and presumptions, he paints a clear but fresh picture.

Joseph C. Palamountain, Jr., *Editor*

PREFACE TO THE REVISED EDITION

The first edition of this book was begun about ten years ago, when it was planned to become one of several separate volumes in a series focusing on the subject of American national government. It was so published in 1965, with only a summary treatment of state and metropolitan judiciaries, preempting ten out of some two-hundred-odd pages of that text. (I had not really been asked to deal with state/metropolitan judicial systems at all in the work; but I then felt that it was essential to say something in order to be able to discuss meaningfully certain aspects of the functioning of the federal court system.) One change in the present edition is that I have eliminated completely the sections that purport to discuss explicitly state and big city courts, and for two reasons.

The best (but an entirely coincidental) reason is that there is now readily available an excellent, brief, and relatively inexpensive book dealing with at least the state court systems.[1] That text can readily be used modularly with this revised edition of the present work, each complementing the other.

The second reason is that the space limitations for the first edition, reflecting the common format for the series, precluded more than a summary treatment of state/metropolitan courts; and even more restrictive limits were imposed upon contributors to a text that combined the previously separate books of the series.[2] The chapters that I contributed to *American National Government* were in effect a second edition of the present book; and for that purpose I had to eliminate the sections on state and local courts. I could have restored that material, brought up to date, in the present edition; but by then I felt that a summary treatment would not suffice under the changed contextual circumstances, because the time and labor necessary to present an adequate and cognate treatment of the other (and far larger and more complex) part of our federal (as distinguished from national) court system would have delayed the appearance of the present revision for at least yet

[1]Henry Robert Glick and Kenneth N. Vines, *State Court Systems* (Englewood Cliffs: Prentice-Hall, Inc., 1973).
[2]Louis W. Koenig, Glendon Schubert, Lloyd D. Musolf, Laurence I. Radway, John H. Fenton, Martin M. Shapiro, and Joseph C. Palamountain, *American National Government: Policy and Politics* (Glenview, Illinois: Scott, Foresman and Company, 1971). Part Four is "Judicial Policy-Making."

another year. So this was a case of half a loaf seeming, to me, to be better than none.

A second change relates to the final chapter. In the first edition this was a discussion of the major perspectives that predominate among political scientists as approaches to the teaching of the subject matter of this book. I have dropped that discussion in both the *de facto* second edition and the present revision, but not because I believe the topic to be any less timely or important. Here also there mushroomed a considerable literature, mostly[3] but by no means exclusively[4] polemical; and any instructor can readily direct his or her students to those aspects of the debate that he or she may think will be most enlightening. What seemed appropriate in 1965 would be stale to do in 1974. So I have substituted instead as Chapter Seven a greatly enlarged and annotated bibliographical guide to the most useful literature on the subjects discussed herein.

A third major change that has transpired during the past eight years is that there are now two other (and excellent) books that focus upon the national court system, and also from the theoretical perspective of systems analysis.[5] Notwithstanding the similarity in perspective, neither of the other two books organizes and discusses the material in a manner that ostensibly duplicates what I have attempted herein; and consequently either of them also can readily be used modularly to supplement the present work.

A fourth change that impresses me, as I look back to the mid-sixties, is the rapid development of both theoretical and methodological sophistication among both teachers of the judicial process and their students, during the past decade. The original edition of the present book was idiosyncratic and conspicuously so in presenting an explicit and consistent theoretical framework as the basis for describing and analyzing judicial systems. Other then-contemporaneous works in the field[6] were organized topically and institutionally, but true to the long-standing traditions of

[3]Kenneth Culp Davis, "Behavioral Science and Administrative Law," *Journal of Legal Education* 17 (1965), pp. 137–154; L. Johnson, "A Defense of Public Law," *Political Studies* 16 (1968), pp. 384–392.

[4]See my "Academic Ideology and the Study of Adjudication," *American Political Science Review* 61 (1967), pp. 106–129.

[5]Sheldon Goldman and Thomas P. Jahnige, *The Federal Courts as a Political System* (New York: Harper & Row, Publishers, 1971); and Richard J. Richardson and Kenneth N. Vines, *The Politics of Federal Courts: Lower Courts in the United States* (Boston: Little, Brown and Company, 1970).

[6]Henry Abraham, *The Judicial Process* (New York: Oxford University Press, Inc., 1962); Herbert Jacob, *Justice in America: Courts, Lawyers, and the Judicial Process* (Boston: Little, Brown and Company, 1965).

public law as a disciplinary orientation they eschewed theory in favor of empirical description. The trend since then has been strongly in the direction of attempts to build a theory of judicial politics, and generally on the foundations of systems analysis.[7]

A fifth change involves a notable concentration of the attention of many political scientists and sociologists of law upon selected aspects of the field of judicial process and behavior,[8] such as the areas now conventionally denoted as "criminal justice"[9] and "impact"[10] studies. Frequently such focuses are associated with a concern for modifying the structure and functions of, or for intervening in the decisional processes of, present judicial operations. The emergence during the past eight years of a specialized journal, *Law and Society Review,* has facilitated and encouraged the publication of a vastly greater body of data and information concerning theory and methodology as well as judicial engineering.

The kind reception that teachers throughout the country[11] have bestowed upon the original edition, even when it continued to speak of the Warren Court while they and their students were confronting the increasingly and impressively different policy outputs of the Burger Court,[12] has encouraged me as well as my publisher to believe that the field of judicial process and behavior has not yet become as mortal as seems to have been intimated by

[7]Jay Sigler, *An Introduction to the Legal System* (Homewood, Illinois: Dorsey Press, 1968); Sheldon Goldman, "Behavioral Approaches to Judicial Decision-Making: Toward a Theory of Judicial Voting Behavior," *Jurimetrics Journal* 11 (1971), pp. 142–164; Charles H. Sheldon, "Structuring a Model of the Judicial Process," *Georgetown Law Journal* 58 (1970), pp. 1153–1184; and Jay Sigler, "A Cybernetic Model of the Judicial System," *Temple Law Quarterly* 41 (1968), pp. 398–428.

[8]For a general discussion of literature in the field, see my "Judicial Process and Behavior, 1963–1971," pp. 73–280 in James A. Robinson, ed., *Political Science Annual: An International Review* Vol. 3 (Indianapolis: The Bobbs-Merrill Co., Inc., 1972).

[9]George Cole, ed., *Criminal Justice* (Los Angeles: Sage Publications, Inc., 1972).

[10]Stephen Wasby, *The Impact of the United States Supreme Court: Some Perspectives* (Homewood, Illinois: Dorsey Press, 1970).

[11]And even in foreign lands, as evidenced by the publication of a Japanese-language translation of the first edition of the present work: Fumio Saito, trans., *Saibansho no Yakuwari* (Kyoto: Horitsu Bunka Sha Ltd., 1973).

[12]See my *The Future of the Nixon Court* (Honolulu: University of Hawaii Foundation, 1972).

the reports of some nay-sayers.[13] Public law may be dying, at least as a subject of political science instruction, and perhaps happily so; but an interest in political analysis of law, courts, judges, lawyers, and persons caught up in social problems with legal implications—all of these evidently are very much alive and well and living in the heartland of academic America. The continuing acceptance of the first edition suggests something else of no little import: that good theory remains relevant long after facts may have become outdated and even misleading. If the present version can stand the test of time with similar resilience I shall be more than gratified.

Nobody writes a book without help, and in many respects rewriting is much more difficult to do than is original composition. (Certainly revision is more tedious, and it entails far less reward in the form of ego gratification.) There are surely many persons who (wittingly or otherwise) assisted me in bringing this task to a tolerable conclusion; and I could not name them all even were I more conscious of who they are. But three persons in particular stand out for their particular aid: Jolyn Brecknock, a social science reference librarian in Hamilton Graduate Library at the University of Hawaii-Manoa, who has been unflinching in her resolve to keep me aware of what I should know that the library has received; Patricia Bieber, a government documents librarian in Sinclair (undergraduate) Library at the University of Hawaii-Manoa, who fought the good fight in an attempt to pry loose what should be deemed to be public information from various judicial bureaucrats in Washington; and Mary Grayson, my secretary during most of this past academic year, who retyped much of the revised manuscript.

Neither the original edition nor the *de facto* second edition was graced with a dedication, due to their respective formats. So now I can indulge the pleasure of making a fresh start in this respect, and I do so by giving the book to my middle daughter: for two full decades of friendship and affection, I owe her more than words can ever say.

Glendon Schubert

---

[13]G. Theodore Mitau, "What Has Happened to the Study of State Public Law by Political Scientists? A Note on Achievements and Lacunae in the Study of State Constitutional Law Since 1950," *Journal of Public Law* 14 (1965), pp. 90–101; Robert G. Dixon, Jr., "Who is Listening? Political Science Research in Public Law," *PS* 4 (No. 1, 1971), pp. 19–26.

INTRODUCTION

Popular sovereignty, while one of the two basic principles of the Constitution, is in practice a complex phenomenon not lending itself to simplistic formulations and often frustrating those who have naive expectations of "pure" or direct democracy. Successful democracy seems to accompany and perhaps require substantial "legitimized elitism," and it is the judicial system of the United States that most amply supports this thesis.

Here, at least on the federal level, we confront a branch of government which at first sight seems remarkably insulated from the pressures and passions of political tumult and popular majorities. Indeed, at the pinnacle of the system, and again at first sight, we seem to perceive a small group of Platonic philosopher-kings whose function it is to explain, refine, and apply our fundamental constitutional philosophy. By their procedures, garb, and method of rendering decisions, they seem closer to the music of the heavenly spheres than to the people and their raucous marketplaces. Yet it is this seemingly remote and insulated few who, in a limited sense as the following chapters show, are the umpires of the entire system with its elements of popular sovereignty and responsiveness and its high degree of pluralistic participation. Again, it is this select elite who in recent years have ordered the full implementation of the fundamental democratic slogan of "one man— one vote."

To be sure, neither the Supreme Court nor lesser courts are as remote or as otherworldly as they may seem at first sight. Even the Supreme Court follows the election returns, albeit sometimes with great time lags. Yet even greater familiarity does not remove the apparent paradox that these elitist groups, with idiosyncratic procedures only dimly understood by the public and usually several stages removed from direct popular pressures, play an often central role in our governmental and even our political systems.

For readers to comprehend fully that role will require them to strike several important and fine balances. The emphasis in this book is on policy making. Consequently, the stress is on the similarities between the judicial and other governmental systems, and between the judges and other official makers of policy. Similarly, there is a stress on the interplay between the judicial system and the other governmental and political agencies. Yet this book singles out the judiciary for separate description and analysis. Why this separate treatment if the judicial system does not function in isolation and if its operations and actors so resemble those of other governmental institutions?

Part of the answer is that the similarities are more fundamental while the differences are largely of surface and of style. Furthermore, the reader approaches the courts with less prior understanding than, say, Congress or the presidency. Secondary education and our communications media present a much dimmer or even a positively misleading picture of the judicial process. This problem of prior understanding is yet further intensified by the fact that the system is operated almost exclusively by members of a "guild," and most guilds find it both flattering and remunerative to shield their operations from popular understanding, whether by esoteric language, ritualistic phrases, archaic procedures, or other devices.

Consequently, while readers may have opened this book with an accurate general understanding of the other branches of the government, their impressions of the judicial system are likely to be misleading or wildly atypical. Thus images may well involve nine black-robed justices descending from Olympus, in response to heaven knows what impetus, suddenly and arbitrarily to decree that schoolchildren must abstain from reciting the Lord's Prayer or board buses for integrated schools; Perry Mason, after much baffling scurrying around and unproductive courtroom maneuvers, quickly using cross-examination like a sabre to disclose the identity of a murderer just before the last commercial; and the media seizing on the latest big murder trial to highlight current problems and inequities facing the American system of justice.

For all of these reasons the judiciary requires separate treatment. Readers must command some familiarity with judicial procedure, forms, and language before they can truly grasp the fundamental similarities underlying the strikingly different surface manifestations. One can take some comfort in undertaking this not easy task from the fact that it is only in the last generation that the similarities were fully comprehended; prior generations only imperfectly, if at all, incorporated the study of the courts within the discipline of political science.

Some patience may be required. To understand the system

itself, how political it truly is, how it makes public policies, and how it interacts with other governmental agencies and political forces, the reader must learn new words or new meanings for old ones, must understand certain basic procedures, and must learn how statistics reveal a reality often quite different from both the ritual and fiction. One must not be intimidated by stumbling on a *certiorari*. Unlike perhaps all but lawyers or political scientists, one must learn that the familiar words "judicial" and "review," when united, have a very special and important meaning. And unlike most citizens, one must learn that most cases never come to court—and what this signifies.

Once having opened the curtains of legal mystique, however, one should find oneself on familiar ground in the political arena, watching the contests out of which emerge public policies. The discussion itself will point out many of the similarities, but the reader, too, should be aggressively hunting them out. Yet, while it is the reader who should be performing the integration that this book enables and the subject requires, a few points can be suggested.

Policy making by other public agencies arises out of struggle, out of competition, and out of compromise. Policy making by judges emerges from what is obviously a similar process. What is perhaps not as obvious is that policies emerging from both spheres are also significantly related to certain norms, values, or principles. This relation is stressed herein, but the reader may profitably, in the light of the judicial example, reflect again upon the relation elsewhere, asking the degree to which such norms really control decisions and the degree to which they are manipulated to legitimize decisions. It will also be necessary to explore, as do Supreme Court justices, the hierarchy of norms and values. To call upon a common example, how high in the hierarchy is the preference for either judicial restraint or activism?

There are other reasons for the separate treatment of the judicial makers of policy. One of them is that judges, lawyers, courts, and their procedures play a uniquely broad role in the American system. (Why this is so should be one of the questions for the reader to ask.) Yet another is that this separation, combined with a relatively small number of actors, permits a more penetrating scrutiny and finer focus than is possible with other branches.

There being only nine justices, most of their significant discussions being explicit and written, and the procedure by which the issues reach them being formal and explicit, it is easier to understand the way in which they reached a particular decision and their rationale than would be the case with most of the policy decisions of nonjudges. (To be sure, this apparent openness and formality can be misleading, the significant steps often occurring off the record and behind the scenes.)

This rich vein is mined to some depth in the pages which follow, and various approaches are employed to see which one best refines the ore. Much light is shed on just how much we can know about decision making.

This sharp scrutiny and fine focus are of course employed to permit the student to reach understandings about the judicial policy-making process. The relatively small number of policy makers and the relative exactness of their procedures enables the author of this book to apply tools of much sophistication and at great depth in this area of judicial policy making. Once again, however, the unity of the discipline must be stressed. The reader should ask how similar analyses could be applied to the other areas of policy formation, and should see this as an example of what can be done elsewhere, albeit often with greater difficulty and narrower assumptions.

While the reader is thus urged to seek out the similarities between the judicial makers of policy and the others who make it, despite the apparent differences of form and of language, yet it is also necessary to be sensitive to the substantive political differences. Are certain kinds of issues more appropriate for judicial handling than others? Do the differences of form and of language, which have been seemingly dismissed as ones of surface rather than of substance, in fact bias or warp the policy outputs? What causes certain groups to seek judicial rather than legislative response? How free are judges to seek out issues on which to enunciate policy, and to what extent can they speak only when spoken to?

More than this, while this book deals directly with many interrelations between the courts and other governmental agencies and political forces, its primary focus necessarily is on the judicial system itself. Therefore, the reader should constantly be reminded that the courts are but part of the total system. The pluralistic nature of our system is obviously amplified and further complicated by the inclusion of the judiciary; and the tactical and strategic options open to groups and agencies are of course extended by the existence of the judiciary.

Finally, and despite the stress on similarities, some of the distinctive and significant characteristics of the judicial system must not escape the reader. As violence became more used as a political tactic, and as concern grew about run-of-the-mill criminal violence, "law and order" has become a political issue. Violence and non-compliance with laws strike at the heart of the system, its assumptions, and those of the discipline. These issues of course relate not exclusively to the courts, but they have a vital relationship to the judiciary. Much of the public views the judiciary as partially responsible for the phenomenon. Are they right?

And while members of the Right view the judges as permissively coddling those resorting to violence, extremists from the other side decline to accept the courtroom rules of the game, and at least one distinguished spokesman from the middle of the road has expressed skepticism that black extremists can receive a fair trial.

Thus while the reader has now been advised on how to promote his understanding of the judicial system, his evaluation, as well as understanding, of that system are also required.

Martin M. Shapiro

TABLE OF CONTENTS

13847

TABLES AND FIGURES

CHAPTER ONE

The Judiciary
in the
American Polity

THE POLITICAL SYSTEM

PUBLIC POLICY

Judges share with legislators, chief executives, and heads of major administrative departments the political power and responsibility to make policy decisions that reflect certain priorities of values. Public policy reflects those values that are preferred, for the time being, by such decision makers. Although public decisions may be enforced by coercion, the coercive aspects are not their most distinctive feature. Rather, public systems of decision making are best distinguished from private systems by the relative heterogeneity of their constituencies and affected clienteles. The greater generality of governmental systems provides some justification for labeling as "public" decisions that usually are directly advantageous only to minorities of the relevant populace.

Governments have no monopoly of either authority or power. Authority is the consensually recognized right to make certain decisions; power is the ability to control the behavior of others through decisions. Authority and power frequently, but not necessarily, coincide; but even when they do, there is wide variation in the proportions of each that may be associated with particular decision-making roles or with specific decision makers, either public or private. Concerning some of these questions, such as the establishment of a national policy of racial integration in public schools, most courts in the United States have little authority *or* power. The federal Supreme Court has considerably more authority than power in this matter: almost a decade after its basic decision in *Brown* v. *Board of Education,* not a single black child attended white public schools in one of the school districts that had been a party to the *Brown* case. On the other hand, courts (like other decision-making systems) may exercise more power than authority; note the federal Supreme Court's abortive attempt in *Dred Scott* v. *Sanford* to resolve the national conflict over slavery. There are some kinds of decisions, such as that to impose capital punishment, which in this country governments have a monopoly of authority (but not of power) to make; there are many others, such as excommunication, which American governments have neither the authority nor the power to make.

Certain functions and facilities, such as taxation and armies, often are suggested as examples of characteristically governmental activities. But only one of the thousands of public governments in the United States maintains armed forces in the form of an army, navy, and air force; and if we turn to armed forces designated as police, capable of undertaking offensive action only against individuals and very small social groups, then many private "governments" (such as the Ford Motor Corporation) also maintain police forces. Public police differ from private police in the broader scope of their responsibility and authority. Most public governments collect taxes, but many private organizations also exact compulsory fees and assessments from their membership. In either case, citizens and members must either pay, suffer pains and penalties for nonpayment, or withdraw from affiliation with the community. Again, the difference is that voluntary expatriation usually involves almost total withdrawal from the normal relationships within a complex society, because it entails a shift in one's physical residence as well as in his psychological allegiance; while the impact upon one's life that results from the resignation of membership in a fraternity or professional society is much more selective and usually is perceived to be so. Many examples can be given, however, of activities that are sponsored jointly or concurrently by public and private governments; the differences among public universities and among private universities certainly are much greater than the differences between them.

When we study policy making by judges, we focus upon a type of activity that is by no means peculiarly governmental. Adjudication takes place in a wide variety of social groups, including the family. It is in governmental systems, however, that courts are most sharply differentiated in structure from other decision-making agencies. This high specialization of judicial structure and function both justifies and necessitates the analysis of judicial behavior as one focal point in the study of public policy making. Since judges play particularly critical roles in the formulation of United States governmental policy, the study of the judiciary is an essential and fundamental part of the study of American government.

SYSTEMS THEORY

This study of the judiciary is based upon an analytical framework known in sociology and political science as "systems theory" or "structural-functional analysis." This basis is chosen in preference to the legal, historical, and institutional categories that in the past have dominated inquiry into the policy-making processes of American government. A major advantage of this strategy is that it diverts attention both from a preoccupation with the substance of judicial policy and from a description of the legal structure of courts in isolation from the rest of the political system. Both of these subjects are relevant to an understanding of judicial policy making; but the use of systems theory can, it is hoped, expand the relevant field of inquiry to the processes and sources of judicial policy making as well as to its results. Thus this mode of analysis should facilitate a more general and more comprehensive examination of American judicial institutions and behavior than would be produced by a less inclusive and less consistent conceptual framework.

Systems analysis focuses upon political behavior and upon empirically observable action. Norms and institutions are relevant only to the extent that they affect the behavior of actors within a system under analysis. A "system" consists of the structure or pattern of interaction among the actors. "Interaction" consists of the ways in which two or more people affect each other's behavior; the participants are called "actors" because we are interested not primarily in their individual idiosyncrasies but rather in the extent to which they conform to their socially defined roles. A "role" is socially defined because it consists of the combined expectations, of both what he *ought* to do and what he is *likely* to do, of an individual actor and of those people with whom he interacts; in a reciprocal manner, the complementary expectations of the individual actor help to define the roles of those other persons with whom he interacts. In sociopsychological terms, an actor's role is his orientation toward political action. The limits that define the universe of data deemed relevant for the examination of a particular system are called "boundaries"; the boundaries, in other words, enclose the variables directly related to the making of decisions within the system. The demands and support that function as stimuli to which the actors within the system react are called "inputs," and the policy-making decisions of the actors are called "outputs." Outputs from one system may be inputs for other systems; when the outputs of a system affect the systems that are its sources of demands and support, the process is known as "feedback." In sum, "political institutions or persons performing political roles are viewed in terms of what it is that they do, why they do it, and how what they do is related to and affects what others do."[1]

One major qualification is in order, however, concerning our use of the systems model. The fundamental metaphor upon which systems theory is based is biological, and it thus reflects the impact of the work of Charles Darwin upon nineteenth-century scientific thinking.[2] It is one thing to hypothesize homeostasis—the tendency for a set of interacting systems to maintain equilibrium—in a living and healthy organism. It is quite another matter to assume that patterns of social organization and behavior, which we analogize to living organisms when we adopt the Darwinian metaphor and speak of social systems, necessarily will seek to maintain a natural balance and remain in some state of equilibrium.[3] Although some

[1]Gabriel A. Almond, "Comparative Political Systems," *Journal of Politics* 18 (1956), p. 393. Cf. Figure 8, p. 140 of this book; William C. Mitchell, *The American Polity: A Social and Cultural Interpretation* (New York: The Free Press of Glencoe, 1962); Talcott Parsons, "The Law and Social Control," and Harry C. Bredemeier, "Law as an Integrative Mechanism," in William M. Evan, ed., *Law and Sociology* (New York: The Free Press of Glencoe, 1962), pp. 56–90; David Easton, *A Framework for Political Analysis* (Englewood Cliffs, N.J.: Prentice-Hall, Inc., 1965); Don Martindale, ed., *Functionalism in the Social Sciences* (Philadelphia: American Academy of Political and Social Science, 1965).
[2]Martin Landau, *Political Theory and Political Science: Studies in the Methodology of Political Inquiry* (New York: The Macmillan Company, 1972), especially Chapters 3, 4, and 5, "On the Use of Metaphor in Political Analysis" (reprinted from *Social Research* 28 [1961], pp. 338–353), "On the Use of Functional Analysis in American Political Science" (reprinted from *Social Research* 35 [1968], pp. 48–75), and "Due Process of Inquiry" (reprinted from *American Behavioral Scientist* 9, No. 2 [October 1965], pp. 4–10).
[3]David Easton, "Limits of the Equilibrium Model in Social Research," *Chicago Behavioral Sciences Publications* 1 (1953), pp. 26–40.

form of homeostasis usually is explicitly assumed by social scientists who have adopted systems theory to guide their analyses, we make no such assumption here. We shall, however, seek to discover the kinds of influences that both shape and lead to changes in judicial systems, and the correlative kinds of influences that judicial systems bring to bear upon other systems, both public and private, with which they interact.

STRUCTURE OF THE AMERICAN POLITY

The American system of government is characterized by a great deal of pluralism and exceptional fragmentation of both authority and power. The Constitution of the United States recognizes no less than fifty-one different governmental subsystems: those of the fifty states remain largely independent of each other and, to a substantial but diminishing degree, independent of the national government as well. This large measure of constitutional independence has become increasingly sublimated in practice, however, by a vast network of policy interaction in such major fields as agriculture, highways, welfare, education, law enforcement, utilities regulation, and taxation. Each of the fifty-one governments accepts the constitutional principle of the "separation of powers": the Constitution of the United States explicitly provides for differentiated legislative, executive, and judicial organizational structures, and all of the state constitutions do likewise. Most of the states substitute what is in effect a plural executive for the unitary executive system authorized by the national Constitution. Most of the institutional patterns that link the national government with the states and the states with each other involve policy interaction among executive systems. Since the adoption in 1913 of the Seventeenth Amendment (which provided for direct election of United States senators by the people rather than by state legislatures), the communication channels linking national and state legislative systems have been minimal, as the direct communication channels among state legislative systems always have been. Judicial (like executive) interaction is relatively extensive between the national and state systems, while interaction among state judicial systems is relatively slight, thus resembling the relationships among state legislatures.

In a similar mode, we can discuss the patterns of policy making that obtain within each state. Both the constitutional and the operating relationships between a state government and its multitudinous units of local government are even more complex than the national-state and interstate relationships summarized above. It is generally true that, except among geographically contiguous units of local government, the horizontal patterns of interaction among either local legislative, executive, or judicial systems are not extensive. The same is true of interaction between the state and local legislative systems. But interaction between the state and local executive and judicial systems is even greater than that between national and state executive systems and between national and state judicial systems.

Legislative systems—national, state, and local—operate in terms of certain common assumptions and attributes. Individuals or small groups of legislators are elected for fixed terms from particular geographic areas defined in constitutions or in statutes, by executive commissions, or by judicial decision. The national legislative system, and that of all but one of the states, includes two independent "houses" of legislators with largely duplicating functions; but local legislative systems usually include only a single structure. Inputs to the system consist of what usually are described as "interests" and "pressures" from other governmental systems (such as executive, judicial, or municipal systems) and from constituents, lobbyists, and political parties (as well as the outputs of other governmental subsystems within the individual legislative districts). On the basis of the estimated support from the same sources for legislative action, the legislature transforms such demands into outputs such as substantive statutory norms, appropriations, taxes, committee and subcommittee investigations, resolutions, and the approval of executive and judicial appointments. Thus the outputs of the legislative system serve as inputs for executive and judicial systems, for nongovernmental systems of decision making (such as those of political parties, corporations, and labor unions), and for other legislative systems.

There is considerably more diversity in the structuring of national and state executive systems and still more in the structuring of local executive systems. The Constitution of the United States provides for a single executive system, whose most conspicuous decision maker is a President who is now selected, in effect, by a national constituency whose votes are tabulated on the basis of fifty-one electoral districts (consisting of the states plus the District of Columbia). From an operational point of view, however, the executive system of the national government is a vast congeries of largely autonomous subsystems with many overlapping functions. Each subsystem depends in fact upon very complex processes of group decision making, although legal authority to "make decisions" typically is vested in individual officials with such status designations as "secretary" (department head), "director" (bureau chief), or "commissioner" (board member). If we inquire concerning the source of outputs to which these various types of administrative subsystems are most responsive, we discover that the constitutional principle of "separation of powers" is a most misleading basis for understanding the primary articulations of administrative subsystems for policy-making purposes. *Departmental* subsystems do interact most closely with each other and with the executive subsystems (e.g., the Executive Office of the President) that function in the name of the President; but many bureau subsystems interact more intimately with their counterpart legislative subsystems (congressional subcommittees) than with the departmental systems of which they are—from a legal point of view—components; and, similarly, the source of policy guidance for many boards (particularly for several of the "regulatory commissions") is first legislative, second judicial, and least executive. However, this brief sketch of some of the most salient aspects of the public policy-making process in the United States makes it evident that judicial systems are structured and function in an environment that is extremely complex and dynamic and that is itself the product of a highly pluralistic political universe.

BOUNDARIES OF THE JUDICIAL SYSTEM

Interaction is extensive and pervasive between the judicial system and the legislative and executive systems, as well as between the judicial system and a vast array of private systems of policy making. The conventional conception of judicial action as consisting of a judge or small group of judges sitting at a bench and presiding over a trial in a courtroom portrays judicial behavior as essentially static, like a still-life portrait. Thereby it sacrifices a concern for what is most significant to a preoccupation with the manifest elements of a ritual which—though not unimportant—is only the most conspicuous scene of a drama with many other acts. As in Shakespearian tragedy, the soliloquies, which are easy to present, occur onstage; the great and decisive battles are fought offstage, and we learn of them only through an occasional clamor from the wings and through the formal announcements of heralds, replete with fanfare and flourishes. Likewise, most politically significant governmental action takes place outside the courtroom. It occurs in the establishment of courts and the selection of judges; in the interplay between judicial, legislative, and executive systems, and between national and state judicial systems; and in the effect of judicial decisions upon society and the economy, and vice versa. It is not possible to learn much about legislative policy making by observing the chamber of the United States Senate from the gallery or to understand presidential decision making by attending press conferences conducted by the President—or even the usual meetings of the cabinet, for that matter. Yet the predominant tendency, until recently, has been to study judges as though they performed their roles in splendid isolation not only from the rest of the political system but from each other as well.[4]

If we are to extend the relevant boundaries of the judicial system beyond the confines of the courtroom, then we must observe the interaction of constituent assemblies, chief executives, and legislatures, with political parties and other private groups, in actions that establish the legal bases of organization for courts. That establishment characteristically takes the form of reorganization of an ongoing judicial structure whose official incumbents invariably evince the most profound interest in such proceedings and claim to be the most expert witnesses available on the subject. The judges themselves, therefore, are either protagonists or major lobbyists in the consideration of any proposals to change their authority and power.[5]

Judges acquire office either by appointment (as in the national system) or by election (as in most of the state systems). To be appointed, a judicial candidate usually must be sponsored by party officials, bar organizations, and legislators in order to receive serious consideration by a chief executive; in subsequent legislative committee hearings on confirmation, private groups frequently lobby to support or to oppose nominations. Similarly, candidates for elective judicial office must be sponsored by political parties and private groups, and frequently by chief executives and legislators as well. Where there are "nonpartisan" systems of election, similar sponsorship usually is worked out covertly, behind the facade of "citizens' committees for good government."

Once selected, judges, like other public officials, have a continuing need for legislative support in the form of appropriations. Legislative-executive norms in the form of statutes provide a constantly shifting redefinition of the substantive content of the public policy framework that generally delimits the field within

[4]But see Jack W. Peltason, *Federal Courts in the Political Process* (New York: Random House, 1955), pp. 1–2; Glendon Schubert, *The Constitutional Polity* (Boston: Boston University Press, 1970); Herbert Jacob and Kenneth Vines, "The Role of the Judiciary in American State Politics," in *Judicial Decision-Making,* ed. Glendon Schubert (New York: The Free Press of Glencoe, 1963), pp. 245–256; and Kenneth N. Vines, "The Judicial Role in the American States: An Exploration," in *Frontiers of Judicial Research,* ed. Joel Grossman and Joseph Tanenhaus (New York: John Wiley & Sons, Inc., 1969), pp. 461–485.
[5]Joseph Alsop and Turner Catledge, *The 168 Days* (New York: Doubleday & Company, Inc., 1938).

which judicial policy making takes place. Criminal cases involve continuing interaction between executive and judicial systems at all levels of government; the more specialized the jurisdiction (such as that of tax courts or courts that handle juvenile delinquency), the more intricate and informal become the processes of boundary interchange between the executive and judicial systems. (An example of "boundary interchange" would be outputs of the executive system functioning as inputs for the judicial system, or vice versa; thus the arrest of a defendant is an executive system output, and it frequently becomes also an input for the judicial system.) Similar complexity of executive-judicial interaction is found also in many civil cases, in which "the government" appears as a direct party litigant, particularly in cases involving commercial, labor, or utilities regulation. Many administrative agencies appear in the dual roles of judge and prosecutor in such cases. Some agencies which exercise initial jurisdiction over such cases function in practice as a part of the judicial system as much as of the executive system. The staffing of nonjudicial positions in judicial systems typically involves direct brokerage with political parties. Civil service reform has had relatively little effect upon judicial patronage, even in those states that established court administrator's offices during and since the 1950s.

These are but selected examples from a broad range of interactions between judicial and other systems. They are, however, sufficient to support the proposition that judicial behavior is best studied in the context of the manifold relationships between judicial and other decision makers. Chapter Five discusses in considerably more detail the inputs and outputs of judicial systems.

THE POLITICAL ENVIRONMENT

CONSTITUTIONAL

The Constitution of the United States specifies that there shall be both a national government and an unstipulated number of state governments; the Constitution has been interpreted to mean that governmental authority shall be in part exercised exclusively by the national government, in part reserved to the state governments for whatever implementation may be authorized by their own individual constitutions, and in part shared by both the national government and the state governments. In addition, certain authority is denied to either the national or the state governments, primarily by means of guarantees of personal and property rights. The procedure for the implementation of such guarantees, which are usually called "civil rights and liberties," is not specified in the Constitution, but traditional expectation and practice has been that it is the function of judges—ultimately of the justices of the Supreme Court of the United States—to determine the meaning of such guarantees by their decisions in specific cases. This was apparently the original understanding of the political generation that adopted the Constitution, and the consistent trend in recent decades has been toward judicial assumption of greater responsibility for the making of policy regarding civil rights and liberties. Certainly the Supreme Court has defined this as its primary role for the past third of a century.

The federal "division of powers" between the national and state governments has in times past provided the basis for another major function of the judiciary, although in this instance primarily of the national (or, as they are usually called, "federal") courts and of the Supreme Court in particular. Because the national (federal) Constitution provides for no other means to resolve conflicts of authority between the national and the state governments, this role was assumed by the Supreme Court relatively early in the nineteenth century. Another result of the federal structure of American government has been the establishment of separate judicial systems in each state, in addition to the national judiciary. Such a result is by no means a necessary consequence of a federal constitutional structure. For example, in Canadian federalism there is one system of courts, all of whose judges (except at the local government level) are appointed by the central government. The United States Constitution explicitly recognizes only the Supreme Court; the establishment of "inferior" national (federal) courts depends upon legislation. Conceivably, Congress and the President might have decided in favor of having no inferior national courts, and the American judicial system might have consisted of one Supreme Court exercising appellate authority over the decisions of state judicial systems, which is the kind of judicial structure found today in Australia. But the decision to establish inferior national courts was made in the first session of the First Congress, and the historical evidence supports the conclusion that this establishment was a part of the initial constitutional consensus.[6]

The Constitution partitions the authority of the national government among three sets of decision makers: a Congress, a

---

[6]Charles Grove Haines, *The Role of the Supreme Court in American Government and Politics, 1789-1835* (Berkeley: University of California Press, 1944), pp. 119–121.

President, and "one Supreme Court, and in such inferior Courts as the Congress may from time to time ordain and establish." Although a system of decision making has developed around each of these nuclei, there is considerably more interaction and less autonomy among the legislative, executive, and judicial systems than appears to have obtained when our general system of national government was first established. The basic constitutional assumption about national policy making, in particular, appears to be a vast oversimplification of current practice. Policy making was a function assigned to the legislative system, while the executive and judicial systems were assigned complementary enforcement roles. Laws made by the Congress were to be "faithfully executed" under the supervision of the President, and disputes about the meaning and administration of the laws were to be resolved by the judiciary.

There were ambiguities—many of which were intentional—even in the constitutional model of the policy-making process, however, and there soon developed a much more complicated structuring of national policy making than that which one would have logically inferred from the abstract principle of separation of powers. The requirement of presidential assent to statutes has eventuated, for example, in a contemporary situation under which an exchange of roles already is well advanced in practice: the President presents his program, subject to congressional veto. On the other hand, the "faithful execution" of many laws now is supervised either by congressional subcommittees or by federal judges. It also soon developed that there was a major policy-making function inherent in the judiciary's role of interpreting the Constitution in relation to the guarantees of personal and property rights and to the federal division of powers. And it has now been well over a century and a half since the Supreme Court, in 1803, first staked out its claim of authority to lay down the constitutional policy—again by interpreting the Constitution—relating to the boundary interchanges between the judicial and the executive and legislative systems. In subsequent decisions, the Supreme Court claimed further authority to define the boundary interchanges between the executive and legislative systems—an issue of constitutional policy in which the judiciary was not directly involved. Judicial review of executive and legislative decision making, in terms of their consonance with constitutional norms (as interpreted by the courts), by no means exhausts the scope of judicial policy making, however. Of increasing importance during the present century has been the policy-making role of the national judiciary in the interpretation of national statutes, including such well-known examples as the antitrust and labor-management relations acts as well as a vast array of others, such as the internal revenue and criminal codes.[7]

The American two-party political system has exerted a major influence upon the judicial system since the days of the Federalists. The use of judicial posts as a source of political patronage began with the appointments by George Washington in the initial staffing of the Supreme Court and of the lower courts under the Judiciary Act of 1789. Particularly during the administration of John Adams, Federalist judges were notorious for the conversion of their courtrooms into forums for political harangues, as in their many charges to juries under the Sedition Act of 1798. Because of such partisan activities, one justice of the United States Supreme Court, Samuel Chase, was impeached when the Republicans gained control of the House of Representatives, although he was acquitted in the Senate, where the Federalists retained sufficient strength to block his removal.

The most celebrated case in American constitutional law, *Marbury v. Madison* (1803), grew out of Federalist attempts to pack the national judiciary through John Adams' appointment of "midnight judges"—so called because their commissions of appointment were rushed through in the waning hours of the outgoing administration. The justices of the Supreme Court, who were solidly Federalist, unanimously declared unconstitutional the Republican attempt to interfere with the Federalist appointments.

The size of the Supreme Court was manipulated no less than seven times in less than seven decades (1801–1869) invariably in order to retain or to gain majority control over the Court. Throughout our political history the parties have waged a continuing battle over the national judiciary,[8] as exemplified by the

---

[7]See, generally, Glendon Schubert, *Constitutional Politics: The Political Behavior of Supreme Court Justices and the Constitutional Policies That They Make* (New York: Holt, Rinehart & Winston, Inc., 1960), pp. 240–251. For several case studies of statutory interpretation, see Glendon Schubert, "Policy Without Law: An Extension of the Certiorari Game," *Stanford Law Review* 14 (1962), pp. 284–327; Martin Shapiro, *Law and Politics in the Supreme Court* (New York: The Free Press of Glencoe, 1964), Chapters 2–6; Martin Shapiro, *The Supreme Court and Administrative Agencies* (New York: The Free Press, 1968); and Arthur Selwyn Miller, *The Supreme Court and American Capitalism* (New York: The Free Press, 1968).

[8]Stuart S. Nagel, "Court-Curbing Periods in American History," *Vanderbilt Law Review* 18 (1965), pp. 925–944.

expansion in the number of federal district judges in 1962, after eight years of Republican staffing under Eisenhower, and again in 1970, after Nixon had come in and the shoe was on the other foot. There are two major reasons for the strong and persistent desire of parties to influence the judicial system: (1) the national judiciary has always been an important source of patronage, and this consideration has become increasingly important as the proportion of patronage positions in the executive system has diminished due to the expansion of the classified civil service; and (2) the federal courts have always (and correctly) been perceived by party leaders as a major instrument for exercising control over the substantive content of public policy.

The structure of the American party system is directly related to the articulation of the political and judicial systems. The structure of each party on a national basis is both incomplete and highly decentralized. National political leadership is dispersed among the executive, legislative, and political party systems. For state and local governments, lack of integration generally is even greater, although some of the elected judges of the judicial systems are included among the party leaders. Indeed, in many units of local government (particularly in rural counties and townships) the judges hold the most important public offices available; they *are* the political leaders of their communities.

Because of the decentralization of the party system, men selected for federal judgeships vary widely in their value orientations. Candidates for federal district judgeships must receive state and local party clearance, and the practice of "senatorial courtesy" in the confirmation process means that any senator of the same party as the President can veto any nomination to a district judgeship within his state. For appointments to the Supreme Court, sectional considerations are not as important as they were during the nineteenth century, but neither are they completely ignored. The crossing of party lines in appointments to the Supreme Court remains exceptional and usually has reflected a presidential judgment that ideological congruity between the President and his appointee was a more important consideration than party affiliation. Usually, crossing has involved conservative Republican Presidents appointing conservative Democrats (such as Taft → White, and Nixon → Powell), or liberal Democratic Presidents appointing liberal Republicans (such as Wilson → Brandeis). Taft's appointments of Edward White and Joseph Lamar, Wilson's of Louis Brandeis, Truman's of Harold Burton, and Nixon's of Lewis Powell have been the norm in crossing situations; the appointment of the liberal Democrat Benjamin Cardozo by the conservative Republican Herbert Hoover remains a unique instance of crossing ideological in addition to party lines.[9] It has been suggested that the recent trend toward promoting lower federal court judges to the Supreme Court betokens not so much a desire to create a career federal judiciary as an attempt to identify safe partisans whose ideological positions have been tried and proven in the minor leagues. Many federal judges have maintained a high level of personal interaction with the party system, as exemplified by Chief Justice William Howard Taft's unabated efforts to influence appointments not only to the Supreme Court but to the federal district and circuit courts throughout the country as well.[10]

SOCIOECONOMIC

The need for courts is a direct consequence of the concentration of people and wealth. In primitive societies, such as that of the nomadic Cheyenne Indians who followed the buffalo herds across the great plains a century ago, the need for organized courts was minimal. Disputes involved primarily obligations arising out of war, hunting, and sexual relationships; these were generally settled by mediation, arbitration, and vendetta without recourse to specialized judicial institutions.[11] But the Barotse of Northern Rhodesia (in pre-World War II colonial Africa), who practiced subsistence

[9]Ira H. Carmen, "The President, Politics and the Power of Appointment: Hoover's Nomination of Mr. Justice Cardozo," *Virginia Law Review* 55 (1969), pp. 616–659.

[10]Walter F. Murphy, "Chief Justice Taft and the Lower Court Bureaucracy: A Study in Judicial Administration," *Journal of Politics* 24 (1962), pp. 453–476; Walter F. Murphy, "In His Own Image: Mr. Chief Justice Taft and Supreme Court Appointments," in Philip B. Kurland, *The Supreme Court Review—1961* (Chicago: University of Chicago Press, 1961), pp. 159–193; David J. Danelski, *A Supreme Court Justice Is Appointed* (New York: Random House, Inc., 1964); and Alpheus T. Mason, *William Howard Taft: Chief Justice* (New York: Simon & Schuster, Inc., 1965).

[11]E. Adamson Hoebel and Karl N. Llewellyn, *The Cheyenne Way: Conflict and Case Law in Primitive Jurisprudence* (Norman, Okla.: University of Oklahoma Press, 1941); Carleton W. Kenyon, "Legal Lore of the Wild West: A Bibliographical Essay," *California Law Review* 56 (1968), pp. 681–700; Donald P. Kommers, "The Emergence of Law and Justice in Pre-Territorial Wisconsin," *American Journal of History* 8 (1964), pp. 20–33; Max Gluckman, *Politics, Law and Ritual in Tribal Society* (Chicago: Aldine Publishing Company, 1965), Chapter 5; Paul Bohannan, ed., *Law and Warfare: Studies in the Anthropology of Conflict* (Garden City: Natural History Press, 1967); and Laura Nader, ed., *Law in Culture and Society* (Chicago: Aldine Publishing Company, 1969).

farming in the flood plain of the Zambezi River, had a well-developed judicial system and process. The most common types of disputes requiring judicial disposition among the Barotse were those relating to the obligations to each other of members of the most basic primary group, the family, or to obligations arising out of sexual relationships between members of different families.[12] Questions of property rights, however, arose more frequently among the relatively civilized Barotse farmers than they did among the Cheyenne huntsmen. Patently, the complexity of legal relationships involving property rights is vastly greater for Manhattan Island today than for Hannibal, Missouri, in antebellum days; and although the difference is not *simply* a matter of either population size or density,[13] the correlation between the complexity of judicial institutions and the concentration of persons and wealth undoubtedly is positive and high.

The nineteenth-century pattern of judicial organization was suited to the needs of a rural, agricultural society and economy. The county courthouse with its acolyte corps of lay justices of the peace could and did resolve most disputes of most people, and a single appellate court completed the judicial system in most states. Throughout the century following *Marbury* v. *Madison,* the United States Supreme Court infrequently decided cases involving claims of personal rights (such as that of Dred Scott). The typical antebellum litigant was a ship, a bridge, a land or canal company, or a bank; after the Civil War it was a railroad, a coal or oil or mining company, or a trust. The subsequent shift to the kinds of questions and litigants now found before the Supreme Court, and the changes that have taken place in the structure of judicial systems have been in substantial measure responses to the great

[12]Max Gluckman, *The Judicial Process Among the Barotse of Northern Rhodesia* (Manchester, Eng.: University of Manchester Press, rev. ed., 1967).

[13]Cf. Hubert Blalock's discussion of the correlation between urbanization and racial discrimination, in his *Social Statistics* (New York: McGraw-Hill Book Company, 1960), pp. 330–332; and Hayward R. Alker, Jr., *Mathematics and Politics* (New York: The Macmillan Company, 1965), Chapters 4–6. Or, to take an example that received much publicity in the autumn of 1969, the National Commission on the Causes and Prevention of Violence argued that although there were high positive correlations between race and crime, and youth and crime, and particularly between black youth and urban crime, race and age were merely intervening variables; the causal independent variable, according to the Commission, was poverty.

changes that have taken place in American society and the American economy during the twentieth century. The major factors to which we can attribute the extent of such changes are industrialization and urbanization. A related factor that has affected judicial organization has been population dispersion: the geographic center of the population of the United States has moved westward every decade since 1790. But the trend toward urbanization has been no simple linear progression from the farm to the central cities of metropolitan areas. Among the conspicuous developments of the post-World War II period was the evacuation of the metropolitan cores, with both residents and retail trade and supporting commercial facilities moving into suburbia and shopping center communities. As was soon demonstrated by the rash of apportionment studies that followed in the wake of the 1960 census and the decision of the Supreme Court in *Baker* v. *Carr,* it was the Republican residents of the suburbs rather than the Democratic dwellers in the core cities who were most discriminated against in legislative representation; and these same persons were also the ones who were least adequately served by the existing structure of state and local judicial services because most judges represent either an urban or a rural—not a suburban—point of view. But the lag between judicial reorganization and changing needs due to shifts in population and industry is even greater than the much more publicized lag in legislative reapportionment.

The Supreme Court conspicuously took the bit in its teeth in forcing reapportionment upon state legislatures throughout the country, and to a lesser extent upon the redistricting of the United States House of Representatives and upon local governmental boards and councils. These are all units of government for which the Supreme Court has no direct supervisory authority or responsibility. The Supreme Court *does* have such authority and responsibility for the federal judicial system; and here the Court has remained, throughout the decade since the decision in *Baker* v. *Carr,* as quiet as a mouse. Of course it is clear that judges do not represent voters in the same sense that legislators do; but it is equally evident that judges do make public policy and they do represent local and other constellations of citizen interests. There is no question of the *fact* of malapportionment, assuming that anything resembling the criteria posited by the Court for legislative representation should be applied also to judicial representation. As Table 1 shows, four of the circuits are within what would probably be consensually acceptable as practical limits of population variation, with levels within ±10 percent of the average of approximately twenty million persons. But three circuits are overpopulated (and

TABLE 1

Malapportionment of the Federal Judiciary

Circuit	1970 Population (in millions)	No. of Federal Circuit and District Judges	No. of Judges per million people	Representation Class**
D.C.	0.8	26	32.5	
5	31.9	88	2.8	Over
9	30.3	71	2.3	
6	26.7	47	1.8	Under
2	21.7	52	2.4	
7	20.7	35	1.7	Under
3	19.6	53	2.7	Over ·
4	18.0	41	2.3	
8	16.0	38	2.4	
1	11.1	16	1.4	Under
10	9.4	27	2.9	Over
Average	(21.6*)	45	2.3*	
Range	(22.5*)	72	1.5*	

NOTES: r = .85
*Not including D.C.
**Blank ⪵ ± 10 percent of average

of these, two by more than 50 percent), while four other circuits are underpopulated (and two by more than 50 percent); and the largest (the fifth) circuit includes over forty times as many people as does the smallest (the District of Columbia) circuit. Clearly the D.C. circuit *does* present special problems (because of its specialized jurisdiction, both in theory and in practice); and the correlation of +.85 between population and the size of judicial cadres demonstrates that a strong attempt has been made to keep these two factors in balance. Indeed, as the representation-class column indicates, there are examples of "over," "balanced," and "under" representation for each of the three categories of overpopulation, modal population, and underpopulation. The question is not whether the rule of "one man, one vote" should apply strictly to the population density of federal judicial districts and circuits— although we should not forget that in most American states the judges *are* elected to office.[14] The question is—and it is the same one that underlay the classic legislative reapportionment suits in states such as Illinois and Tennessee, during the period of litigation that resulted in *Baker* v. *Carr*—to what extent, how, and how frequently, should patterns of political (in this instance, judicial) structure, which reflect the needs and political compromises of past eras, be projected into a present and probable future for which it is increasingly apparent that needs and interests are very different from those of the past? It is really a matter of *mortmain*—the persistent influence of the past upon the present—and the continuing problem of dealing with it through judicial reorganization is a social problem, and not merely one of administrative efficiency.

There is some evidence that the Supreme Court may elect to proceed under its power of statutory policy initiation, rather than through case law (as it did for legislative reapportionment), by having the Judicial Conference[15] approve a reorganization plan for the lower federal judiciary, which could then be introduced by members (probably by the respective chairmen) of the judiciary committees of the House and Senate, for statutory action by the Congress and President. The question is being given serious consideration, as evidenced by a statement in the 1970 annual report of the director of the Federal Judicial Center:[16]

E. CIRCUIT REORGANIZATION

At the request of the judicial conference, the Center has undertaken to provide research support on the issue of geographical reorganization of the circuits. The Center has recognized that its special abilities do not extend to those controversial areas. In that light, the Center has prepared a design for supportive research in this extremely important but very sensitive area. (See Appendix I.)

[14]Cf., however, *Wells* v. *Edwards,* Docket #72–261, 41 L.W. 3374 (1973), a decision of the Burger Court affirming a lower court decree approving malapportioned judicial electoral districts for the Louisiana state courts.
[15]See Chapter Two, p. 49, for a description of the Judicial Conference.
[16]*Third Annual Report of the Federal Judicial Center* (Washington, D.C.: 91st Cong., 2d Sess., House Doc. No. 91–411, November 16, 1970), pp. 10, 64–67. Judge Alfred P. Murrah is the second and incumbent director of the Center, having succeeded former Supreme Court Justice Tom Clark upon the latter's having reached the compulsory retirement age of sixty-five. See also the monthly newsletter, *The Third Branch,* published jointly since 1969 by the Administrative Office of the U.S. Courts and the Federal Judicial Center.

Working closely with advisors drawn from the Federal judiciary, the Center will delineate the issues involved in geographic organization, the various factors bearing on those issues, the constraints that must be observed in responding to the issues, and the values to be served in building a geographic structure. The Center will collect and analyze a substantial base of information bearing on all the points developed by the design. The objective of this information collection and analysis will be to provide the judicial conference all the information possible on the effect of various proposals for geographic reorganization of the circuits.

The "Appendix I" mentioned is the staff report which appears below; it should be noted that this memorandum, which quite appropriately places the question of population variance within the broader context of several other at least equally relevant considerations, is distinguished by its candor, and its provision incidentally of some insight into the administrative process of judicial policy making:

APPENDIX I

APRIL 24, 1970.

To: Judge Murrah.
From: William B. Eldridge.
Subject: Geographic reorganization of the circuit courts.

It is imperative to give some very hard thought to the whole question of a study of circuit court reorganization before taking any major steps in this connection. In my view we certainly do not have at this point a sufficiently clear idea of what such a study would be about to enable us to look for someone to conduct it. The conversations at staff meetings last week—in connection with this project and other matters—suggest very strongly that we do not need Charles Alan Wright or anyone remotely like him to perform what the Center should do in this area. Professor Wright would provide a superb rationale in supporting argument for adopting a particular approach to reorganization. That is a very valuable service, but not the one the Center should be offering.

The obvious first question in this connection is the objective of a geographical reorganization. The answer to that question is not at all obvious. We can speak easily of "improving judicial administration" or "making the administration more efficient." Immediately a number of questions arise such as: (1) What would an efficient structure be if we had no constraints on how we would draw it? (2) What are the characteristics to be considered in preparation of such a model structure? (3) What constraints, apart from efficiency considerations, will shape the actual decisions that will be made in implementing a model proposal?

To some extent from the literature, but particularly from the discussion I have heard among judges, the impression is that the circuits should be redrawn to equalize them. Exactly what attributes of the circuits that are not now equal should be equalized in any reorganization is never quite clear. Let's consider what some of them might be:

(1) Space: This might appear to be a frivolous inclusion since trees and buildings are not entitled to a day in court any more than they are entitled to a ballot during elections. But space does enter into the efficiency of an administrative structure. Further, taken together with population, space is a determinant of density which doubtless has pervasive effects on the workload of courts.

(2) People: Since people bring lawsuits, the number of people involved in a circuit will have a very significant effect on its workload. We may expect the correlation between the number of people and the number of cases to vary depending upon the kinds of cases. That is, we might expect to find a strong correlation between the number of people and the number of criminal appeals. On the other hand, certain kinds of civil cases might show no correlation whatever with the number of people.

(3) Cases: Cases constitute the work of the court but it is doubtful that equalizing numbers of appeals would equalize work. We need to know a great deal more about the kinds of appeals and the burden that the various kinds of appeals impose. That is to say, a form of weighted caseload for appellate courts.

(4) Judges: Aside from the ratio of judges to the number of cases in the workload of the court, the number of judges is an important element in itself. A circuit with only three judgeships is at the mercy of a not always benign providence. While senior judges always offer some resource pool, the number available in a very small circuit is quite limited. A death or sustained illness may have very deleterious effects. Similarly a circuit of 15 judges faces great

difficulty in seeing itself as "a court." Jokes are made about the Fifth Circuit sitting in three tiers for en banc hearings. I suspect a more serious problem is involved in the court seeing itself as a single functioning unit in the overall picture of the Federal judicial system.

(5) Administrative units: In our system the courts of appeals are much more than another layer of the judiciary providing opportunity for the vindication of rights. It is, or at least it should be, the most critical unit in the administration of the entire Federal judiciary. If that is true or if it is expected at some time to become true, circuits should be drawn with a major consideration given to the administrative efficiency of the resulting structure. This means that when a circuit is drawn all of the units that affect the administration of that circuit should be taken into account so that the potential for administrative efficiency is maximized. Thus we would take into account the number of district courts to be encompassed by each circuit, the number of judges involved in those districts, the number of statutory sitting places, and the business generated in each of those sitting places and the total business of the districts.

We must also ask what are the constraints imposed by considerations other than efficiency. I wish to exclude at this point (though certainly not permanently) consideration of what are usually called political realities. By this I mean whether or not an ideal plan could be enacted. There are, however, some constraints growing out of political subdivisions that must be considered. For example, drawing circuit lines along State boundaries probably would have no relevance in terms of efficiency but the recognition of political subdivision is a reality that doubtless must be considered in the course of assessing possible reorganization structures. I would not put absolutely beyond consideration the splitting of a State, but a great many considerations militate against it.

Another constraint on the development of efficiency oriented models would be the need for stability in the law. Suppose, for example, the efficiency experts tell us that we should have 20 circuits so that no circuit is ever called upon to supervise more than five districts. The answer might be that 20 circuits would introduce a greater uncertainty in the law than the system can tolerate and would impose a greater burden on the Supreme Court than it could meet.

In an enterprise such as this, there will be inevitable trade offs among the various things competing for prominence among the factors to be considered. Those decisions will ultimately be made by the judges of the federal system, but it is our job to develop the information to make sure that all aspects of those decisions are as fully identified as possible and that the potential effects and impacts of those decisions are as completely anticipated as possible. At least, that is my view of the responsibility of research in this area. It is not a thing to be done in the isolation of a research cloister but in as full contact as possible with advisory representatives of the ultimate decisionmakers.

I recommend that an ad hoc committee be appointed to consult with the center on the operation of this project.

The first task of the project would be to identify the factors that should be considered in developing reorganization alternatives and in choosing among those alternatives. The staff would consult fully with this ad hoc committee in identifying those factors.

Second, the center would develop the fullest possible information about each of those factors. This would include the five things listed above and all others that grow out of the staff-committee consultation.

Third, the committee would advise staff concerning constraints that are likely to be considered indispensable by the policymakers who will make ultimate choices. These would be matters that would have to be taken into account in developing alternatives for the policymakers to consider.

Fourth, the Center, with whatever contracted services that might be required, would develop a fully [sic] array of alternatives, taking into account the basic considerations and the constraints developed by the advisory committee and the staff.

Fifth, the board of the Center, when the project had met its requirements, would report the project to the Judicial Conference for policy decisions among the alternatives.

Sixth, the Center would stand ready to offer any further assistance required by the Judicial Conference to develop information needed by them for exercising their policymaking function.

Another demographic factor of significant implications relates to the rise of the megalopolis. The metropolis is distinguished by a surrounding hinterland of rural territory; but already emergent in the United States are giant urban complexes which extend for hundreds of miles, as from Arlington, Va., to beyond Boston, from

Milwaukee to Albany, from San Diego to San Francisco. The adequacy of the fifty relatively static, independent state judicial systems to meet the needs of dynamic population growth and shifts has increasingly been challenged by the concentration of the national population in these interstate urban complexes. One immediate consequence is that the workload of the federal courts is increased, and this in turn increases both the pressures upon and the difficulty of access to the Supreme Court. The Court now dockets over 4500 cases in each term; it can decide on the merits—that is, on the substantive questions presented by the litigants—of only about a tenth of these cases, given its present basis of organization and operational procedures. The seventy-three new federal judgeships established in May 1962 and the forty-five more added in 1966 expanded the national judiciary by over one fourth. Such a rapid expansion was certain to result in changes in the national judicial system, and all but a dozen of the 119 new federal judges appointed by President Kennedy during his first year in office were Democrats. Because of these new judges, who were added to federal district courts and courts of appeals in the metropolitan areas of rapid growth, litigants in federal trials during the 1960s were more likely to have their cases heard by a Democratic judge—and the trial is the stage of litigation at which most questions in a case are conclusively foreclosed. Moreover, appellants from the decisions of trial courts were then much more likely to draw a court of appeals panel with a Democratic majority—as were certain of the government agencies which are required to defend their own decisions before such panels. A major shift in the balance of partisan representation in the federal judiciary results in important qualitative differences in the kinds of socioeconomic values supported by the national judicial system.

On the other hand, the election of Richard Nixon in 1968 portended corresponding redress in the balance of partisan representation in the judicial system. Most obviously there was, of course, his almost immediate opportunity to substitute Warren Burger for Earl Warren in the chief justiceship, followed by his appointments of Blackmun, Powell, and Rehnquist, all during his first term. But there were also the fifty-eight permanent (plus three temporary) new federal district judgeships, which provided him with the opportunity to make no less than 177 federal district and circuit judge appointments by the end of 1972.[17] Nixon's partisan-

---

[17]From the point of view of sexual equality, the group included 176 males and one female. On racial equality see Beverly Blair Cook, "Black Representation in the Third Branch," *Black Law Journal* 1 (1971), p. 260.

TABLE 2

Four Decades of Appointments to the Federal Judiciary, 1933–1972*

Appointing President	District and Appeals Judges		U.S. Supreme Court Justices	
	Total	% same party as President	Total	% same party as President
FDR	194	97	9	72
HST	125	93	4	75
EISEN	174	95	5	80
JFK	122	91	2	100
LBJ	168	95	2	100
RMN	177	93	4	75
Totals	960	94	26	84

*Cf. the table "Judgeships as Patronage," *Congressional Quarterly Almanac* 27 (1971), p. 117, and the article "The Judiciary: Nixon Nearing Record on Nominees," *Congressional Quarterly Weekly Report* 30 (Dec. 16, 1972), pp. 3158–3161.

ship in making these judicial appointments was in no way different from that of any of his five most immediate predecessors; as Table 2 shows, Republican and Democratic Presidents alike have done their best to pack the federal courts with lawyers who were fellow partisans. If anything, Nixon appears in the table to be perhaps slightly *less* partisan than John Kennedy and Lyndon Johnson, because Nixon did appoint a Democrat to the Supreme Court—but such an inference is rather misleading. Lewis Powell, Jr., is a very conservative *southern* (Virginia) Democrat; and similarly, in all twelve of Nixon's Democratic appointments to the lower federal courts, there were strong partisan reasons to support the choices that he made.[18] Nixon's former law partner and 1968 campaign manager, John Mitchell, was the attorney general who, through his then deputy Richard Kleindienst, arranged these appointments,

[18]See *Congressional Quarterly Weekly Report* 30 (Dec. 16, 1972), p. 3159.

which included an ex-G.O.P. National Committee vice-chairman who became a federal appeals judge; half a dozen Republican state chairmen who became federal district judges; plus two unsuccessful gubernatorial candidates, a former state governor and United States senator, a pair of former congressmen, and assorted other party veterans. Perhaps the crowning irony—but inevitable consequence of the appointment system—is that one of these federal district judges was Charles A. Richey (a protegé of Vice-President Spiro Agnew) whose duty it became to preside over the early Watergate trials—which were postponed until after the 1972 election.

The transition to an industrial economy took place during the closing decades of the nineteenth century; and with the lag of about a generation between changes in the social and economic systems and corresponding accommodations in the legal system, the Supreme Court remade the Constitution in the image of Social Darwinism and in support of the interests of big business.[19] This remained the official policy of the Court until the advent of the Great Depression and the New Deal, which resulted—after a lag which was stopped only by Franklin Roosevelt's attack upon the Court—in a dramatic reversal of the values supported by a majority of the justices and in the received meaning of the Constitution. For example, the decision in *Baker* v. *Carr* followed closely on the heels of the 1960 census and focused attention upon the implications for political representation in American legislatures of the new patterns of urbanization. There was then sufficient congruity between the values upheld by a majority of the justices and the apparent interests of a preponderant majority of the American people to impel the Court to make a policy decision that it had refused to make as recently as 1946, when the proportion of urban residents was only about 58 percent instead of 70 percent as in 1960; by the end of the next decade (and the 1970 census), this percentage had risen, though less sharply, to 73.5 percent.

[19]Walton H. Hamilton, "The Path of Due Process of Law," in *The Constitution Reconsidered,* ed. Conyers Read (New York: Columbia University Press, 1938); Wallace Mendelson, *Capitalism, Democracy, and the Supreme Court* (New York: Appleton-Century-Crofts, Inc., 1960), Chapter 4; Arnold M. Paul, *Conservative Crisis and the Rule of Law: Attitudes of Bar and Bench, 1887–1895* (Ithaca, N.Y.: Cornell University Press, 1960).

PROFESSIONAL

Although many state constitutions now include a "closed shop" provision for judges, adopted at the behest of the organized bar, the Constitution of the United States does not require that federal judges shall be lawyers. The politics of judicial selection long have made it necessary, however, for a candidate for a federal judgeship to have had legal training, although no previous experience either as a judge or as a practicing lawyer is required. All of the men who have been justices of the Supreme Court have had some type of legal training. Almost all the earlier justices learned their law under the apprenticeship system; the late Robert Jackson, who died in 1954, probably will prove to have been the last person appointed without a law degree, and the trend increasingly has been for justices to be graduates of Ivy League law schools, such as Harvard, Yale, and Columbia,[20] but only about a fourth of some four hundred federal circuit and district judges, appointed during 1952 to 1966, were graduates of prestige law schools.[21]

Since 1945 the American Bar Association's Standing Committee on the Federal Judiciary has participated actively in evaluating nominees to federal judgeships. This committee rates nominees in terms of their "legal qualifications"—that is, their status in the legal guild. The committee's reports are considered by the Deputy Attorney General who chairs the Department of Justice committee on judicial selection and who also receives the reports of field investigations, conducted by the Federal Bureau of Investigation, of the nominees' loyalty, sobriety, and sexual orthodoxy. On a four-point scale ranging from 4 (not qualified) to 1 (exceptionally well qualified), 15 percent of a group of one hundred newly appointed federal district and circuit court judges during the sixties received scores of 1 from the ABA; 50 percent scored 2; 28 percent scored 3; and 7 percent received the lowest score. The average score for all one hundred judges was 2.27, which means that the ABA evaluated their average competence as between "qualified" and "well qualified." Translated into the familiar sym-

---

[20]John R. Schmidhauser, "The Justices of the Supreme Court: A Collective Portrait," *Midwest Journal of Political Science* 3 (1959), pp. 24–25.

[21]Sheldon Goldman, "Characteristics of Eisenhower and Kennedy Appointees to the Lower Federal Courts," *Western Political Quarterly* 18 (1965), pp. 755–762 at Table I; and Harold W. Chase, "The Johnson Administration: Judicial Appointments, 1963–1966," *Minnesota Law Review* 52 (1968), p. 964.

bols of academic evaluation, this was a *B–* group—from the point of view of the ABA. Clearly, other considerations than professional status were instrumental in the selection of these men; but clearly also, the institutionalization of the advice of the organized bar makes it improbable that persons who are *persona non grata* to the legal guild will receive appointments to the federal judiciary.

The interest of the bar in the selection of one of the key groups of decision makers with whom lawyers must interact is both substantial and understandable. Obviously, it is important for the bar to screen the selection of judges to assure that judges will meet at least minimal standards of technical expertise and personal morality; and it is quite rational that the bar should make some attempt to exclude incompetents, drunks, and crooks (from among its own membership) from positions of authority and power in the judicial system. In addition, there are other and perhaps less obvious reasons that reinforce the bar's interest in judicial selection.

There is always explicit consideration, in hearings of subcommittees of the Senate Judiciary Committee on the confirmation of presidential nominations to federal judgeships, of the "judicial temperament" of the nominees. But it is difficult to give concrete meaning to this vague concept; it becomes apparent that from the viewpoint of an individual who is a member of or a witness before the subcommittee passing upon the qualifications of a nominee, persons with whom he is in fundamental ideological agreement are blessed with "judicial temperament," and those with whom he disagrees lack it. In particular, spokesmen for the bar—whether in the role of witness, of co-opted member of the subcommittee, or of built-in (through committee membership as senators) institutional advocate—are in a position to manipulate the notion of "temperament" so as to attempt to minimize the selection for the federal bench of persons other than conservative supporters of established values and institutions.

Since its organization in 1878, the American Bar Association, through the speeches of its leaders and the opinions expressed in its journal, has consistently supported the most conservative ideas of the times. During the 1880s and 1890s, doctrinaire laissez-faire ideology was the "party line" of the ABA, as exemplified both in direct representation by ABA leaders before the United States Supreme Court and in the principal speeches at ABA national meetings.[22] In particular, the ABA was a bulwark of support for

[22]Benjamin Twiss, *Lawyers and the Constitution* (Princeton, N.J.: Princeton University Press, 1941).

the United States Supreme Court until 1937; but for the next three decades, while the Court has played a much more liberal role, the ABA became its persistent and virulent critic, leading to the resignation in 1959 of Chief Justice Earl Warren from the organization, after twenty years of affiliation.

A necessary consequence of the conservatism of the ABA has been the tendency of its Standing Committee on the Federal Judiciary to equate "judicial temperament" with ideological conservatism as an attribute of candidates it deems qualified to become federal judges.[23] Consequently, the relations between the Supreme Court and the ABA hierarchy took a turn for the better after Warren Burger became chief justice in 1969; and unlike Warren, who opted for a role of substantial independence from the organized bar, Burger became the first chief justice in forty years—since Taft—to exploit conspicuously the instrumental possibilities of the bar for use both in restructuring the courts and in developing better integrated control over judicial policy making at all levels.[24] But the portended rapprochement was at least partially frustrated for several years by Nixon's persistence in next trying to appoint arch conservatives irrespective of their professional distinction. Peace between the White House, Capitol Hill, and the ABA came only after an agonizing period in which the United States Senate rejected the nominations of Southerners Clement Haynsworth and G. Harrold Carswell;[25] and then the ABA com-

[23]John R. Schmidhauser, *The Supreme Court: Its Politics, Personalities, and Procedures* (New York: Holt, Rinehart & Winston, Inc., 1960), p. 19 and Chapters 2 and 4, passim; Joel B. Grossman, *Lawyers and Judges: The ABA and the Politics of Judicial Selection* (New York: John Wiley & Sons, Inc., 1965); Harold W. Chase, "Federal Judges: The Appointing Process," *Minnesota Law Review* 51 (1966), pp. 185–221; and Sheldon Goldman, "Views of a Political Scientist: Political Selection of Federal Judges and the Proposal for a Judicial Service Commission," *Journal of the American Judicature Society* 53 (1968), pp. 94–98.

[24]See James F. Simon, *In His Own Image: The Supreme Court in Richard Nixon's America* (New York: David McKay Co., Inc., 1973), especially pp. 94–96; Arthur R. Landever, "Chief Justice Burger and Extra-Case Activism," *Journal of Public Law* 20 (1971), pp. 523–541; and cf. Peter Alan Bell, "Extrajudicial Activity of Supreme Court Justices," *Stanford Law Review* 22 (1970), pp. 587–617.

[25]Edward N. Beiser, "The Haynsworth Affair Reconsidered: The Significance of Conflicting Perceptions of the Judicial Role," *Vanderbilt Law Review* 23 (1971), pp. 263–291; and James A. Thorpe, "The Appearance of Supreme Court Nominees Before Senate Judiciary Committee," *Journal*

mittee refused to approve either Herschel Friday (a conspicuously antidesegregation attorney from Little Rock) or Mildred Lillie (a female but pedestrian county judge from Los Angeles), resulting in the first open, public, and vociferous disagreement in thirty-five years between the ABA and the presidency in regard to Supreme Court appointments.[26] Lawrence E. Walsh, a Wall Street lawyer with impeccable professional qualifications and the chairman of the ABA Standing Committee on the Judiciary, reacted to the counter-attack emanating from the Nixon–Mitchell–Kleindienst axis and allied administration stalwarts, by issuing a series of white (position) papers, variously to the *New York Times,* radio and TV reporters, and in an article published in the ABA's official journal of most general circulation.[27] With the "bipartisan" appointment as an associate justice late in 1971 of Lewis Powell, Jr., not only a conservative southern Democrat but also a former national pre-sident of the ABA (who had been Phi Beta Kappa and first in his law school graduating class, with a Master of Laws degree from Harvard, and so forth), there began a new era of good feeling between the bench, the bar, and the Nixon administration.[28]

TRADITIONAL

The traditions of his court constitute one of the most pervasive aspects of the environment in which a judge makes policy. These

of Public Law 18 (1969), pp. 371–402. Indeed, James Simon reports that according to Washington columnist Art Buchwald, other sons of the old South were available too, and awaiting the President's call. One such was "Judge Caleb E. Lee of the Fifth Circuit Juvenile and Bankruptcy Court of Juniper County, Alabama. Judge Lee had no investments in stocks and bonds. It was reliably reported, in fact, that Lee's holdings were limited exclusively to slaves, which the judge contended should not give rise to any conflict of interest questions. 'Ah don't know how owning a few darkies could affect the way ah decide the constitutional issues,' drawled Judge Lee. 'Besides, you have to have some balance on the Court, and right now it's heavily weighted in favor of the antislave forces.' " Op. cit., p. 115.

[26]"Nixon's Court: Its Making and Its Meaning," *Time* 98, No. 18 (November 1, 1971), pp. 14–20.

[27]Lawrence E. Walsh, "Selection of Supreme Court Justices," *American Bar Association Journal* 56 (1970), pp. 555–560.

[28]For a discussion of the professional image of the Supreme Court, see Edward N. Beiser, "Lawyers Judge the Warren Court," *Law and Society Review* 7 (Fall 1972), pp. 139–149.

traditions are unwritten social norms that have an important influence upon how a judge makes his decisions, for they control many of the specific applications of the procedures employed in judicial policy making. Because they tend to vary considerably from court to court, we shall focus our discussion upon the court whose traditions are probably of longest standing and best understood.

Even such a seemingly basic aspect of judicial behavior as the public reporting of voting disagreement among Supreme Court justices depends upon custom that has varied throughout the history of the Court. Initially, the Court followed the English practice, and each justice delivered his own individual opinion in each decision. Then, under John Marshall's influence, the general practice was to "mass the Court" in support of unanimous opinions, read by the chief justice in important cases. Since the days of Roger B. Taney (1835–1864), the custom has been for justices to join in the opinion (usually, of the majority) that announces the decision of the Court; to write or to join in independent concurring opinions if they vote with the majority but wish to articulate a different or an additional rationale; or to write or to join in dissenting opinions if they vote against the majority decision of the Court. The writing of the opinion that announces the decision of the Court is assigned by the chief justice, if he votes with the majority; otherwise, the senior associate justice voting with the majority makes the assignment. Each justice decides for himself whether he will join in the opinion of the Court or in a concurring or dissenting opinion written by another justice, or whether he will write an independent opinion of his own—in which other justices might then decide to join. Many other appellate courts follow quite different practices. In the Michigan Supreme Court, for instance, cases are assigned among the justices by rotation, but any other justice may write an independent opinion; then, at the conference at which a vote is taken, all opinions that have been prepared are circulated for signature, and the opinion that attracts the largest number of signers becomes the opinion of the Court, assuming that a majority are agreed upon the disposition of the case.

In the United States Supreme Court, the voting division in each decision can be determined only inferentially. That is, reports of the Court's decisions do not explicitly state the vote of each justice; instead, the reports show who wrote the opinion of the Court, who wrote concurring opinions and who dissented, and who failed to participate in the decision. Given the known membership of the Court at any particular time, the justices who joined in the opinion of the Court can be inferred. The decisions of almost all other American appellate courts explicitly specify the votes of individual judges.

Six is now the statutory quorum for decision making by the United States Supreme Court, and decisions are determined by the vote of a majority of the participating justices. Thus the size of majority voting groups can vary from four to nine, depending upon the number of participants, while the size of dissenting voting groups never can exceed four justices. Ties of three-to-three and four-to-four can occur, if the number of nonparticipants is odd, in which event the Court announces no opinion and the decision of the court that last handled the case is affirmed pro forma.

Each Supreme Court justice decides for himself whether to disqualify himself from participating in any decision. The presumption is that all justices will participate in all decisions; but illness may prevent a justice from hearing the oral argument or from attending the conference at which a vote is taken, and in such cases a justice customarily disqualifies himself. Similarly, a recently appointed justice may disqualify himself from the substantive decisions in cases on which arguments and conferences were held before he joined the Court. Throughout most of the last eleven (and busiest) weeks of the 1961 term, for instance, there were only seven participating justices, because of Justice Frankfurter's illness, and because the recency of Justice White's appointment prevented him from participating in more than a dozen of the forty-four decisions on the merits during this period. It is assumed, also, that there are grounds—however nebulous—of propriety on the basis of which a judge, because of either real or putative conflict of interest, will decline to sit in particular decisions; some of the most famous controversies surrounding the justices have stemmed from charges that individual justices have been reluctant to drop out when colleagues or political critics have asserted that they should have acted like Caesar's wife.[29] Thus, a justice who has had any personal relationship to a case during its previous litigation usually

[29]For example, see the detailed *apologia* filed by Justice Rehnquist in justification of his refusal to disqualify himself—when directly challenged to do so by the party against whom he had voted in a 5–4 reversal of a lower court—notwithstanding his earlier relationship, as a high official of the Department of Justice, to the litigation. See his Memorandum Opinion concerning *Laird* v. *Tatum* (Docket No. 71–288), dated October 10, 1972, in *Law Week* 41 (10–17–72), pp. 3208–3211. See also the Note, "Justice Rehnquist's Decision to Participate in *Laird* v. *Tatum*," *Columbia Law Review* 73 (1973), pp. 106–124.

will refuse to participate in its decision by the Supreme Court. In recent decades, for example, many justices who earlier had served as attorney (or solicitor) general have disqualified themselves in cases to which the national government was a party and for which they had had official responsibility during earlier stages of litigation. Yet another example is Justice Stewart's decision to disqualify himself in *Ohio ex rel. Eaton* v. *Price,* in the decision of which the remaining eight justices divided equally; the reason for Stewart's nonparticipation was that his father had participated in an earlier decision on the case as chief justice of the Ohio Supreme Court. But justices of the federal Supreme Court have not always adhered to such rigorous criteria of putative bias; it was common in the early days of the Court for justices to participate in the decision of cases in which they had direct and sometimes large financial interests. In *Marbury* v. *Madison* the Secretary of State whose negligence initially resulted in Marbury's failure to receive his commission as a justice of the peace was none other than John Marshall himself, the Chief Justice who wrote the unanimous decision of the Supreme Court in the case. Indeed, Marshall had held both posts simultaneously during the closing weeks of the Adams administration.

Many courts have given up the ancient practice of reading in full all opinions written in cases decided on the merits. The Supreme Court continues to allocate several days each month to the ceremony of opinion-reading,[30] although some justices have not agreed with the custom; Justice Frankfurter, for instance, preferred to present oral summaries of his often lengthy opinions. This procedure has led to some public controversy among the justices, while they have been sitting at the bench in open court. Chief Justice Warren once accused Frankfurter of including in his oral presentation arguments that had not appeared in his written opinion. Warren's concern was that other justices could have no opportunity to consider and—if they so chose—to rebut arguments that were withheld from the written opinions (which are circulated among all of the justices prior to the announcement of decisions); a justice who departed from the custom thus would have an unfair advantage.

Tradition has a very important bearing on the decision-making process of the Court in many other ways. The secrecy of the conference[31] forces the justices to engage in petty clerical

[30]David L. Grey, *The Supreme Court and the News Media* (Evanston, Ill.: Northwestern University Press, 1968).
[31]See Arthur S. Miller and D. S. Sastri, "Secrecy and the Supreme Court," *Buffalo Law Review* 22 (Spring 1973), pp. 799–823.

activities that few decision-making groups of similar responsibility and authority—and there are few—continue to tolerate. The most recently appointed justice, for instance, serves as the doorkeeper for the conference, and any information that goes into or out of the conference room while the court is in session there requires his personal attention; thus Oliver Wendell Holmes, as a freshman justice at the age of sixty-one, served for a year as the messenger boy for the group. The decisions themselves are generally well-kept secrets, although a few celebrated leaks occurred during the nineteenth century.

The judges of the federal and most of the state supreme courts wear robes while on the bench, but in several states they appear in business garb. There has been some speculation that the wearing of judicial robes encourages the laity to believe that judges are able to suppress their personal attitudes, thus permitting them to indulge their biases with less fear of being detected.[32] There is, however, little empirical evidence available concerning psychological and other effects that the wearing of robes may have upon judicial decisions.[33]

No written rule defines the extent to which the justices of the United States Supreme Court give reasons in support of their decisions. It is customary for the Court to report an assigned opinion to justify the decisions in most of the cases for which the justices have heard oral argument, although in several such cases each term only brief and anonymous (per curiam) opinions are reported. Either stereotyped reasons that communicate little or nothing (viz., "want of jurisdiction" or "lack of a substantial federal question") or—most of the time—no reasons at all are reported for the Court's decisions to refuse to decide cases on the merits. Many (but by no means all) other appellate courts follow the same practice.

The postulated norm of *stare decisis* (i.e., that a court shall follow its own previous decisions, or those of higher courts in the same system, on the same policy issue) presumably is a fundamental aspect of the judicial decision-making process. But for justices of the United States Supreme Court, institutional *stare decisis* does not have even the status of the customary norms

---

[32]Jerome Frank, "The Cult of the Robe," *Saturday Review* 28 (October 13, 1945), pp. 12–13, 80–81; and *Courts on Trial* (Princeton, N.J.: Princeton University Press, 1949), pp. 254–261.

[33]See Stuart S. Nagel, "Off-the-Bench Judicial Attitudes," in *Judicial Decision-Making,* ed. Glendon Schubert (New York: The Free Press of Glencoe, 1963), pp. 41–42; and Robert A. Kessler, "The Psychological Effects of Judicial Robes," *American Imago* 19 (1962), pp. 35–66.

discussed thus far.[34] The Court's practice is that each justice decides for himself the extent to which he believes there should be consistency between the Court's past and present policy making. Individual decisions are much less apt to be based upon an undefined and abstract obligation to follow precedents than to be a function of the considerations relevant to judicial activism and restraint, that is, to be related to whether the justice believes that the Court should play an active part in interpreting the Constitution or defer to legislatures and executives.[35] But the manipulation of precedents in support of decisions is an indispensable judicial skill, since it is the basic tool for the process of rationalization in opinion–writing;[36] and judicial activism proffers a less persuasive theory of decision-making behavior than does the theory of ideology that we shall consider in Chapter Six, below.

[34]William O. Douglas, "Stare Decisis," *Record of the Association of the Bar of the City of New York* 4 (May 1949), pp. 152–179; and Walter V. Shaefer, "Precedent and Policy," *University of Chicago Law Review* 34 (1967), pp. 3–25.

[35]See particularly the distinction between "traditional" and "personal" *stare decisis* discussed in Reed C. Lawlor, "What Computers Can Do: Analysis and Prediction of Judicial Decisions," *American Bar Association Journal* 49 (April 1963), pp. 337–344; and also Lawlor's "Personal *Stare Decisis,*" *Southern California Law Review* 41 (1967), pp. 73–118; Glendon Schubert, "Civilian Control and *Stare Decisis* in the Warren Court," Chapter 3 in *Judicial Decision-Making,* ed. Schubert (New York: The Free Press of Glencoe, 1963), and Fred Kort, "Content Analysis of Judicial Opinions and Rules of Law," Chapter 6 in ibid.; S. K. B. Asante, "*Stare Decisis* in the Supreme Court of Ghana" *University of Ghana Law Journal* 1 (1964), pp. 52–67, and N. A. Ollennu, "Judicial Precedent in Ghana," ibid., 3 (1966), pp. 139–164.

[36]The most useful (if incremental) steps in the direction of constructing a behavioral theory of *stare decisis* have been taken by Martin Shapiro: see his "Toward a Theory of *Stare Decisis,*" *Journal of Legal Studies* 1 (1972), pp. 125–134; and "Stability and Change in Judicial Decision-Making: Incrementalism or *Stare Decisis,*" *Law in Transition Quarterly* 2 (1965), pp. 134–157. For a lexicon of what stereotyped judicial language really means, see Richard M. Evans, "Judicial Cop-Outs: A Freshman's Primer," *Student Law Review* 16 (February 1971), pp. 5–27.

Federal
Judicial Structures

GENERAL STRUCTURE

In the formal or constitutional view, there are fifty-one different judicial systems within the American polity: a national ("federal") system and a separate system for each of the states. This view is
more formal than real because of the high positive correlation
between the population of a governmental unit and the complexity
of its judicial system. The judicial systems of many of the less
populous states are smaller and show less differentiation of both
structure and function than do the judiciaries of the twenty-six
metropolises with populations of over half a million persons.
Indeed, by 1970 the ten largest cities (including the District of
Columbia) all had populations in excess of seven hundred and fifty
thousand, while there were the same number of whole states with
smaller populations. Many of these municipal judicial systems are
almost as autonomous within the state judicial systems as the latter
are within the federal system. From a functional point of view, it
would be more correct to say that there are over a hundred
different major judicial systems in the United States, including
those of all of the states, those of the fifty largest cities, and that of
the national government.

THE FEDERAL JUDICIAL SYSTEM

When Richard M. Nixon began his second term as President in January 1973, there were more than six hundred and fifty judges in the federal judicial system. They included a chief justice and eight associate justices of the United States Supreme Court; about one hundred chief judges and circuit judges of the eleven courts of appeals—50 percent more than in 1960; and some four hundred chief judges and district judges of the ninety-two district courts; plus almost a hundred and fifty "senior" (i.e., semi-retired) judges.[1] These federal judges constituted the principal cadre of the "regular" or "constitutional" federal judiciary, so-called because of the now obsolescent legal presumption that Congress had, in establishing these courts, acted under the authority of Article 3 (the judiciary article) of the Constitution. Another forty-odd federal judges are members of federal courts that are specialized on the basis of function rather than area, as we shall discuss in greater detail below. Most of these latter courts originated as administrative boards, which after a time were redesignated by statute as courts. Beginning in the middle 1950s the Supreme Court acquiesced in further legislation that reclassified some of the special courts—the Court of Claims, the Customs Court, and the Court of Customs and Patent Appeals—as "regular" constitutional courts, with the first and third being assimilated to the level of courts of appeals, and the Customs Court to the salary and status level of the federal district courts. In the late 1960s bills were introduced that would have reclassified the Tax Court in a similar manner; but their consideration was delayed by opposition from several committees (made up of lawyers and federal judges) of the Judicial Conference of the United States.[2] At issue was whether almost all internal revenue appeals would be settled finally by the Tax Court itself (save for a very occasional appeal to the Supreme Court), or whether (as now) several hundred decisions of the Tax Court would be reviewed each year by the courts of appeals. In addition to the fourteen judges of the Tax Court, the forty-odd who now comprise the Superior Court and the municipal Court of Appeals

---

[1]This includes the District of Columbia and Puerto Rico, but not the Canal Zone, Guam, American Samoa, or the Virgin Islands. It represented an overall increase of well over 50 percent in the size of the entire federal judiciary since 1954. The number of district judges increased by 55 percent; circuit judges also increased by 55 percent; but there has been no change in the number of Supreme Court justices since 1837, except for half a dozen years (1863–1869) when the size of the Court was manipulated by Unionists during the Civil War and Reconstruction periods.

[2]See p. 49 for further discussion of the federal judicial conference.

of the District of Columbia, the three judges of the Court of Military Appeals, and the half dozen judges assigned to noncontiguous territorial district courts (in the Canal Zone, Guam, Puerto Rico, and the Virgin Islands) constitute the "nonconstitutional" federal judiciary. Historically, this peculiar status was a *modus vivendi* during the transition from territorial government to statehood, but that problem is no longer with us. Since the justification has disappeared, and because there are administrative advantages to having a single status floor for all federal judges, it seems likely that John Marshall's distinction between constitutional and legislative courts, having outlived its purpose, will disappear. More meaningful now is the distinction between federal courts with a diversified function and those with a specialized policy-making function.

COURTS WITH A DIVERSIFIED FUNCTION

The United States district courts are the trial courts of general jurisdiction in the federal judicial system. There is at least one district court in each state, and there is one in each of the five more important remaining national territories—the District of Columbia, Puerto Rico, the Virgin Islands, the Canal Zone, and Guam. The number of courts assigned to each state reflects past partisan choices of Congress more than it does present needs. The correlation between state population and the number of district *courts* is much higher for the years immediately prior to the Civil War than it is now, but the same comment does not apply for the correlation between state population and the number of federal *judges.* California, New York, and Texas are each divided into four judicial districts; nine states (Alabama, Florida, Georgia, Illinois, Louisiana, North Carolina, Oklahoma, Pennsylvania, and Tennessee) are divided into three each; thirteen states have two districts; and the remaining twenty-five states have one each. However, the ten most populous states, ranked according to 1970 populations, were in 1973 assigned federal district judges as follows: California, 33; New York, 41; Pennsylvania, 33; Texas, 22; Illinois, 17; Ohio, 13; Michigan, 12; New Jersey, 9; Florida, 15; Massachusetts, 6. Evidently, the correlation between population and number of federal judges is very high and positive and statistically significant. The corresponding correlation between state area and the number of federal judges is, however, low and, though positive, not statistically significant.

The number of judges assigned to district courts ranged from one to twenty-seven. Barely half a dozen districts now have only a single judge, and but eight districts had ten or more judges: New York, Southern (Manhattan), 27; Pennsylvania, Eastern (Philadelphia), 19; California, Central (Los Angeles), 16; District of Columbia, 15; Illinois, Northern (Chicago), 13; California, Northern (San Francisco), 11; and Pennsylvania, Western (Pittsburgh), and Michigan, Eastern (Detroit), each 10. Most common were districts with two judges; there were about twenty-seven such districts in 1973. In many of the less populous states having, nevertheless, more than one district, at least one of the judges is assigned to two, or even to three, different districts, in an attempt to equalize workload differentials within the state. Moreover, temporary transfers are frequent. During the fiscal year 1970–1971, for example, 121 judges undertook 342 visiting assignments involving a total of about 3036 days of participation. Almost three fifths of such temporary assignments were between courts within the same circuit. However, during an eight-and-a-half-year period extending from March 1960 to September 1968, 432 temporary intercircuit assignments of visiting judges were made, of which two thirds were from district courts in the eighth and ninth circuits to district courts in the fifth and second circuits; over a third of these intercircuit assignments were undertaken by senior (semi-retired) judges. But this pattern had changed by the early 1970s; by then the principal exporters of judicial services were the third, eighth, and tenth circuits; while the leading importing circuits were the first, fourth, and fifth—especially the latter, which in fiscal 1970 received 520 days of visiting service from other circuits but donated none to others. The ninth was the most active circuit, with a net balance of seventy-four imported days on top of 870 days of intracircuit transfers. Although it occurred earlier during the 1950s, the celebrated Little Rock school integration trial was presided over by Visiting Judge Ronald N. Davies from Fargo, North Dakota.

The term "circuit" is a semantic vestige of the earlier appellate system, under which there was a circuit court for each state, usually composed of a specially designated circuit judge and one of the district judges, participating together. They were joined during part of each year by the Supreme Court justice who was assigned to the regional grouping of states—the circuit—of which the state was a part. Supreme Court justices and circuit judges alike "rode the circuit" until the 1890s, although by then no longer on horseback. Just before the turn of the century, the present system of permanent (and fixed) courts of appeals was substituted. Although each Supreme Court justice still is assigned to one or more circuits, his major duty today consists of hearing emergency motions that arise in his circuit during the Court's summer vacation.

Each of the courts of appeals decides cases that are (in effect) appealed from the-so-called independent federal regulatory commissions (particularly the National Labor Relations Board) and

TABLE 3

States and Territories in Each of the Federal Circuits

First:	Maine, Massachusetts, New Hampshire, Rhode Island, Puerto Rico
Second:	Connecticut, New York, Vermont
Third:	Delaware, New Jersey, Pennsylvania, Virgin Islands
Fourth:	Maryland, North Carolina, South Carolina, Virginia, West Virginia
Fifth:	Alabama, Florida, Georgia, Louisiana, Mississippi, Texas, Canal Zone
Sixth:	Kentucky, Michigan, Ohio, Tennessee
Seventh:	Illinois, Indiana, Wisconsin
Eighth:	Arkansas, Iowa, Minnesota, Missouri, Nebraska, North Dakota, South Dakota
Ninth:	Alaska, Arizona, California, Hawaii, Idaho, Montana, Nevada, Oregon, Washington, Guam
Tenth:	Colorado, Kansas, New Mexico, Oklahoma, Utah, Wyoming
D.C.:	District of Columbia

from the Tax Court of the United States, as well as from the district courts in the circuit. There is also a United States Court of Appeals for the District of Columbia Circuit, which supervises the decision making of the federal district court, and a municipal Court of Appeals for the City of Washington, which in turn receives appeals from a new Superior Court that was established in 1970 to replace the former Court of General Sessions, Juvenile Court, and municipal Tax Court. The U.S. Court of Appeals for the D.C. gets far fewer appeals from the U.S. Tax Court than do the courts of appeals for the numbered circuits, and it reviews a smaller proportion of the decisions of the National Labor Relations Board than do most of the other courts of appeals; but it reviews considerably more appeals from the other administrative regulatory agencies than any other court of appeals.

In both the courts of appeals and the district courts, the chief judge is the judge under the age of seventy with the greatest seniority. The number of circuit judges assigned to the courts of appeals ranges from three in the first circuit to thirteen in the ninth and fifteen in the fifth, with the other eight circuits having seven to nine each. There were a total of approximately one hundred circuit judges in 1973, plus almost fifty "senior judges" who had retired but were available for part-time work. With few exceptions, however, the decisions of courts of appeals are made by "panels" (subgroups) of three judges. Such panels vary in composition from case to case, so that in the larger courts of appeals any one of many subgroups might make the decision in the name of the court. Because subgroups do not always agree on what should be the policy position of the court, it is necessary from time to time to resolve intracourt (interpanel) conflicts by having all of the judges assigned to the court decide the issue by majority vote in what is called an *en banc* decision.[3]

Individual circuit judges do not make decisions for their court except in procedural matters, but in the district courts almost all decisions are made by individual judges, who act in the name of their respective courts. Out of some 143,000-odd decisions in civil or criminal cases made by the district courts in the fiscal year ending June 30, 1972, only 310 were made by so-called three-judge district courts—and this was typical of recent years. Such panels, consisting (usually) of two district judges and one circuit judge, are part of a special procedure established by a few statutes, originally in order to expedite judicial review of certain decisions of the Interstate Commerce Commission. In legal theory it was assumed that there was a particular public interest in settling policy in such matters, so the statutes provide that cases will be tried by specially convened three-judge courts, with appeals direct to the Supreme Court—thus bypassing, of course, the courts of appeals. In recent years, there has been relatively frequent use of such special district courts in cases where the policy issue has been racial equality and there were 166 such hearings in 1972; review of ICC orders required fifty-two hearings; and next most frequent (thirty-two) was state legislative reapportionment, an issue for which three-judge courts were frequently used during the early 1960s, but which had required only two such courts by 1970–1971. A committee of law professors and other legal experts, appointed by Chief Justice Burger, recommended late in 1972 that all three-judge federal district courts (and therefore, all direct Supreme Court review of their decisions) be abolished.

The circuit judges and the judges of the ninety-one district courts in the fifty states and in the District of Columbia (and of

---

[3]See Burton M. Atkins, "Decision-Making Rules and Judicial Strategy on the United States Courts of Appeals," *Western Political Quarterly* 25 (1972), pp. 626–642. In 1972, for example, only three of the eleven courts of appeals met *en banc*, for a total of only twenty (out of 5748) decisions.

those special courts that have been assimilated to them) now are appointed for terms of life. Their commissions of appointment read "for good behavior," but the chances of any federal judge's being removed by impeachment, the only authorized means, are very remote. No circuit judge ever has been impeached. Of the six district judges who have been, three were acquitted; an insane and alcoholic Federalist was removed in 1803 by a Senate dominated by Jeffersonians; a border-state supporter of the Confederacy was removed on grounds of sedition by the Union Congress in 1862; and Judge Ritter of the Southern District of Florida was removed in 1936. About ten judges have resigned under threat of impeachment, including Supreme Court Justice Abe Fortas in the spring of 1969. A judge appointed for good behavior cannot successfully be removed merely for partisan reasons, for simple neglect of duty, or for incompetence.

The formal method for appointing federal judges is for the President to present nominations to the Senate. If the Senate "confirms" (concurs) by a majority vote, the President directs that a "commission" (certificate of appointment) be issued to the candidate, who accepts his appointment by his oath at a "swearing in" ceremony. The functional considerations channeled through the formal conduit are these: the senator (or senators) of the President's party—or, if there are none, those representatives of the President's party from districts within the jurisdiction of the court to which the appointment is to be made—suggests candidates. Additional suggestions are received from a wide variety of other sources, including national, state, and local political party leaders. There is now an institutionalized clearance process under which the deputy attorney general functions as a clearinghouse for the collection and evaluation of information concerning the qualifications of all proposed appointments of legal personnel to the Department of Justice including United States attorneys and marshals, as well as federal judges. The deputy attorney general receives investigative reports from the F.B.I., as well as from the American Bar Association, and this information is pooled so that a supporting record accompanies nominations submitted to the Senate. The Senate Judiciary Committee then conducts hearings on the nominations, at which witnesses testify for and/or against the candidates, and makes its recommendations, which the Senate almost always follows.[4] The influence that a single senior senator can have in the appointment of a federal judge is suggested by the

[4]See Harold W. Chase, "Federal Judges: The Appointing Process," *Minnesota Law Review* 51 (1966), pp. 185–221; and Joel B. Grossman, *Lawyers and Judges: The ABA and the Politics of Judicial Selection* (New York: John Wiley & Sons, Inc., 1965), Chapter 2.

case of Sarah T. Hughes, a Dallas lawyer who was appointed to the Northern District of Texas in 1962. At the time of her confirmation, Judge Hughes was sixty-six years of age and was rated as "not qualified" by the ABA,[5] but she had the support of Lyndon Johnson, the Texan who presided over the Senate and who for years had been its most influential leader. When President Kennedy was assassinated in Dallas on November 22, 1963, it was Judge Hughes who administered the presidential oath of office to her long-time personal and political friend, Johnson. On the other hand, however, when Johnson as President attempted to stand behind the nomination, sponsored by the Kennedy family, of Francis X. Morrissey, Senator Ted Kennedy's best efforts—which included the support of the Speaker of the House of Representatives (McCormack of Massachusetts) and of the president of the Massachusetts (State) Bar Association—were not enough to overcome the determined opposition of the ABA Committee, whose public attacks upon his character forced Morrissey to ask that his name be withdrawn and Kennedy to move that the nomination be recommitted to (i.e., pigeonholed in) the Senate Judiciary Committee.[6]

The district judges in four of the five national territories have even more diversified functions to perform than do the federal district judges in the states, because to a greater or lesser extent these territorial courts exercise jurisdiction equivalent to that of a state court, in addition to the ordinary jurisdiction of a national district court. This is maximally so for the district courts in the Canal Zone, in Guam, and in the Virgin Islands, where there is no other court of record than that of the federal district judge. In the District of Columbia, there is a municipal (but not a state) court system which in 1970 was reorganized after the model of (and with the expressed intent that it henceforth perform more like) a state judicial system; but in the Commonwealth of Puerto Rico there is a state type of judicial system. All of the territorial district judges are appointed in the same way and are paid the same salary as other federal district judges. However, only those in the United States District Court and Court of Appeals—not the municipal Superior

[5]Her advanced age accounted for the rating. Bernard G. Segal, Chairman of the American Bar Association's Committee on the Federal Judiciary, has stated that there are two principal reasons for rating a prospective judge as not qualified: (1) if he is over sixty-five years of age, or (2) if he lacks significant trial experience, either as a judge or as a practicing attorney. See the discussion of the Hughes case in Grossman, ibid., at pp. 150, 179–180.

[6]For a discussion of the Morrissey case, see Harold W. Chase, "The Johnson Administration: Judicial Appointments, 1963–1966," *Minnesota Law Review* 52 (1968), pp. 980–986.

Court or Court of Appeals—of the District of Columbia are appointed for life terms; the tenure for the others is eight years.

SPECIAL COURTS

There are five other adjudicative agencies that Congress has designated as courts, each of which works in a special area of public policy. The judges of three of these agencies (the Court of Claims, the Court of Customs and Patent Appeals, and the Customs Court) are appointed for life terms; the judges of the Court of Military Appeals have terms of fifteen years; and the judges of the Tax Court of the United States have twelve-year terms. All are appointed by the President, with confirmation by the Senate. The judges of the Customs Court and those of the Tax Court are at the same status and salary level as district judges. The judges of the Court of Claims, the Court of Customs and Patent Appeals, and the Court of Military Appeals are assimilated to the level of circuit judges. Supreme Court review of the decisions of the courts of appeals, though discretionary, does occur on a regular if limited basis; but Supreme Court review of the decisions of the Court of Claims is relatively infrequent, review of the decisions of the Court of Customs and Patent Appeals is rare,[7] and there is no provision for direct review by the Supreme Court of the decisions of the Court of Military Appeals.[8]

The Court of Military Appeals is exclusively concerned with questions of criminal law, and the other four courts are exclusively concerned with questions of civil law. Indeed, they so specialize in particular kinds of property rights that Supreme Court Justices

---

[7]For such a rare example, see *Gottschalk* v. *Benson and Tabbot,* 41 L.W. 4015 (November 20, 1972).

[8]In recent terms, the Supreme Court has considered on the merits an average of only about two cases per term from the Court of Claims, while denying or dismissing certiorari in over 90 percent of the petitions for review. During the period 1917–1945, the Supreme Court did accept jurisdiction in fourteen customs cases; but it has apparently reviewed only one such decision of the Court of Customs and Patent Appeals since then, just as since 1930 it apparently has granted certiorari in only one patent case on direct review from the Court of Customs and Patent Appeals. Both of these decisions were clustered within a week of each other in the latter part of March 1966: *Brenner* v. *Manson,* 383 U.S. 519 (the patent case), and *Clayton Chemical and Packaging Co.* v. *United States,* 383 U.S. 821 (the Customs [reappraisal] case). Similarly, the Supreme Court had not yet reviewed any decision of the Court of Military Appeals, until June 1969, in *O'Callahan* v. *Parker,* 395 U.S. 258. For a useful discussion of the military court system, see S. Sidney Ulmer, *Military Justice and the Right to Counsel* (Lexington, Ky.: University of Kentucky Press, 1970).

Douglas and Black argued that it was a denial of the constitutional rights of the accused for a retired judge of the Court of Customs and Patent Appeals to have presided by special assignment over the trial by the district court for the District of Columbia of a defendant who was convicted of armed robbery.[9]

Three of these courts are concerned with the administration of tax collection: the Tax Court specializes in internal revenue, and the Customs Court and the Court of Customs and Patent Appeals in external revenue. Only a part of the internal revenue code comes within the purview of the Tax Court, which functions through divisions, one for each of its judges. It works in the field, establishing terms and dockets in the larger cities where taxpayers have claims (against the Internal Revenue Service and vice versa) that remain unresolved after the extensive processes of administrative adjudication within the Treasury Department have been exhausted. The Customs Court conducts trials in New York City, and in other major ports. It is concerned primarily with reviewing appeals from administrative review of the decisions of customs collectors in regard to the amount of taxes due on imported merchandise. The Customs Court decided over 33,000 cases in 1971; a majority of these protested administrative decisions classifying goods (i.e., specifying the applicable tax rates), while most of the remainder protested appraisals (i.e., administrative assessments of the economic value of goods). The extent to which the Customs Court succeeded in performing its basic function—to settle the conflicting claims of taxpayers and the government—is in part suggested by examining how many of its cases remain undecided at the end of each year: the ten Customs Court judges had a backlog of 403,059 pending cases in June 1972. In the nineteenth century the path to modernization was seen as converting what had begun as a bureaucratic process into an explicitly judicial one; today modernization is found in a return to the administrative process. Retired Supreme Court Justice Tom Clark, reporting for the Federal Judicial Center in 1969 on a special study that had been made for the Judicial Conference, "noted that the tremendous backlog of cases before the Customs Court resulted from the enormous rise in imports and customs disputes, with which, he said, the [Customs] Court [ought] to deal using the procedures of an administrative agency, not those of a court."[10] He proposed a reduction in the number of cases filed, the consolidation of issues to be decided, the substitution of one-judge for three-judge trials, and the elimination of written opinions justifying decisions in most cases.

[9]*Lurk v. United States,* 360 U.S. 530, 589 (1962).
[10]*Congressional Quarterly Almanac,* 25 (1969), p. 913.

The Customs Courts Act of 1970 (Public Law 91-271), effective October 1, 1970, provides for a single judicial proceeding, known as a civil action, in which all issues, including both the classification and valuation of imported merchandise, may be presented. A civil action is commenced by the filing of a summons and the payment of a filing fee. Civil actions are tried and decided by a single judge, except when constitutional issues are involved or when there are broad and significant issues concerning the interpretation or administration of the customs laws. In such cases, and when so designated by the chief judge, a civil action may be heard and determined by three judges. Appeals from decisions in civil actions go directly to the Court of Customs and Patent Appeals.[11]

During fiscal 1972, the five judges of the Court of Customs and Patent Appeals decided less than two hundred cases in all—forty-seven cases on appeal from the Customs Court and over three times as many on appeal from the Board of Appeals (which acts for the Commissioner) of the Patent Office of the Commerce Department. The patent cases take the form of claims by inventors that the Patent Office wrongfully refused to issue to them the legally approved monopolies that they sought. Like the customs cases, they reach the Court of Customs and Patent Appeals only after extensive prior administrative adjudication. The district court of the District of Columbia provides an alternative forum for appeals on the question of patentability; and, in addition, there were scattered among the district courts in 1972 some 885 other patent litigations—conflicts over infringement in which the question of patentability often was raised as a defense, thus constituting what lawyers call a "collateral attack" upon the patent.[12]

There are many claims against the national government which allege that plaintiffs have suffered wrongs either (1) due to injuries, called "torts" (usually caused by the carelessness of governmental employees) or (2) due to the failure of governmental employers to carry out obligations to which the government previously had agreed in (usually, written) contracts. Under present legislation, most of the claims for property damages of less than $10,000 are settled by administrative adjudication by the executive departments most directly involved, while the district courts and the Court of Claims have concurrent jurisdiction to decide claims involving larger amounts and also appeals from the departmental

---

[11] *Annual Report of the Administrative Director for United States Courts for the Fiscal Year Ending June 30, 1971* (Washington: G.P.O., 1971), p. 394n.5.
[12] See Martin Shapiro, "The Supreme Court and the Patent Office," Chapter 3 in his *The Supreme Court and Administrative Agencies* (New York: The Free Press, 1968).

adjudications. In 1970–1971, the seven judges of the Court of Claims decided 382 cases, and had 179 others decided by commissioners, leaving over 1900 cases pending on the court's docket and about the same number pending on the commissioners' dockets. Most of these cases were concerned with tax, contract, or civilian pay claims. Notwithstanding the relatively wide publicity given to the handful of cases that the Supreme Court has decided during the past generation relating to the claims of Indian tribes for fair compensation for their long-lost hunting grounds, in 1970–1971 the Court of Claims decided only five such cases—which was only 1 percent of the total of its decisions for the year.

Since World War II the Court of Military Appeals, staffed by three civilian judges, has become the court of last resort within the system of military courts for appeals which used to go (at least in principle) directly to the President as commander in chief. This court has obligatory appellate jurisdiction on questions of "law" (policy) only—in all cases involving either (1) persons with the rank of brigadier general (or its equivalent) or higher, or (2) any person sentenced to execution. It also hears cases which the chief legal officer of each of the armed services wants reviewed, as well as cases it chooses from among petitions filed by defendants who have been sentenced by military courts to more than one year of imprisonment.

THE UNITED STATES SUPREME COURT

The Chief Justice of the United States and the eight associate justices of the United States Supreme Court are appointed for life terms by the President, with confirmation by the Senate, at salaries (currently, of $60,000 per year with an extra $2500 plus a limousine for the chief justice) second only to those of the President, and about the same as those for the Vice-President, members of the President's cabinet, and the Speaker of the House of Representatives. The Court convenes, exclusively *en banc*, from early October through the end of June, in the District of Columbia. Since the 1961 term, it has refused to review, by denying applications for writs of certiorari or by dismissing appeals, over two thousand cases annually; and by the early 1970s the yearly total of jurisdictional denials was more than 4000. About two thirds of the cases in which its review is sought come on petition for certiorari from the courts of appeals, as do almost a third of the cases that it selects for decision on the merits. A fourth of the latter are federal district court appeals; while about 40 percent are appeals or certioraris from state courts. Both "certiorari" and "appeal" are technical terms for the discretionary procedures by which the

Court selects the relatively much smaller number of cases—usually now about 350 per term—that it chooses to review; of these, about half are decided unanimously. The Court occasionally decides a case under what is called its "original" jurisdiction, and sometimes—as in the Tidelands Oil Cases of 1947 and 1950—such decisions are of considerable importance for the public policies at issue; but they constitute only a fraction of 1 percent of the cases on the Court's dockets in any term. There are also other procedures (certification and extraordinary writs) under which cases occasionally—usually, much less than 1 percent per term—are reviewed.

A clear majority of the Court's decisions consist of denials of certiorari to review the decisions of the courts of appeals and of state supreme courts in cases where the petitioners cannot pay the costs of review and therefore have filed *in forma pauperis,* a category which distinguishes those cases—now averaging several thousand per term—in which prisoners in national (and in recent years, to an even greater extent, in state) penal institutions seek to be released on the claim of illegalities in their trials. The celebrated case of Clarence Gideon, a penniless convict who sent directly to the United States Supreme Court a petition that he had scrawled with pencil and paper in his Florida jail cell, asserting that he had been denied counsel in his trial for having broken and robbed the cigarette machine of a pool hall in which he was employed, exemplifies but hardly typifies the grist of the Miscellaneous Docket mill. Gideon was one of the few needles that are discovered in that haystack; and the Supreme Court not only decided to hear his case, but it also assigned to represent him one of the best known, most successful, and reputedly brightest luminaries of the Washington bar—Abe Fortas. Fortas won a reversal for Gideon from the Supreme Court, which used this decision as a vehicle for the pronouncement of a new and liberalized norm of constitutional policy: that rich and poor defendants alike are entitled to be represented by a lawyer in state criminal trials. Subsequent by-products included the popularization of Gideon's trial by Anthony Lewis, the Pulitzer Prize-winning *New York Times* reporter who had since 1955 made the Supreme Court his "beat."[13] And although other considerations such as his long-standing and close friendship with President Lyndon Johnson certainly were involved in Fortas'

---

[13]*Gideon* v. *Wainright,* 372 U.S. 335 (1963); Anthony Lewis, *Gideon's Trumpet* (New York: Random House, Inc., 1964). Gideon had been convicted of a felony; another by-product came almost a decade later when provision of counsel was extended to include misdemeanor cases in which the defendant could be imprisoned: *Argersinger* v. *Hamlin,* 407 U.S. 25 (1972).

appointment to the Supreme Court in the year following the publication of Lewis' book (and two years after the Gideon decision), the favorable publicity that focused upon Fortas because of his successful representation of Gideon helped to make him seem a particularly attractive candidate for the Court in 1965. (It seemed inconceivable then that Fortas could become—as he was, in less than four years—the first Supreme Court justice ever forced to resign under fire.)

SUPPORTING ADMINISTRATIVE STRUCTURES

It is evident to anyone who visits the sumptuous marble palace in which the Supreme Court has worked since 1935, located on "the Hill" little more than the length of a football field from the Capitol, that there are many supporting players in addition to the nine stars who fill the most conspicuous public roles. Each justice has a secretary, and each has been allotted (since 1969) three administrative assistants or "law clerks," in most instances young honor graduates of the leading law schools.[14] The principal administrative officer is the Clerk of the Supreme Court. There are also the librarian, the marshal, the reporter, and their staffs, messengers, bailiffs, and custodial employees. The custodial staff for the new building remained stable at thirty-three persons during the years 1957–1972, while the administrative staff of the Court (which had more than doubled during the two decades from 1937 to 1957 following the move) had grown to over two hundred and fifty by 1972. It would be impossible for each of the nine justices to participate in deciding almost five thousand cases each year without the assistance of the administrative staff and the physical facilities made available with the help of the custodial staff. For each justice, there are on the average about twenty-five persons in the supporting administrative structure.

For the other federal courts, there are over 8000 supporting personnel in the administrative category alone; and in a broader sense, the entire Department of Justice provides a supporting administrative structure for the federal courts. Beyond that, there are thousands of private attorneys throughout the country who, having been admitted to practice before the federal courts, technically are considered to be "officers of the court." These private

[14]The most recent discussions appear to be Chester A. Newland, "Personal Assistants to Supreme Court Justices: The Law Clerks," *Oregon Law Review* 40 (1961), pp. 299–317; and *Report of the Study Group on the Caseload of the Supreme Court* (Washington: The Federal Judicial Center, December 1972), pp. 43–45.

attorneys (together with the United States attorneys) assume most of the initiative in the process of judicial decision making, particularly in the trial courts. The bar tends to specialize, on a subject matter and/or a geographical basis[15] (for practice in the district courts and courts of appeals) and on a functional basis (for practice before the courts with specialized functions). Thus there are lawyer-specialists who comprise the tax bar, the customs bar, the claims bar, and the patent bar—although many of the practitioners of the patent bar are formally educated as engineers rather than as lawyers. Finally, the even larger number of laymen who enter into court proceedings in the roles of litigant, witness, juror, and audience should be considered a part of the supporting administrative structure for judicial decision making.[16]

THE JUDICIAL CONFERENCE OF THE UNITED STATES

The principal policy-making group for the national judiciary is the Judicial Conference of the United States, which was authorized by statute in 1922 and has met at least once a year since then. The conference is composed of both ex officio and elected members: (1) the fourteen chief judges of the Supreme Court, the courts of appeals, the Court of Claims, and the Court of Customs and Patent Appeals; and (2) eleven district judges, one of whom is elected by each of the analogous circuit judicial councils. The Chief Justice of the Supreme Court chairs the conference in his capacity as Chief Justice of the United States. Most of the other ex officio members of the conference are in effect selected on the basis of seniority, since the chief circuit judges are so selected. Conferences typically last for one or two days and are held in the District of Columbia, in recent years semiannually. Their agenda ranges from the broadest questions of policy (e.g., disapproving a proposed revision of the federal Administrative Procedure Act) to the minutiae of judicial administration (e.g., raising from $200 to $500 the salary of the part-time magistrate at Rutland and Brattleboro, Vermont). Verbatim transcripts of proceedings are not published; instead, there is a summary of the decisions, which tends to suggest—doubtless quite falsely—that all decisions are reached not

[15]See, for example, Charles Horsky, *The Washington Lawyer* (Boston: Little, Brown and Company, 1952); Erwin O. Smigel, *The Wall Street Lawyer* (New York: The Free Press of Glencoe, 1964); and Martin Mayer, *The Lawyers* (New York: Harper & Row, Inc., 1966).
[16]Delmar Karlen, *The Citizen in Court: Litigant, Witness, Juror, Judge* (New York: Holt, Rinehart & Winston, Inc., 1964).

only consensually but also unanimously. These summaries, together with a transmittal statement from the chief justice to the
Congress, emphasizing the conference's policy recommendations
for legislation, are published in the same volume with the annual
report of the director of the Administrative Office of the United
States Courts.

A more general legislative function of the conference is its role
in the formulation of rules of procedure for the federal courts.
The conference is a major decision-making group but since 1958
has been only one among many in the widespread process of
consultation that is associated with this particular policy-making
function. The formulation or revision of such "rules" (which is the
term lawyers use to describe the legal norms, analogous to statutes,
that are made by judges or executive agencies) is preceded by the
establishment of study groups consisting of committees of technical
specialists, including practicing attorneys, judges, and law professors; such professional organizations as the Association of American Law Schools, the American Judicature Society, and the American Bar Association and its state affiliates cooperate with the
conference in staffing the study groups. The Federal Judicial
Center, the Administrative Office of the United States Courts, the
Department of Justice, and state attorneys general present their
views to the study groups, whose published recommendations to
the conference are given broad circulation among the legal and
related professions prior to action by the conference. After the
conference has approved a set of rules, those rules are sent to the
Supreme Court—the statutory rule-making agency—for its (pro
forma) approval and then transmitted to Congress. Initially, the
rules of civil procedure and of criminal procedure were transmitted through the attorney general, but now this is done directly
by the chief justice. Unless Congress disapproves, they become
effective at the end of ninety days. Congress has not yet adopted
any such disapproving resolution, and in view of the widespread
process of antecedent professional consultation, it seems very
unlikely that the conference would recommend a rule so controversial that it would be politically possible to get Congress to
nullify it. Moreover, lawyers constitute the principal occupational
group in Congress, and there is immense prestige (at least among
lawyers) associated with the work of the conference. Both that
prestige and the factors of inertia that make it difficult to get any
kind of resolution through two houses of Congress within ninety
days make such disapproval most unlikely, quite apart from the
substantive merits of any particular rule.

The rules of procedure for both the lower federal courts and
the Supreme Court are published along with the decisions of the

Supreme Court in the *United States Reports*[17] and with the statutes of Congress in the *United States Code.* This arrangement suggests the ambivalent status of the rules—structurally an output of the judicial system, but functionally most analogous to the acts of Congress which (in terms of their substantive content) they have tended to displace. The Supreme Court's rules were generally revised as recently as 1967, although the Court from the outset has made its own rules of procedure under a delegation of authority in the Judiciary Act of 1789. The areas of policy making for the lower federal courts and the dates on which the Supreme Court first exercised the powers transferred to it by Congress are indicated in the following: "Rules of Practice in Admiralty and Maritime Cases" (1854); "General Orders and Forms in Bankruptcy" (1898); "Rules of Civil Procedure for the United States District Courts" (1938); and "Rules of Criminal Procedure for the United States District Courts" (1945).

At least twice a year there is convened in each circuit a judicial council, which discusses many of the same policy questions that come before the national conference, as well as matters of primary interest to a particular circuit. Such councils, presided over by the chief circuit judges assigned to the circuit, consist of the district and circuit judges assigned to the circuit, and sometimes selected members of the bar. Almost a generation after the position of state judicial administrator had become common, action finally was taken (by statute, late in 1970) to authorize the appointment of a "circuit court executive" to assist each chief circuit judge in carrying out his administrative and managerial functions. A similar bill to provide an administrative assistant to the chief justice of the Supreme Court passed the House in 1971, but died in the Senate the following year.

[17]For examples of the promulgation of ninety-day rules, see the "Federal Rules of Appellate Procedure" effective July 1, 1968, 389 U.S. 1063; the "Amendments to the Rules of Civil Procedure for the United States District Courts" effective July 1, 1966, 383 U.S. 1029, and July 1, 1968, 389 U.S. 1121; and the "Amendments to the Rules of Criminal Procedure for the United States District Courts" effective July 1, 1966, 383 U.S. 1087, and July 1, 1968, 389 U.S. 1125. However, certain other rules (such as the bankruptcy rules and those applying to magistrates trying minor offenses) go into effect (like the Court's own rules) directly upon promulgation by the Supreme Court, instead of being reported to Congress with a delay of three months before they become effective; for examples, see the "Revised Rules of the United States Supreme Court" effective October 2, 1967, 388 U.S. 927, and the "Federal Rules of Procedure for United States Magistrates" effective May 19, 1969, 395 U.S. 989.

THE ADMINISTRATIVE OFFICE OF THE UNITED STATES COURTS

The Administrative Office was established by Congress in 1939 as a direct consequence of President Franklin Roosevelt's political attack upon the Supreme Court in 1937, when he accused the Court of administrative inefficiency, caused by the superannuation of the justices. The Supreme Court appoints the director and the deputy director of the Administrative Office. This is intended to assure that the justices will be able to maintain policy control over the Administrative Office, which is designated by the statute to be an agency of the Judicial Conference of the United States. The question of who exercises policy control over whom is of some interest, considering the scope and depth of the "housekeeping functions" that the Administrative Office has come to exercise for the courts of appeals and district courts. Except for the Supreme Court, for which similar functions are performed by its own clerk's office, the Administrative Office centrally directs and manages many court operations. It controls the hiring and compensation of subordinate personnel, i.e., all except the judges. It collects and analyzes information concerning dockets and workload; compiles and distributes to the chief circuit judges reports for purposes of statistical control over decision-making activities; supervises the pay of the judges and provides office facilities and supplies for the lower national courts; administers an annuity system for judicial retirees; and supervises the preparation of budgets by court clerks and audits their accounts. It also supervises the accounts of federal probation officers and federal administrators appointed under the Bankruptcy Act. (The federal district judges act, in effect, as foremen for the administration of the national probation and bankruptcy systems.) It submits annual public reports to the Judicial Conference, the Congress, and the attorney general; and it publishes, in cooperation with the Bureau of Prisons of the Department of Justice, the journal *Federal Probation,* which is devoted to "correctional philosophy and practice." It has also arranged seminars in which experienced federal judges orient newly appointed judges.[18] These seminars were in addition to sentencing institutes, which the Administrative Office helped to arrange in the early 1960s on an individual or a joint-circuit basis. In effect, the Administrative Office came to perform the general function of a brain for the national judicial system. However, many of the functions of research, innovation and development, plan-

---

[18]Beverly Blair Cook, "The Socialization of New Federal Judges: Impact on District Court Business," *Washington University Law Quarterly* (1971), pp. 253–279; also her "Perceptions of the Independent Trial Judge Role in the Seventh Circuit," *Law and Society Review* 6 (May 1972), pp. 615–629.

FIGURE 1

The Judicial Dollar

Obligations Incurred*-Fiscal Year 1972

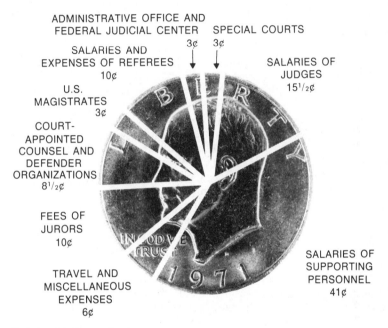

ADMINISTRATIVE OFFICE AND
FEDERAL JUDICIAL CENTER   SPECIAL COURTS
3¢   3¢
SALARIES AND
EXPENSES OF REFEREES   SALARIES OF
10¢   JUDGES
U.S.   15½¢
MAGISTRATES
3¢
COURT-
APPOINTED
COUNSEL AND
DEFENDER
ORGANIZATIONS
8½¢

FEES OF
JURORS
10¢
SALARIES OF
SUPPORTING
TRAVEL AND   PERSONNEL
MISCELLANEOUS   41¢
EXPENSES
6¢

*Exclusive of the Supreme Court

Source: Administrative Office of the United States Courts, 1972 *Annual Report of the Director*, p. 212.

ning, continuing judicial education, and training of other than judicial personnel of the federal courts, which the Administrative Office had been carrying out, were transferred to a new Federal Judicial Center, established late in 1967. The Judicial Center will increasingly assume, it is presumed, the function of principal staff agency for the Judicial Conference of the United States, thereby returning the Administrative Office to such housekeeping functions as assuring adequate court facilities and supplies, paying salaries and travel expenses, and processing associated fiscal records. Figure 1 indicates the overall allocation of costs for the operations of the federal judiciary (except for the Supreme Court) during the 1972 fiscal year.

THE DEPARTMENT OF JUSTICE

The Attorney General of the United States is the political

administrator of a large organization, most of whose activities are indispensable to the functioning of the federal courts. In fiscal 1971, the department included over 43,000 people whose activities involved the expenditure of over one and a quarter billion dollars. Its organization chart depicts four levels of administrative structure: (1) a primary level, consisting of the attorney general and deputy attorney general and their offices, the solicitor general, the legal counsel, the pardon attorney, and the Public Information Office; (2) a secondary level, consisting of eight divisions (administrative, tax, civil, lands and natural resources, antitrust, criminal, civil rights, and internal security), each headed by an assistant attorney general; (3) a tertiary level, consisting of four bureaus (investigation, narcotics and dangerous drugs, prisons [and the related Federal Prison Industries, Inc.], and the Immigration and Naturalization Service) plus the Community Relations Service and the Law Enforcement Assistance Administration; and (4) a fourth level, including the Board of Parole, the Board of Immigration Appeals, and the United States marshals and attorneys.

From a functional point of view, however, the department is better conceptualized as three subsystem structures. The major function of one of these subsystems is political; that of the second is direct police operations; and that of the third is interaction with the national courts. The political subsystem can be further subdivided in terms of external and internal orientation. Thus the Community Relations Service (CRS) is almost exclusively oriented outside of the department; while the Office of Legal Counsel (until 1972 headed by William Rehnquist, who is now a Supreme Court justice) is concerned mostly with giving legal advice to the President and other executive agencies, although it also provides house counsel for the Department of Justice. The administrative division is primarily concerned with intradepartmental activities, and both the attorney general and the deputy attorney general have dual responsibilities. The second or police subsystem is concerned with the surveillance, apprehension, and custody of persons who, as suspects in cases of either ordinary or political crime, are deemed to constitute an actual or potential danger to national order and security. This subsystem consists of the four bureaus, which conduct direct—primarily field—operations; the criminal and internal security divisions; the Law Enforcement Assistance Administration; and the two appeals boards (parole and immigration) and the pardon attorney. The courts subsystem includes the solicitor general, five divisions whose job is litigation management in behalf of the national government (tax, antitrust, lands, civil, and civil rights), and the United States attorneys and marshals (who are officers of the district courts throughout the country).

The relative importance that is attached by Congress to these various functions is suggested by the amounts of their respective budgets. In 1968 the lion's share of the departmental budget, some $195 million or about 44 percent of the total, went to the Federal Bureau of Investigation, whose director, J. Edgar Hoover, was, at the time of his demise in 1972, rounding out almost fifty years of continuous service as F.B.I. chief. But this had changed within three years to such an extent that the F.B.I.'s share, although $100,000 larger than in 1968, was no longer the biggest within the department but had dropped to less than a fourth of the total budget for Justice. Meanwhile the Law Enforcement Assistance Administration escalated from less than 2 percent in 1968 to over half a billion dollars (over 42 percent) in 1971—because, of course, it functioned primarily to channel massive federal grants to state and local governments, under the Omnibus Crime Control Acts of 1968 and 1970. Two of the three other bureaus, the Immigration and Naturalization Service and the Bureau of Prisons, received $122 million (10 percent) and $125 million (also 10 percent) in 1971; while notwithstanding the sharp rise beginning in the late sixties, in both the use of narcotics and arrests for their illegal use (Figure 2), less than 4 percent went to the Bureau of Narcotics and Dangerous Drugs, established in 1968 by the consolidation of two bureaus, from Treasury and from Health, Education and Welfare. The remaining 10 percent went to pay the costs of all of the rest of the department: general administration and legal activities, the seven divisions, the attorneys and marshals in the field, the fees and expenses of government witnesses, the Community Relations Service, and the other boards and offices that comprise the superstructure of the departmental organization. Evidently, the detection of crime and the incarceration of criminals are the most costly functions of the department, while those of interaction with the judicial and administrative and political systems at all levels of government are relatively inexpensive to support.

The attorney general's principal function is to represent the Department of Justice in relations with the President, the Congress, the Supreme Court, other political administrators both outside and inside the department, and the public—that is, to represent the department in interactions at the policy level with other actors in the major subsystems of the national political system. In effect, these functions of representation are divided among the attorney general's principal associates: the assistant attorney general who is legal counsel works with the Executive Office of the President and with other administrative agencies; the solicitor general represents the department before the Supreme Court; the assistant attorney general in charge of the administrative division is concerned with interrelationships among the administrative units of the department; and the deputy attorney

FIGURE 2

Narcotic Drug Law Arrests

Rate Per 100,000 Population

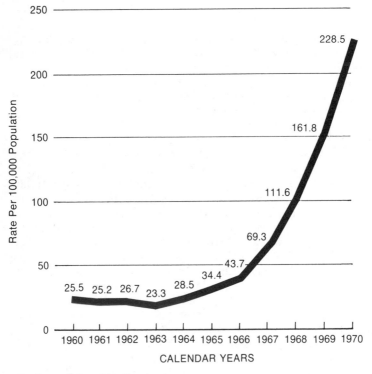

Data Source: Uniform Crime Report

Source: *Annual Report of the Attorney General of the United States for the fiscal year 1971*, p. 125

general shares much of the attorney general's responsibility for interaction with Congress, particularly in regard to interstitial procedures that have become routinized.

In a sense, the deputy attorney general is the department's chief lobbyist with the national legislative system, just as the solicitor general is the chief lobbyist with the national judicial system and the legal counsel with the national administrative system. It is the deputy attorney general who handles the screening of all nominations for the federal judiciary, and it is he who presents the department's policy views, for which there are several thousand requests annually, on the clearance of pending and enrolled bills. He also supervises the activities of the United States attorneys, and the United States marshals, while the assistant attorney general in charge of the administrative division provides both groups with supporting administrative services; there is an attorney and a marshal (plus their staffs) attached to each district court. An example of such supervision is the direction of the activities of the task force of marshals who were assembled and flown to Oxford, Mississippi, in September 1962 to enforce James Meredith's claim of constitutional right to enroll as a student of political science at the University of Mississippi. A quite different and considerably less well publicized responsibility of the deputy attorney general is the department's recruitment program for honor law graduates.

The legal counsel prepares formal opinions of the attorney general, provides informal opinions and legal advice to the agencies of the national administrative system, and reviews various kinds of executive legislation, such as executive orders, presidential proclamations, and presidential regulations. The administrative division conducts the business management operations of the department, including budgeting and auditing, personnel, records control, and the departmental library.

The courts subsystem of the department interacts primarily with the rest of the federal judicial system, of which it must certainly be considered an integral component. The solicitor general personally argues certain cases before the Supreme Court, in order to emphasize their policy significance, while members of his staff represent the federal government in all other Supreme Court cases to which the United States is a party litigant. He also can and does intervene, through what are called *amicus curiae* (friend of the court) briefs, to present the administration's policy views in cases between private parties. Moreover, he has an important influence in deciding which private interest groups will be permitted to present their own policy views to the Court through *amicus* briefs and oral argument. The federal government participates in almost half of all of the cases that the Supreme Court decides on the merits of the substantive issues presented, and in the 1970 term, for example, the "United States" participated in three fifths (89 of 151) of the argued cases. Therefore, the career staff of the solicitor general's office has come to acquire a considerable advantage over private counsel in terms of experience, expertise, and prestige. The solicitor general also is in a much better position than private counsel to pick and choose the time, place, and circumstances under which he will push a policy issue to decision by the Supreme Court. The latter advantage stems from the solicitor general's power to manipulate the issues that will be considered by appellate courts; without his approval, the federal government can appeal to a higher court no case to which it is a party. The appellate sections of the departmental divisions exercise a prior veto over both appeals in such cases from district courts to the courts of appeals, and federal agency requests for appellate judicial review; and the Office of the Solicitor General rejects two fifths of the requests for Supreme Court certiorari that are recommended by the appellate sections. In 1962, for example, the solicitor general's office authorized 930 appeals (of which about a third were granted) from district courts to courts of appeals, while in 1968 the Supreme Court granted two thirds of the certioraris that the solicitor general approved from lower courts. An earlier study showed that in the 1950s the Court granted only about 6 percent of the petitions filed by private litigants, while approving over half of those petitions supported by the solicitor general.[19] During the 1970s as had been true also in the 1960s, the solicitor general's staff (1) participated in over a third of *all* cases docketed by the Supreme Court; (2) participated in well over half the cases that went to oral argument; and (3) was successful in about two thirds of the cases decided on the merits. Thus the solicitor general is by far the most frequent, as well as one of the most successful, of the lobbyists with the Supreme Court. The details of his current record of wins and losses are reported in the latest issue of the attorney general's *Annual Report*.

The courts subsystem of the Justice Department includes five divisions. Antitrust deals primarily with the control of monopolistic business organizational structures and practices, partly through litigation but to an even greater extent through negotiated settlements. Many of the antitrust prosecutions that do go to litigation result in policy decisions at the level of the Supreme Court, but there are exceptions. In February 1961, for example, the district court for the Pennsylvania Eastern District (Philadelphia) made an unreported[20] decision approving an antitrust decree against the

[19]Joseph Tanenhaus, Marvin Schick, Matthew Muraskin, and Daniel Rosen, "The Supreme Court's Certiorari Jurisdiction: Cue Theory," Chapter 5 in *Judicial Decision-Making*, ed. Glendon Schubert (New York: The Free Press of Glencoe, 1963). Cf. S. Sidney Ulmer, William Hintze, and Louise Kirklosky, "The Decision to Grant or Deny Certiorari: Further Consideration of Cue Theory," *Law and Society Review* 6 (May 1972), pp. 637–643; and S. Sidney Ulmer, "The Decision to Grant Certiorari as an Indicator to Decision 'On the Merits,'" *Polity* 4 (Summer 1972), pp. 429–447.

[20]See p. 116 for an explanation of the reporting of federal judicial decisions.

heavy electrical equipment industry for conspiracy to combine to fix prices. In the following year, over 1700 private suits for treble damages were filed against the industry by customers in thirty-three different federal judicial districts located in twenty-four states and the District of Columbia.

The civil division deals with a miscellany of policy issues, including the following categories of cases: admiralty and shipping; tort and contract claims against the government; fraud; patents; customs; and the defense of suits to avoid military service. During 1968, civil division attorneys and members of the ninety-three United States attorneys' staffs were involved in thirty-one thousand general civil litigation cases (in addition to custom and alien property matters), of which some 736 were decided in federal appellate courts (with the civil division "winning" 85 percent of these).

The tax division's primary function is to represent the Internal Revenue Service (IRS) of the Treasury Department in civil and criminal litigation in both the state and federal courts (except for the United States Tax Court, in which attorneys of the Treasury Department's Office of General Counsel represent the IRS). Tax division attorneys closed over 10,000 cases in 1971, winning over three fourths of the 1000-odd that were pursued to judgment, in both the district courts and the courts of appeals. The land and natural resources division traditionally has been concerned with the very slow and complicated litigation relating to claims for and against government ownership of real property, Indian lands, water rights, and other natural resources. The federal government claims title to some 768 million acres of land, about a third of all the land in the United States, and each year the aggregate of funds the federal government pays in settlements and judgments in land condemnation cases *exceeds* what it expends for *all* other settlements and judgments in federal courts. To protect the government's large financial interest in this field of policy and litigation, the land and natural resources division employs over a hundred lawyers in Washington and half a dozen or so in the field (where the land is located). By 1968 this division had begun to take a more active interest in problems of interstate air and water pollution; and by 1970 the land and natural resources division had established a pollution control section, and, for the first time since the enactment of the Refuse Act of 1899, undertook to abate the pollution of navigable waters by filing during 1971 over fifty civil suits and almost two hundred criminal prosecutions. The division also enforces such related legislation as the National Environmental Policy Act of 1969.

The other division in the courts subsystem is the civil rights division, which initiated and sponsored the litigation of many of the most important Supreme Court decisions in the two decades after the end of World War II. Among the components of judicial policy that the civil rights division helped to shape are (1) elections and the right to vote, as this relates both to legislative reapportionment and to racial nondiscrimination, and (2) other aspects of racial nondiscrimination, e.g., schools and hospitals receiving funds from the national government, interstate transportation facilities such as airports and railroad and bus terminals, sit-ins, and employment discrimination. The Department of Justice has defined its mission in regard to civil rights as "to work toward the day when the quality of American life will no longer be marred by discrimination against any of our people on account of their race, color, national origin, sex, or religion."[21] The division had been reorganized in 1968 so that its efforts and resources—which had previously been largely concentrated on discrimination in voting, public accommodations, and public school systems in southern states—could be more fully directed to civil rights problems in the northern and western areas of the country, such as employment discrimination in cities outside of the South. Then the division's staff was increased, by more than 50 percent in 1971 (above the 1968 levels) to more than three hundred persons of whom over half are lawyers; and the program areas that received particularly rapid expansion were housing, voting, and interference with civil rights; much more modest development took place for the areas of housing and public accommodations and facilities, while there was a one-third decrease in the number of employment cases filed. Over half of the approximately two hundred new civil rights cases in which the division became involved in 1971 concerned the first group of issues, which had comprised less than a fifth of the one hundred new cases filed in 1968. The Community Relations Service differs from the Civil Rights Division not in goals but in methods: while the division employs the more traditional techniques of litigation, the CRS has a frankly political role, which it plays by undertaking negotiations with, and mediation among, blacks and other groups involved in race-related conflicts and disputes, particularly in urban slum areas. Thus CRS attempted to minimize the friction and violence associated with the Poor People's Campaign and the March on Washington of 1968; and CRS during 1971 provided, for 335 cities in twenty-seven states, conciliators in 836 crisis situations arising out of problems in police-

---

[21]Attorney General of the United States, *Annual Report, 1968* (Washington, D.C.: United States Department of Justice, 1968), p. 59.

community relations, unemployment, housing, and school desegregation. CRS claimed (for example) to have been instrumental in blocking the demolition of 3500 homes with consequent massive relocation of the persons who lived in them, incident to the planned construction of a crosstown expressway in Philadelphia that was viewed by minority residents as a device to build a buffer between themselves and the downtown business community. Instead, HUD (the Department of Housing and Urban Development) was persuaded to expedite the grant of three million dollars in Neighborhood Development Program funds to upgrade the district as a place of residence instead of converting it to a roadway for automobiles.

The police subsystem preempts the greater part of the department's fiscal and personnel resources: over half a billion dollars (43 percent) of the budget and over three fourths (over thirty thousand) of all departmental employees. This subsystem is built around the activities of the three large operating bureaus. The thousands of special agents and supporting personnel of the F.B.I. are mostly decentralized among some sixty field offices and over four hundred suboffices. The substantive concerns of the F.B.I. range from certain ordinary crimes (bank robbery, interstate transportation of stolen motor vehicles, income tax evasion, and so forth), to organized racketeering, the protection of civil rights, and investigation of what the late J. Edgar Hoover's valedictory report referred to as "The Extremist New Left" (which had displaced, at least temporarily, the Communist party as the focus for F.B.I. extirpation of subversion). The F.B.I. is also concerned with the training of state and local police employees, the maintenance of a national laboratory for scientific crime detection (which contains a nationwide fingerprint identification clearing house, sponsors research in the forensic sciences, etc.), and the publication of such documents as *Uniform Crime Reports,* a national compilation of statistics on the detection of crime and the arrest of suspects. In its crime detection work, the F.B.I. places considerable reliance upon a network of mostly paid but undercover agents. In 1971 the F.B.I. claimed 13,357 convictions based on its investigations, and the recovery of over $475 million returned to the government in fines, savings, and other recoveries.

The two divisions that work most closely with the F.B.I. are criminal and internal security, which specialize in the prosecution of "ordinary" and of "political" crime, respectively. The criminal division enforces national criminal law, including acts of Congress and administrative regulations and decisions of the federal courts relating to organized racketeering, interstate commerce (such as concerning aircraft highjacking), the postal business, government officials (viz., bribery), national territories and maritime jurisdiction, frauds against the government, national banks, stock exchanges, and taxation. The internal security division is concerned with espionage, seditious activity, the Communist party and its various "front" organizations, and other organizations with extremist political goals or methods of operations. Thus, for example, the criminal division was responsible for enforcement of the Gun Control Act of 1968, as a consequence of which firearms prosecutions increased more than 300 percent during fiscal 1970 and 1971, while in the latter year alone some 2200 indictments were filed leading to more than 1200 convictions of gun violations. The internal security division, on the other hand, was concerned with such matters as the prosecution of the Ellsberg-*Times-Post* cases in regard to the disclosure of the "Pentagon [Position] Papers" on United States participation in the Vietnam war, the prosecution of the Phillip Berrigan group on charges of plotting to blow up the House Office Building and kidnap Kissinger, and violations generally of the selective service acts.

Approximately twenty thousand—a population level that remained relatively stable—federal prisoners were confined, in 1971, in some thirty-odd correctional facilities: five for long-term adults, five others for intermediate-term adults, and seven for short-term adults; seven for young adults and three for juvenile and youth offenders; two for female offenders; one medical center and eight community treatment centers. Two camps for minimum custody offenders were added in 1971. In recent years, the Bureau of Prisons has placed increasing emphasis upon rehabilitation as the overriding goal of confinement. It has, for example, moved away from traditional classroom instruction and toward individual instruction specifically prescribed for each inmate, using learning laboratories, team teaching, and other up-to-date educational media and techniques. Increasingly, the Bureau has become influenced by the social sciences, particularly sociology and psychology, and by social work concepts and approaches,[22] as evidenced by the planning for a behavioral research center (for mentally disturbed and violent offenders) which the Bureau expects to open in Butner, N.C., in 1975. The current treatment of inmates who are narcotic addicts includes confinement in institutions that provide specialized treatment programs and units. A work-release program begun in 1965 makes it possible for approximately 10 percent of the inmate population to hold regular jobs in communities during

[22]See C. Ray Jeffery, *Crime Prevention Through Environmental Design* (Beverly Hills, California: Sage Publications, Inc., 1971).

the day, returning to institutions for confinement at night. The community treatment centers provide, for offenders who are nearing release, a supervised environment and programs to help them make a successful readjustment in their home communities. The Bureau also operates an employment placement program which finds jobs for approximately five thousand of the prisoners released annually.

About half as many offenders as are kept under some form of confinement are permitted to complete their sentences under parole supervision. The decisions as to whether a confined offender should be released on parole and how long his parole status should be continued are made by the Board of Parole and its staff, a Department of Justice organizational unit that is independent of the Bureau of Prisons but works in close cooperation with the Bureau. The Parole Board also works with the United States Probation Service (a subdivision under the director of the Administrative Office of the United States Courts) because it is the probation officers who provide such parole services as prerelease investigations, supervision of released prisoners in the community, and reports to the Board concerning the progress of parolees.

During fiscal 1972 the 640 federal probation officers made some 67,607 investigations, of which over 40 percent were done for presentencing purposes, while an additional 28 percent were made for other needs of the federal district courts. The remainder were carried out for the federal Bureau of Prisons and the Board of Parole, or for United States attorneys in juvenile cases. Notwithstanding the considerable emphasis upon noninstitutional community care of convicted criminal defendants, and the ideal of rehabilitative justice, both of which have received much nationwide publicity in recent years, the number of field probation officers remained unchanged from 1967 to 1971, and was only about a sixth larger in 1971 than it had been a decade earlier. Moreover, the average number of supervised cases per officer, and also the average number of presentence investigations per officer, *both* were *smaller* in 1971 than a decade earlier, despite the remarkable stability in the size of the field probation staff. A couple of dozen positions finally were added in 1972, for the entire country; but this less than 4 percent increase in personnel was more than compensated for by the 16 percent increase in caseload. One can only wonder how the rehabilitation of no longer institutionalized federal offenders was taking place—and who was doing the job.

Yet another channel for politico-legal reconsideration of the convictions of federal offenders is provided by the Office of the Pardon Attorney, which is attached directly to the Office of the Attorney General. Throughout the Eisenhower and most of the Kennedy-Johnson administrations the pardon attorney had recommended that the President exercise "executive clemency" by pardoning, or by commuting the sentences of, about a third of the six hundred-odd convicted federal offenders who annually sought this form of review of their status. But the ratio of affirmative exercise dropped suddenly to less than 4 percent in Lyndon Johnson's last year in office, and he and Richard Nixon then combined to set some sort of modern (at least) record for non-clemency, as 505 requests were denied and *none* was granted, for either pardon or commutation, during fiscal 1969. In fiscal 1971 Nixon granted 157 pardons and sixteen commutations, which together comprised 21 percent of the total requests upon which he acted in that year.

The fourth bureau, the Immigration and Naturalization Service, deals with the admission, exclusion, and deportation of nonresident aliens and with the naturalization of resident aliens. In 1971 about 300,000 aliens were denied entry, while 370,000 others were admitted as permanent residents, and over 100,000 persons of 146 different nationalities became naturalized American citizens.

The Board of Immigration Appeals is in effect an administrative court, composed of persons who do not have the formal status of judges but whose function—and, increasingly, procedures—are very similar to those of courts. In 1968, for example, the Board of Immigration Appeals decided some 1900 cases, in about a third of which it disagreed with the action taken by the Immigration and Naturalization Service. (The volume of litigation had increased to over 3200 by 1971; but by then the Board no longer saw fit to publish the extent to which its decisions were in agreement with those of the Immigration and Naturalization Service.) These were cases relating to the status of aliens, and the typical question was whether a specific nonresident alien should be deported from the country. In all such cases, there were extensive hearings and investigations undertaken by the Immigration and Naturalization Service before this relatively small proportion of the total caseload of the bureau—considerably less than 1 percent—was appealed to the board. Thus the function of the board is hardly distinguishable in a procedural sense from that of such specialized national courts as the Customs Court or the Tax Court. We might well infer that the Board of Parole and the Board of Immigration Appeals represent an intermediate evolutionary stage, and the Tax Court of the United States a later stage, of a process of institutional development which, at a still later stage, is recognized as having culminated in a full-fledged court such as the Customs Court. Certainly such an inference is perfectly compatible with the known natural history of these and other adjudicatory subcomponents of the national judicial system.[23] (This analogy was extended, and perhaps further supported, by the "modernization" of the Customs Court in 1970 which, as previously noted, in the present stage of its evolution is emphasizing an *administrative* approach to its workload problems—and hence a step toward reverting to its origins and youth as a subordinate administrative bureau.)

[23]Several studies have been made of adjudicatory processes in administrative agencies, using theories and methods of analysis that were developed in research into judicial behavior: Bradley C. Canon, "Voting Behavior on the FCC," *Midwest Journal of Political Science* 13 (1969), pp. 587–612, covers the period during the sixties when Judge Loevinger was a commissioner, and therefore the analysis includes his voting behavior; William P. Yohe, "A Study of Federal Open Market Committee Voting, 1955–64," *Southern Economic Journal* 32 (1966), pp. 396–405, is a similar inquiry into voting behavior in one of the principal policy-making groups of the Federal Reserve System.

CHAPTER THREE

Federal
Judicial Functions

INTERCHANGE BETWEEN FEDERAL AND STATE SYSTEMS

The continuously expanding scope of policy making by the federal courts, particularly during the present century, has been primarily a reflection of the expansion in the policy-making responsibilities of the legislative and administrative systems of the federal government. It was probably inevitable that, once the other two major subsystems of the national political system were committed to a course of big government, with substantially greater public management of both the economy and society, the judicial system would be forced to accept and accommodate to such major changes. It was not inevitable, however, that the federal judiciary in general, and the Supreme Court in particular, should have emerged in mid-century as the most dynamic force for socio-politico-economic change—in such major policy fields as racial equality and fair procedure—to which the national legislative and executive-administrative systems as well as the state political systems would have to accommodate *their* own actions.

Notwithstanding this sharp increase in policy making by the federal courts, it remains true that in terms of both qualitative and quantitative criteria, an even greater amount of policy is made by the fifty state judicial systems.[1] The volume of decisions made by the state courts is many times greater than the output of the federal courts, and it is the state judicial systems—not the federal—which have the function of resolving most of the litigational problems that arise in the lives of most of the people in the United States. These problems include (but are by no means limited to) conflicts involving marriage, divorce, the custody of children and the mentally ill, and other legal aspects of domestic relations; petty and grand theft, embezzlement, assault, robbery, breaking and entry, homicide, rape, forgery, auto theft, disorderly conduct, and other common crimes and misdemeanors; real property, negotiable instruments, sales, torts, contracts, and other business relationships; vagrancy, inebriation, sexual deviance, gambling, narcotics, and other "morals" offenses; industrial accidents, workmen's compensation, motor vehicle accidents, and other kinds of personal injury and property damage; and labor-management relations, corporate organization, competitive practices, and other aspects of business practice.

The subject categories of the cases typically decided by the federal judicial system will be analyzed later in this chapter. Some of the categories relate to conflicts that rarely if ever are decided in state judicial systems; they constitute what lawyers call the "exclusive jurisdiction" of the federal courts. Examples are suits between two or more states, or between a state and the United States, a petition of a federal regulatory commission asking a court to decree the enforcement of the commission's decisions, or a prosecution for a violation of the federal criminal law. State courts do not decide questions of "exclusive federal jurisdiction," except occasionally through what lawyers call "collateral attack" (in cases over which a state court otherwise has jurisdiction such as the settlement of an estate, against which another state or the United States has a tax claim).

The converse of this proposition, however, is not true. Almost any question of "state jurisdiction" can—and a small proportion do—become redefined as a matter of federal jurisdiction, because of the overlapping bases of national jurisdiction. The jurisdiction of the federal courts is defined partly in terms of "parties" (i.e., who is suing or being sued by whom), and partly in terms of "subjects" (i.e., maritime, bankruptcy, taxation, and so forth). Moreover, as

[1]For an excellent and comprehensive discussion, see Henry R. Glick and Kenneth N. Vines, *State Court Systems* (Englewood Cliffs, N.J.: Prentice-Hall, Inc., 1973); and in particular regard to metropolitan criminal courts, see Martin A. Levin, "Urban Politics and Judicial Behavior," *Journal of Legal Studies* 1 (1972), pp. 193–221.

Congress, the presidency, and the Supreme Court have redefined the boundaries between the federal and the state constitutional systems, the jurisdiction of the federal judicial system has also expanded.

The subject-matter scope of federal "diversity jurisdiction" extends to most of the civil categories characteristically resolved by state judicial systems,[2] since the primary test of diversity jurisdiction is that the parties to a case be resident in different states—irrespective of the substance of their conflict. Congress has added specific requirements that must be met before the federal district courts can accept a case in diversity jurisdiction, including the prerequisite that the economic value involved in the dispute must be at least $10,000. Under the current procedural policy of the United States Supreme Court, federal judges are supposed to invoke the same substantive norms that they think would be followed by the appropriate state court if it were deciding a diversity case.[3] But there would still be differences in the rules of procedure followed, and there might also be significant differences in the location of the two courts, in the policy predilections of the judges, or in the probable bias of the jury composition in the state as compared to the federal court. It may therefore make a considerable difference to the parties (or to their respective counsel) whether a case is to be tried in a state or a federal court, notwithstanding the legal presumption that the "law" is the same in both of these courts.

Plaintiffs are free to elect whether to begin a qualified diversity suit in a state or a federal court, and litigants also have a choice between state and federal systems of adjudication in those areas of policy making in which the functions of courts and administrative agencies substantially overlap. For example, many states have enacted labor legislation that purports to regulate aspects of labor-management relations over which the National Labor Relations Board (NLRB) has inchoate jurisdiction—that is, the NLRB has not chosen to exercise the authority to regulate certain industries or relationships which it might claim to control but which remain in the meantime under state jurisdiction. In states that provide for judicial rather than for administrative enforcement of such state labor acts, the plaintiff might have a choice between

---

[2]Cf. *Dick* v. *New York Life Insurance Co.,* 359 U.S. 437 (1959).

[3]*Erie Railroad Co.* v. *Tompkins,* 304 U.S. 64 (1938). During the preceding century, however, the national courts were supposed to develop a body of national policy independent from that of the states or of any particular state. See *Swift* v. *Tyson,* 16 Peters 1 (1842). Before 1842, the presumption was similar to the one now obtaining.

initiating action in a state court or trying to persuade the NLRB to accept jurisdiction. Conversely, the choice may lie between a national district court and a state administrative agency. Louisiana and Virginia and other southern states, for instance, established elaborate systems of administrative adjudication—designed, apparently, to wear out litigants who are supposed to "exhaust their administrative remedies" before taking their cases to court—in regard to such aspects of racial equality as pupil placement and voter registration. Typically, it was futile to pursue the state "remedy" in such cases, because by the time the plaintiff had gone through the several stages of state appellate administrative review and then three or four levels of the state judicial system, his child had grown up or the election was long past. Yet attempts to invoke the jurisdiction of a federal district court may be rejected as premature if no effort has been made to use the state system of administrative adjudication to challenge an adverse administrative decision. Such situations present difficult questions of lego-political tactics.

The other way in which the federal and state judicial systems most commonly articulate is through Supreme Court appellate review of the decisions of state judicial systems. Usually, such decisions are those of the state supreme courts. In many states where there is an intermediate appellate court, appeals to the state supreme court are almost completely discretionary with that court, and in some cases state law makes no provision for appeal of any kind. In such instances, the Supreme Court will sometimes directly review whatever purports to be the final decision made within the state judicial system; indeed, of the 147 cases in which the Supreme Court reviewed state judicial decisions during the 1968 term, over a fifth came directly from lower state courts. The United States Supreme Court was, for example, the only court to review a misdemeanor case that had been tried by a municipal court in Kentucky.[4]

There are two principal methods by which the Supreme Court exercises jurisdiction to review the decisions of lower courts, including state courts. These methods are the statutory procedures for *appeal* and for *certiorari*. Certiorari petitions are by far the most common type of review process, and denials of certiorari are by far the most common type of jurisdictional decision. If the Court accepts jurisdiction, then it grants the writ of certiorari and schedules the case for oral argument, unless the case is decided summarily on the merits at the same time that the jurisdictional

---

[4] *Thompson* v. *City of Louisville,* 362 U.S. 199 (1960), on certiorari to the Police Court of Louisville, Kentucky.

decision is announced. Technically, the writ is an order to a lower court directing that it transmit to the Supreme Court the record of the proceeding before the lower court. A summary decision of the Court, on the merits of the question or questions that the Court was asked to decide in the certiorari petition, is one in which the Court acts on the basis of the information in the certiorari briefs (pro and con) plus the record of antecedent court action, without the benefit (as the phrase goes) of having heard oral argument. Presumably, the issues presented in cases decided summarily are so clear that oral argument would not change the voting alignment of the justices. The most usual function of the certiorari grant with summary affirmance or reversal is to decide "satellite" cases by per curiam order (i.e., by an anonymous statement of the decision for "the whole Court"). The "satellites" are cases docketed at about the same time and raising the same policy issue as some other case that the Court has decided formally (i.e., on the merits after oral argument and with an assigned opinion for the Court written by a designated justice).

The other common process for review by the Court involves the jurisdictional statement (with accompanying brief) for an appeal. Appeals from state courts are now handled by the Court much as if they were certiorari petitions. In certiorari cases, the Court "grants" the writ, while if the Court decides to accept an appeal for decision on the merits, the jurisdictional decision that it announces is to "note probable jurisdiction" in the case, which means that the case then is scheduled for oral argument. Most appeals from state courts, however, are "dismissed" (rather than "denied," as are certiorari petitions) with a stereotyped reason that is no more informative than the silence that accompanies certiorari denials.

A majority of all appeals from the national courts came directly from three-judge district courts in the 1971 term. In order to appear to adhere to the principle that there shall be at least one stage of appellate review for all cases, the Supreme Court must seem to make decisions "on the merits" in all such cases. Most such decisions, however, are summarily made and most are summary affirmances; that is, the Court notes probable jurisdiction and then proceeds, without hearing oral argument or entertaining briefs from the parties on the substantive merits of the issues, to announce its affirmation of the decision below.

The Court has available and utilizes three alternative forms of mandate in order to signify summarily its agreement with the decisions of lower courts. Which form it invokes depends upon the type of review process (certiorari or appeal) and the type of lower court (state or national) associated with the case. In certiorari cases, the Court frequently expresses summary agreement by denying the writ; in appeals from state courts, the Court accomplishes the same purpose by dismissing the jurisdictional statement; and in appeals from United States district courts, the Court summarily affirms, on the merits, the decision of the lower court.

There is, however, one manifest difference in the form in which jurisdictional decisions are made, as between certiorari cases and appeals cases. The certiorari decisions are listed in what is now called the "Orders" category, which means that they are collected at the rear of each volume of the *United States Reports*. Although it is surely not customary for dissenting justices to announce their voting position, neither is it uncommon; and occasionally a dissenting or concurring opinion may accompany the announcement of such jurisdictional decisions. The per curiam decisions, however, have since 1957 all (instead of selectively, as was true earlier) been reported among the formal decisions—i.e., decisions on the merits, after oral argument, with signed opinions of the Court—and now per curiams are grouped in clusters which alternate with clusters of the formal decisions that comprise the greater bulk of each volume.

The per curiam decisions generally may be characterized as follows: (1) each is accompanied by an anonymous opinion "for the whole Court," and it seems probable that most per curiam opinions are written either by the chief justice or for him by one of his four law clerks; (2) although the per curiam decision sometimes is used for cases that have gone through oral argument, this is unusual, since it is primarily used in order to dismiss state appeals and to affirm appeals from the federal district courts; (3) per curiam decisions (rather than "orders") are used for jurisdictional and jurisdictional/summary appeals dispositions in order to maintain the fiction that all appeals cases are decided on the merits, since appeals are stated (in the act of Congress authorizing the Supreme Court to exercise such appellate jurisdiction) to be a legal right; (4) summary certiorari decisions are made per curiam, irrespective of whether they come from national or from state courts; and (5) dissenting and concurring opinions are filed in the nonjurisdictional and nonsummary per curiam decisions to about the same extent as in formal decisions.

In legal theory, a party to a case has a right to have the United States Supreme Court review his appeal from a state court decision which either (1) declares unconstitutional some provision of national law or (2) upholds the validity of some provision of state law against a claim that it is contrary to the Constitution of the United States. In practice, however, the Supreme Court notes probable jurisdiction in (i.e., accepts) for formal decision only about a fourth of such cases, disposing of an even smaller fraction on the merits but per curiam, and dismissing a majority of the appeals because of "want of a substantial federal question" or simply "for lack of jurisdiction."[5] Of course, such reasons are worthless, and the Supreme Court as a matter of policy chooses to refuse to explain why it accepts some appeals from state courts and rejects others. Furthermore, the Administrative Office of the United States Courts did not report for appeals (as it did until 1971 for all other forms of Supreme Court review) the percentage of cases in which the Court accepted jurisdiction. It also failed to publish the number of Appellate Docket appeals granted or dismissed or denied. These omissions apparently reflected deliberate policy rather than oversight, because they had been pointed out to the Administrative Office. Any student, interested in the question to what extent the Supreme Court itself complies with congressional efforts to control by statute the Court's appellate jurisdiction, must make his own observations directly from the *United States Reports.*[6]

Certiorari is used in those cases where a petitioner seeks review by the United States Supreme Court of a state court judgment but can invoke neither of the two grounds for appeal mentioned above. His counsel can file with the Supreme Court a petition which should—although it frequently does not—focus upon *why* it is a matter of substantial public importance that the Court should decide the question of public policy that his case raises, instead of focusing on the claim that the court below erred in its disposition of his case. The Supreme Court typically denies certiorari—it refuses, that is, to hear oral argument or to consider a more lengthy written brief which *would* focus upon the merits of the petitioner's side in the case—in about 97 percent of these state cases. Consequently, both processes of review of the decisions of state judicial systems are discretionary with the United States Supreme Court; the Court is free to pick those few cases that raise the policy issues it wishes to consider, when it wishes to consider them, and the particular factual contexts in which it wishes to decide the issues. The "legal right" of appeal, as distinguished from the avowedly discretionary certiorari process, is not without significance, however. The odds against a litigant's getting the Supreme Court to reconsider a state court decision are about 30 to 1 in certiorari, but they drop sharply to only about 4 to 1 if his counsel has been able to import into the

---

[5]Glendon Schubert, *Quantitative Analysis of Judicial Behavior* (New York: The Free Press of Glencoe, 1959), pp. 49–55.
[6]Ibid., p. 38 n. 15. Cf. Walter F. Murphy and Joseph Tanenhaus, *The Study of Public Law* (New York: Random House, Inc., 1972), p. 62 n. 56.

record of his case either of the two constitutional grounds to make at least a *prima facie* showing of the right to appeal.[7] Once he gets there, however, it makes little difference which route he took; the odds then shift to his favor, since in decisions on the merits the Supreme Court tends to reverse state courts in about four fifths of both certiorari and appeals cases. In the 1970 term, the Court upheld the federal government in almost two thirds of the formal cases to which it was a party, while upholding state governments only half as often (i.e., one third of the time).

FUNCTIONS OF THE FEDERAL JUDICIAL SYSTEM

Many discussions of the federal courts in general, and of the United States Supreme Court in particular, tend to create the impression that the primary function of federal judges is to consider the constitutionality of acts of Congress, state legislatures, national administrative agencies,[8] and, from time to time, even of the President himself.[9] Judicial review, thus defined, is said to uphold the constitutional principles of separation of powers and of federalism by keeping within their assigned systemic orbits the two "political branches of the national government" and the states. As the overseer of the judicial branch of the national government, the Supreme Court, according to this interpretation, also sees that lower court judges keep within their assigned rotations and revolutions around the axis that constitutes The Law, as defined in the

[7]In recognition of the increasing anomaly of the various special statutory exceptions that purport to justify both state and federal appeals to the Supreme Court, and in particular the special demands that they make upon the time of the Court—in the 1971 term, for example, appeals constituted only a tenth of the cases docketed, but they produced one third of all cases decided after oral argument and with signed opinions, thus reflecting the persistence of some effect by the statutory jurisdictional norms—the Study Group on the Supreme Court's caseload recommended in 1972 that discretionary review by certiorari be substituted (necessarily, by act of Congress) for all of the present statutory rights of appeal to the Supreme Court.

[8]In regard to judicial review of administrative agencies, see Martin Shapiro, *The Supreme Court and Administrative Agencies* (New York: The Free Press, 1968).

[9]See Glendon Schubert, *The Presidency in the Courts* (Minneapolis: University of Minnesota Press, 1957). A recent example is the unanimous decision of the Burger Court (with Rehnquist not participating) in *United States* v. *United States District Court for the Eastern District of Michigan, Southern Division*, 407 U.S. 297 (1972), which rejected Nixon's claim of direct constitutional power for the President to order wiretapping for internal security purposes, even with the consent of Congress, if there had been no explicit judicial approval prior to the wiretap.

decisions of the Supreme Court. The Supreme Court thus emerges as something more than the superego of the American constitutional polity; its role is even more majestic, since the Court is expected to play God for the American political universe by preventing tyranny, upholding the union, preserving democracy, and (incidentally) righting all legal wrongs—or at least all those that rise to constitutional stature—to boot.

A principal difficulty with such an idealized conception of the function of the Supreme Court is not so much what it says but what it leaves unsaid. Judges would have to be demigods to live up to the expectations of the stated ideal, which demands that they function like Plato's philosopher-kings; but American judges are only too human.[10] To take as an example those who scintillate as the "most dazzling jewel in the judicial crown of the United States," as one writer puts it,[11] Supreme Court justices sometimes bicker with each other at oral argument or when opinions are being read (to say nothing of what they say in their written opinions, for posterity to read). Several of them have looked upon the Court as merely a stepping-stone to higher political office—and have guided their behavior as justices accordingly. Others have clung to the office long after blindness, senility, or terminal and incapacitating illnesses have rendered them unfit to continue. They have stayed too long for a variety of very human reasons, ranging from the felt responsibility for the support of relatives (in either an economic or a psychological sense) to the fear that the incumbent President might appoint an extremist from the other political party as their successor. Still others have perished, in Byronesque fashion, quite literally in the arms of their mistresses. Such human failings, however, are not well known among the general public, and at any rate the general standard of deportment of the justices has been very high. Consequently, the United States Supreme Court is a model that many of the rest of the nations in the Western world—and even some of the new political societies of Africa and Asia—seek to emulate in their own judicial systems. Among the countries that have been particularly influenced by the American Supreme Court model are India, Japan, Norway, and the Philippines.[12]

[10]As exemplified, perhaps, by the resignation of Abe Fortas, in May 1969.
[11]Henry J. Abraham, *The Judicial Process* (New York: Oxford University Press, 1968), rev. ed., p. 171.
[12]See my "Judges and Political Leadership," Chapter 8 in Lewis Edinger, ed., *Political Leadership in Industrialized Societies: Studies in Comparative Analysis* (New York: John Wiley & Sons, Inc., 1967), pp. 220–265; and cf. Carl J. Friedrich, *The Impact of American Constitutionalism Abroad* (Boston: Boston University Press, 1967), Chapter 3.

FIGURE 3

Judicial Review in the Middle Third of the Twentieth Century:
Decisions of the United States Supreme Court,
Holding Acts of Congress to be Unconstitutional, 1937–1972

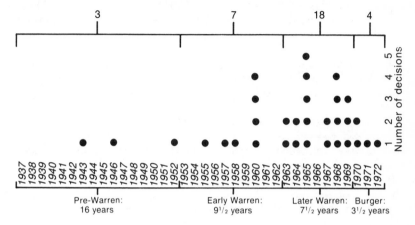

Pre-Warren: 16 years
Early Warren: 9½ years
Later Warren: 7½ years
Burger: 3½ years

Legend to Figure 3: The list of decisions that comprise the data for Figure 3 include:

No.	Date	Decision		Subject
1	1943	*Tot v. United States,*	319 U.S. 463 FP	(stat. presumption; firearms)
2	1946	*United States v. Lovett,*	328 U.S. 303 PF	(legis. firing of civil servants)
3	1952	*United States v. Cardiff,*	344 U.S. 174 RP	(food & drug inspection of business)
4	1955	*Toth v. Quarles,*	350 U.S. 11 CE	(military trial of civilian)
5	1957	*Reid v. Covert,*	354 U.S. 1 CE	(military trial of civilian)
6	1958	*Trop v. Dulles,*	356 U.S. 86 CE	(expatriation for military crime)
7	1960	*Kinsella v. Singleton,*	361 U.S. 234 CE	(military trial, civilian dependent)
8	1960	*Grisham v. Hagan,*	361 U.S. 278 CE	(military trial, civilian employee)
9	1960	*McElroy v. Guagliardo,*	361 U.S. 281 CE	(military trial, civilian employee)
10	1960	*Wilson v. Bohlender,*	361 U.S. 281 CE	(military trial, civilian employee)
11	1963	*Kennedy v. Mendoza-Martinez,*	372 U.S. 144 CE	(involuntary expatriation; sel. svc.)
12	1963	*Rusk v. Cort,*	372 U.S. 144 CE	(involuntary expatriation; sel. svc.)
13	1964	*Schneider v. Rusk,*	377 U.S. 163 CE	(involuntary expatriation; for. res.)
14	1964	*Aptheker v. Secretary of State,*	378 U.S. 500 CE	(right to travel; Communist citizens)
15	1965	*Lamont v. Postmaster General,*	381 U.S. 301 PF	(mail censorship; Communist publica.)
16	1965	*Fixa, Postmaster v. Heilberg,*	381 U.S. 301 PF	(mail censorship; Communist publica.)
17	1965	*United States v. Brown,*	381 U.S. 437 PF	(Communists as labor union officials)
18	1965	*Albertson v. Subversive A. C. Bd.,*	382 U.S. 70 PF	(registration of Communist party)
19	1965	*United States v. Romano,*	382 U.S. 136 FP	(stat. presumption; bootlegging)
20	1967	*Afroyim v. Rusk,*	387 U.S. 253 CE	(involuntary expatriation; for. vot.)
21	1967	*United States v. Robel,*	389 U.S. 258 PF	(Communist employment; def. industry)
22	1968	*Marchetti v. United States,*	390 U.S. 39 FP	(self-incrimination; bookie tax & reg.)
23	1968	*Grosso v. United States,*	390 U.S. 62 FP	(self-incrimination; bookie tax repts.)
24	1968	*Haynes v. United States,*	390 U.S. 85 FP	(self-incrimination; gun registrat.)
25	1968	*United States v. Jackson,*	390 U.S. 570 FP	(capital punishment; kidnapping)
26	1969	*Washington v. Legrant,*	394 U.S. 618 E	(econ. underdog; indigent migration)
27	1969	*Leary v. United States,*	395 U.S. 6 FP	(stat. presumption; marihuana)
28	1969	*Powell v. McCormack,*	395 U.S. 486 VE	(Cong. membership; rt. to representat.)
29	1970	*Schacht v. United States,*	398 U.S. 58 PF	(free speech by impersonating soldier)
30	1970	*Oregon v. Mitchell,*	400 U.S. 112 N	(youth suffrage in S/L elec., bef. 26th Am.)
31	1971	*Tilton v. Richardson,*	403 U.S. 672 RF	(time limit on preclusion of rel. use of fed. grant)
32	1972	*Chief of Cap. Police v. J. Rankin Brig.,*	409 U.S. 972 PF	(free assembly & petition on U.S. Capitol grounds)

NOTE: Subject codes are: CE=civic equality; FP=fair procedure; PF=political freedom; RP=right to privacy; VE=voting equality; E=economic liberalism; N=nationalism; RF=religious freedom. For a list of 76 decisions prior to 1937, see Wilfred C. Gilbert, *Provisions of Federal Law Held Unconstitutional by the Supreme Court of the United States* (Washington: U.S. Government Printing Office, 1936).

The Supreme Court does occasionally argue on constitutional grounds its disagreement with statutory policies of Congress, but such decisions declaring acts of Congress invalid have averaged less than one per year during the past third of a century, although the rate did increase sharply during the 1960s as Figure 3 shows. Their policy impact was confined to the status and rights of national citizenship, especially in the context of civil-military and foreign relations, until 1965 when the Court began to uphold in such decisions political freedom for communists and fair procedure for criminal defendants. Decisions announcing the unconstitutionality of national statutes constituted a very small proportion of the workload of the lower national courts and tended to have slight effect upon the political system—in part because the Supreme Court's decisions from 1937 through 1970 were based almost exclusively upon civil liberties grounds, and the then generally more conservative judges of the lower national courts tended to uphold the constitutionality of the challenged legislation; in part because of the limited territorial jurisdiction of the lower courts; but most importantly because lower court decisions are almost always subject to Supreme Court review. Cases such as the steel seizure decision of 1952 are few and far between. In that instance, the Supreme Court approved a ruling by David Pine, a United States district judge for the District of Columbia, that President Truman had violated the Constitution by placing certain steel mills under [symbolic] governmental control to prevent a labor strike which would have crippled defense production during the Korean War. The most effective restraints upon both the presidency and Congress have been those imposed by such other components of the national political system as the political parties and major interest groups.

Judicial review of administrative action is, however, primarily a function of the lower federal courts, and the Supreme Court at least purports to intervene primarily in order to lay down new policy guidelines for federal courts of appeals. On the other hand, it has been the Supreme Court itself that has been most active in making policy for the states in cases raising claims of civil liberties under the national Constitution. Such questions of civil liberties reach the Supreme Court less frequently through the lower federal courts, usually doing so when plaintiffs ask a United States district court to enjoin state officials from acting in a manner that is claimed to violate national civil rights. In what were formerly the major policy fields of racial equality and legislative reapportionment, cases raising the most important questions have reached the Supreme Court through both state and federal court channels, including "direct appeals" from three-judge district courts. The enforcement of such policies, however, quite clearly has not been a function of either the Supreme Court or the state judicial systems but, rather, has been a major job of the national courts of appeals and district courts.[13] The Warren Court was equally active in reviewing state court decisions to persuade the states to liberalize their policies in regard to such varied questions as police methods of search and seizure; the rights of indigent criminal defendants to counsel and to appellate review of trial court decisions; and the disestablishment of religious influence in the public schools. It is in the review of civil liberties claims against the states that the Supreme Court has come closest to living up to the ideal portrait with which we introduced the present discussion.

By far the larger function of the federal courts, certainly in terms of the number of decisions and perhaps in terms of impact upon the American polity as well, lies not in constitutional interpretation but in the judicial interpretation of national statutes,[14] administrative regulations and decisions, judicial regulations (such as the procedural rules for the federal courts), and judicial decisions. In legal theory, the analogous forms of state lawmaking are interpreted by the state's own courts, not by the national courts. This may help to explain, in part, why the Supreme Court employs constitutional interpretation actively in regard to state law but rarely in regard to national law. The various forms of national law all can be reinterpreted by the Supreme Court to have a meaning consistent with the policy views of a majority of the justices. This obviates the necessity for the more open and direct clash between the Court and other major national decision makers, while at the same time accomplishing the same result as judicial review: the substitution of the Court's policy for the one initially made by another decision maker.

---

[13]On the enforcement of the Supreme Court's racial equality policies, see Kenneth N. Vines, "Federal District Judges and Race Relations Cases in the South," *Journal of Politics* 26 (1964), pp. 337–357, and his "The Role of Circuit Courts of Appeals in the Federal Judicial Process: A Case Study," *Midwest Journal of Political Science* 7 (1963), pp. 305–319; Jack W. Peltason, *Fifty-Eight Lonely Men* (New York: Harcourt Brace Jovanovich, Inc., 1961). On the enforcement of the Court's reapportionment and redistricting policies, see Glendon Schubert, ed., *Reapportionment* (New York: Charles Scribner's Sons, 1965), and Edward N. Beiser, "A Comparative Analysis of State and Federal Judicial Behavior: The Reapportionment Cases," *American Political Science Review* 62 (1968), pp. 788–795.
[14]Martin Shapiro, *Law and Politics in the Supreme Court: New Approaches to Political Jurisprudence* (New York: The Free Press of Glencoe, 1964).

A QUANTITATIVE ANALYSIS

Table 4 presents some of the data that bear upon the processes and sources of appeals to the Supreme Court, for the term that ended in June 1972.

The table differentiates the appellate cases docketed during that term by three variables: (1) whether the process is certiorari or statutory appeal, (2) what is the court immediately below, whose decision is reviewed, and (3) whether the case is civil or criminal in form. The columns of Table 4 define the review processes; the rows of the table specify the courts below; and each cell of the table is bifurcated by a diagonal, with civil cases indicated above and to the left of the diagonal, and criminal cases below and to the right of it. Contrary to what we shall observe below in regard to the allocation of the time of the lower federal courts as between civil and criminal cases, the Supreme Court clearly apportions most (60 percent) of its docket to the consideration of criminal cases. More than twice as many cases come from the federal courts of appeals as from state courts; and only about 5 percent are reviewed directly and in the aggregate from single-judge federal district courts, three-judge courts, and specialized federal courts. Furthermore most of the seventy-four appeals from single-judge federal district courts were in fact disposed of jurisdictionally, as we shall see presently. So Table 4 confirms that over 90 percent of the Supreme Court's appellate cases now arise through certiorari from either federal courts of appeals or state supreme courts; and for criminal cases, the proportion is almost 98 percent. Of the four thousand certioraris docketed in the 1971 term, over 80 percent were decided during the term, the rest being carried over for screening during the summer and fall of 1972; and of these between 5 and 10 percent represented certiorari grants (followed by, with rare exceptions, decisions on the merits) while the rest were certiorari denials (and therefore only jurisdictional). It is not possible to say, on the basis of any of the published discussions of this term, to what extent there may be differences in the rate of certiorari grants for federal as distinguished from state cases; but it is clear that the Court followed up its major formal decision regarding capital punishment with a single per curiam appeal (vacating and remanding to the Supreme Court of Massachusetts),[15] and that this latter brief decision then became the peg upon which were hung no less than 133 certiorari trailers (plus half a dozen trailers that arose in appeal). The Court summarily vacated by memorandum decision the death sentences that had been upheld by the courts below in all

[15] *Furman* v. *Georgia,* 408 U.S. 238 (1972), and *Stewart* v. *Massachusetts,* 408 U.S. 845 (1972).

TABLE 4

Sources of, and Supreme Court Review Processes for Considering, Appellate Cases (1971 Term)

Lower Court	Review processes:			Sums
	Certiorari	Appeals	Totals	
Federal Courts of Appeals	1066 / 1718	12 / 3	1078 / 1721	2799
State Courts	340 / 843	105 / 53	445 / 896	1341
Three-judge federal courts and federal district courts	3 / 0	193 / 3	196 / 3	199
Other federal (special) courts	31 / 0	1 / 0	32 / 0	32
Totals	1440 / 2561	311 / 59	1751 / 2620	4371
Sums	4001	370	4371	

LEGEND   Type of case:

civil / criminal

of these cases; and in view of the circumstance that otherwise the Court granted certiorari in only a total of 184 other cases of all types throughout the entire term, it is readily understandable that these 133 death sentence trailers account for the range specified above for certiorari grants during this particular term: without them, it is a normal 5.8 percent; counting them it rises to an abnormally high 9.6 percent. There was a difference also between the rate of success of petitioners who could pay their own appellate costs, and those who had filed *in forma pauperis:* certiorari grants for the former were 8.9 percent, while (again, excluding the 133 death sentence trailers) only fifty-six other indigent defendants, out of a total of 1720 petitioners, for a rate of 3.3 percent, persuaded the Burger Court to review their claims.

Neither the official nor the acolyte discussions in the law reviews and political science journals reveal what the Court did in the disposition of appeals cases. The official source (i.e., the Clerk of the Supreme Court, who supplies the minimally and selectively quantified data upon which the Director of the Administrative Office used to rely, until he ceased providing any relevant information after 1970) always has disguised the Court's practice in the handling of appeals, evidently because of the sharp and increasing gap between what the Supreme Court does and the "black letter" law of the now almost fifty-year-old statute that the Court is supposed to be following. But unlike the four thousand certioraris, there are only a couple of hundred or so appeals cases to be dealt with, so these were classified and counted for present purposes. The results are given in Table 5, which shows a total of 239 cases whereas the report of an officially sponsored study group with full access to the Court's own data resources indicates a total of 253.[16] Evidently the tabulation made for present purposes, utilizing the sets of reports available locally, errs by about 5 percent in the direction of undercounting, having missed seven of the decisions on the merits after oral argument, and seven of the (probably) memorandum decisions. In all likelihood the decisions missed were the docket numbers of additional cases that were grouped for decision with ones that *were* observed and counted; it is unlikely that their inclusion would change in any material way the generalizations that we shall base upon the table, which should be considered to represent, however, an excellent sample rather than the complete universe of the appeals data for the 1971 term.

Table 5 distinguishes among three variables in terms of which the appeals cases have been classified. The columns differentiate the types of opinion that were employed to justify decisions. The rows indicate whether decisions were on the merits or jurisdictional only; and if on the merits, whether or not the Court heard oral argument. The cell diagonals separate federal appeals (above and to the left) from state appeals (below and to the right). What the table shows is that very few if any appeals are found in a majority of

---

[16]*Report of the Study Group on the Case Load of the Supreme Court* (Washington, D.C.: Administrative Office of United States Courts, December 1972), Table VI, p. A10.

TABLE 5

Appeals Decided by the Supreme Court (1971 Term)

Type of Decision	Type of Opinion:				
	Signed	Per curiam	Memo-randum	Totals	Sums
Argued, on merits	26 / 8	3 / 0	0 / 0	29 / 8	37
Not argued, on merits	1 / 1	7 / 3	60 / 10	68 / 14	82
Jurisdictional	0 / 0	2 / 0	26 / 92	28 / 92	120
Totals	27 / 9	12 / 3	86 / 102	125 / 114	239
Sums	36	15	188	239	

LEGEND   Type of court:

state / federal

six of the nine cells of the table; and only thirty-four were decided formally, on the merits after oral argument with a signed opinion for the Court. This compares with approximately three times as many such formal decisions in certiorari cases, a conclusion that we can deduce from the knowledge that (as reported by the Clerk of the Court) there were 143 formal cases in all, and only eight cases decided in original jurisdiction—of which some were probably signed opinions and others per curiam.

Otherwise almost two thirds of all of these appeals fall in only two categories: memorandum dispositions of federal appeals, decided on the merits but summarily without oral argument; and memorandum jurisdictional decisions which dismiss state appeals. Because these are all memorandum dispositions, we can eliminate one of our variables and reorganize the data for the relevant two cells of Table 5, into the format of Table 6. The latter is a four-fold table which can readily be tested for statistical significance by means of a common nonparametric statistic, chi square, in order to guide our decision on the question whether the concentrations of appeals in the two categories specified above—i.e., in cells *a* and *d* of Table 6—are significantly greater than what we ought to expect might happen by chance if there were no relationship between the two variables, source of case (federal/state) and type of disposition (merits/jurisdictional). The relationship is to some extent blurred empirically in the table, because in cell *c* there are a couple of dozen dismissed appeals from the federal courts of appeals (from which cases get reviewed by the Supreme Court almost exclusively by certiorari rather than appeal, although a few litigants and their lawyers keep trying the appeal route every term—and almost always in vain), and also the presence in cell *b* of ten state appeals that were vacated for reconsideration in the light of other (and usually intervening) decisions of the Supreme Court. Nevertheless, the piling up of what are mostly affirmances of single-judge federal

TABLE 6

How the Supreme Court Disposed Jurisdictionally of Federal and State Appeals (1971 Term)

Type of decision:	Type of court:		
	Federal	State	Totals
Affirmance, reversal, or remand	60 a	b 10	70
Dismissal	c 26	d 92	118
Totals	86	102	188

$X^2 = 69.2445$

district courts, in cell *a*, and of what are without exception refusals to hear appeals from state (mostly supreme) courts, in cell *d*, are of such magnitudes that the relationship is highly statistically significant (with $X^2 = 69.245$). This finding confirms the persistence of a trend first noted almost twenty years ago, in the early days of the Warren Court:[17] that the Supreme Court disposes of appeals by *affirming* federal district courts and *dismissing* state court decisions —and that whatever may be their differences *de jure*, these are equivalent modes of jurisdictional decision making *de facto*. Consequently, the datum reported by the Study Group on the Supreme Court's caseload, that 82 percent of the total universe of appeals is disposed of without oral argument, is about as close as we can come to a generalization that is equivalent to our previous observation: that about 94 percent of the total universe of certioraris is denied. And if we combine the two sets of data, taking into consideration the considerable difference in their respective sizes (i.e., 209 of 253 appeals, and 2969 of 3153 certioraris), then we can arrive at the best overall estimate of the extent to which the Supreme Court accepts review under its appellate jurisdiction: 93 percent get turned down, and conversely only 7 percent are given more than preliminary screening consideration by the Court.

Both district courts and courts of appeals decide civil and criminal cases, and this constitutes, in one sense, their most important function. In addition, the courts of appeals have a specialized function of administrative supervision. The district courts have a different function of administrative supervision, as well as many primarily administrative tasks.

Table 7 shows the number of cases, in each of these categories, that were decided during the 1972 fiscal year. The naturalization of aliens and the approval of passport applications, which constitute the largest number of items for the district courts, are direct administrative functions that require only a small amount of judicial time. During the period 1955–1972, the annual number of passport applications more than doubled to over 370,000— reflecting, no doubt, the increasing affluence of Americans—while the number of aliens naturalized was halved to about 95,000 annually. At that, the federal district courts processed one hundred thousand fewer applications in 1972 than the year before, and this decrease was directly attributable to the expansion of passport offices operated by the United States Postal Service by then, in

[17]Glendon Schubert, *Quantitative Analysis of Judicial Behavior* (Glencoe, Illinois: The Free Press, 1959), pp. 56 and 65, which reports an empirical test of an hypothesis suggested in the anonymous "Note" by a law student, *Harvard Law Review* 69 (1956), pp. 712–713.

TABLE 7

Major Components of Decision Making of Lower National Courts (1972)

Type of case	District Courts	Courts of Appeals
United States civil	26,116	2,512
Private civil	69,065	5,399
Total civil	95,181	7,911
Criminal	48,101	3,799
Total, civil and criminal	143,282	11,710
Administrative appeals	—	1,448
District of Columbia Court of Appeals	—	15
Bankruptcy	187,714	307
Probation	49,023	—
Naturalization of aliens	95,842	—
Passport applications	370,953	—

eighty of the ninety-four federal judicial districts. Bankruptcy and probation are the next most numerous, and together they constitute slightly more than half as many cases (approximately 237,000) as are in the direct administrative category. Bankruptcy and probation cases require administrative supervision by the district courts and consume, relatively, considerably more judicial time. The judges appoint referees to supervise the management of estates in bankruptcy and approve their decisions. Probation supervision is closely related to the sentencing of convicted criminals, either under the more traditional system in which the judge determines sentences or under the newer "flexible" procedures of indeterminate sentencing through which the judge delegates much of his discretion to parole and probation (administrative) officials. The major sources of the approximately 49,000 probation cases are: by court sentence of a district judge or magistrate, about three fourths; on parole from penal custody, about a fifth; and mandatory release to probation from penal custody upon completion of partial sentence in confinement, about 4 percent. Very few of the administrative functions of the district courts, whether direct or supervisory, are reviewed by the courts of appeals. Even in the bankruptcy cases, which are among the exclusive functions of the federal court system, less than two tenths of 1 percent are appealed beyond the district court level.

The district courts docket over a dozen times as many civil and criminal cases as do the courts of appeals, but only about 12 and 16 percent in each category, respectively, go to trial; the remainder are resolved by negotiation and agreement between the parties. There were 10,962 civil trials in 1972, of which a third were tried with a jury.

Almost two thirds of the 7818 criminal cases that went to trial involved the participation of petit juries. The greater average allocation of the time of the district courts nevertheless is in favor of the civil cases. The courts of appeals affirmed about three fourths of the 8537 decisions below that it reviewed in 1972, but with differential rates of approval ranging from a high of 83 percent in criminal cases, with 72 percent approval of administrative appeals, to 68 percent for civil cases and a low of 65 percent for bankruptcy appeals.

Some indication of the accelerated pace of change during the sixties is provided by noting that of the seven United States courts of appeals with more than 1100 appeals each during 1972 (and the range was up to a maximum of almost 2900), none had had more than 600 in 1960; the total of appeals filed in all federal circuits increased from less than 4000 (in 1960) to more than 14,500 (in 1972).[18] Contrary to what had happened during the sixties, in 1972 the courts of appeals reviewed a slightly higher proportion of criminal (70 percent) than of civil (63 percent) appeals from the district courts. But because most of these appeals were civil, the ratio of civil to criminal cases decided by the courts of appeals also was about 2 to 1 (4948 to 2664). Criminal appeals constitute over a fourth of the *total* caseload of the courts of appeals, but their disposition requires a much smaller proportion of the time of these appellate courts. The point is that both the district courts and the courts of appeals give most of their time and attention to civil cases—i.e., to what are ostensibly questions of property rights rather than of personal rights. However, as we shall see below, many of these appellate civil cases are actually concerned with appeals of criminal convictions.

During the decade 1962–1972, the volume of cases decided by the courts of appeals increased by well over 300 percent, from 4167 to 13,828; while during the same period, the increase in the cases decided by the district courts was only a fifth as much, or about 63 percent. Among the major kinds of appeals in "United States civil"

[18] *Annual Report of the Director of the Administrative Office of the United States Courts* (Washington: Government Printing Office, 1972), Table B3.

cases were federal prisoner motions (to vacate sentences), tax suits, and habeas corpus and related petitions filed in the federal district courts by both federal and state prisoners, in their attempts to gain release from custody. (The sharp rise in the numbers of such petitions filed, during the period 1961–1972, is shown in Figure 4.) Indeed the quantitative increase of petitions (by over 600 percent during that dozen years) was accompanied by qualitative changes of at least sweeping magnitude. According to the Director of the Administrative Office of the United States Courts,

> both state and Federal prisoners appear to have turned away from commencing suits against law enforcement officials or judicial procedures. Instead they are turning to Federal courts to attack as a civil rights issue the organized regimen of prison life which, often for security and safety reasons, must strongly control liberties taken for granted by the general public. Complaints vary from requests for relaxed mail privileges to censorship of the mail, from general housing accommodations to size of cell, from general dissatisfaction with the food to requests for special dietary supplements due to religious or philosophical reasons, from refusal to accept medical care to requests for more medical care. . . . [19]

The principal sources of appeals in "private civil" cases were habeas corpus and related motions by state prisoners, contract actions and personal injury claims based on diversity of citizenship, and civil rights actions. For federal criminal cases, the leading sources of appeals were from defendants convicted of narcotics offenses, robbery and burglary, Selective Service Act, larceny and theft, and fraud. During 1972 the courts of appeals conducted 5748 hearings, of which only twenty were *en banc* while the remainder (99.7 percent) were held by three-judge panels.

About seven eighths of the cases reviewed by the courts of appeals came in 1972 from the district courts, but the remaining eighth constituted many of the most complicated and important policy questions. The latter come under the rubric of what lawyers call "administrative law," and they are appealed directly from the so-called regulatory commissions,[20] from one of the specialized national courts, or from the executive departments. For example,

[19]Ibid., p. II–28.
[20]See Lee Loevinger, "The Administrative Agency as a Paradigm of Government—A Survey of the Administrative Process," *Indiana Law Journal* 40 (1965), pp. 287–312.

FIGURE 4

Petitions Filed by State and Federal Prisoners in United States District Courts

Fiscal Years   1961–1972

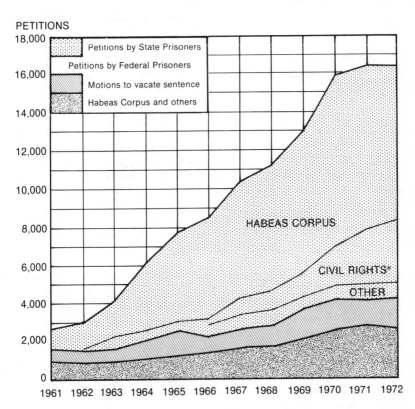

PETITIONS

Legend:
- Petitions by State Prisoners
- Petitions by Federal Prisoners
- Motions to vacate sentence
- Habeas Corpus and others

HABEAS CORPUS

CIVIL RIGHTS*

OTHER

*"Civil Rights" prior to 1966 are included in "Other Prisoner Petitions".

Source: Administrative Office of the United States Courts, 1972 *Annual Report of the Director* ,p. 118.

about 5 percent of all the cases docketed with the courts of appeals come from the National Labor Relations Board, either as Board petitions to have a court order the enforcement of the Board's decision or as petitions from private litigants who seek to have a court declare invalid an order or proposed action of the Board. Another 4 percent of the cases docketed with the courts of appeals consist of appeals from a large variety of other regulatory commissions and administrative agencies, including the Civil Aeronautics

Board, the Federal Communications Commission, the Federal Power Commission, the Federal Trade Commission, the Department of Agriculture, the Securities and Exchange Commission, the Immigration and Naturalization Service, and the Court of Tax Appeals of the District of Columbia.

Most appeals from the Interstate Commerce Commission (ICC), it will be recalled, do not come to the courts of appeals at all but have gone instead to special three-judge district courts; this procedure has had the nominal effect of "expediting" the disposition of such cases and the practical effect of maximizing the probability that the Supreme Court would review the trial courts' decisions in such cases, because the decisions of three-judge district courts are not subject to review by the courts of appeals but only by the Supreme Court. But late in 1972 a committee appointed by Chief Justice Burger proposed, in conjunction with its advocacy of a new intermediate-level "National Court of Appeal" to serve as a further buffer between the Supreme Court and the lower courts, that the three-judge district courts be abolished along with any direct review by the Supreme Court of district court decisions in antitrust cases and in regard to orders of the Interstate Commerce Commission. Because the Warren Court had a more liberal orientation than the great majority of the panels of the courts of appeals, the effect of bypassing the courts of appeals in most ICC (and other three-judge district court) cases was, during the 1950s and 1960s, to provide a more liberal base for policy making in appellate review than obtained generally for the other administrative law cases, which had to be filtered through the courts of appeals. On the other hand, given the fortuity that Nixon was in a position to recast the policy orientation of the Supreme Court[21] much more rapidly and radically than he was able to transform the balance of ideologies in the much larger bureaucracy of the lower federal courts, the no doubt unintended effect of forestalling direct Burger Court review was—at least in the short run—a relatively liberalizing one. But the corresponding proximate effect of the proposed National Court of Appeals (assuming that Congress accepts it) will be strongly conservative because Chief Justice Burger will have (according to the proposal) a predominant voice in making the special assignment of circuit judges to the new super appeals court.

[21]See my *The Future of the Nixon Court* (Honolulu, Hawaii: University of Hawaii Foundation, 1972), passim.

FIGURE 5

Civil Cases Commenced in United States District Courts

Fiscal Year 1972

TOTAL CIVIL CASES   96,173

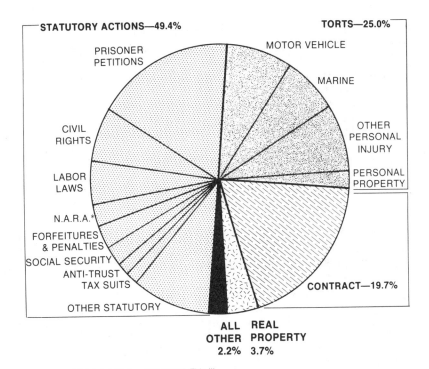

*Narcotic Addict Rehabilitation Act of 1966, Title III.

Source: Administrative Office of the United States Courts, 1972 *Annual Report of the Director* .p. 113.

As Figure 5 indicates, almost half of the civil cases filed in the federal district courts are based upon statutory rights of action, including (of course) many of those that involve judicial review of federal administrative agency action (i.e., questions of administrative law). Between a fourth and a third are tort suits concerning claims for compensation for injuries, many of which arise in federal courts only because they involve either diversity or maritime jurisdiction or persons employed in certain transportation industries. The contract suits generally are based on various particular federal statutes. The "United States" (viz., the seven divisions of the courts subsystem plus three of the "Services" and the U.S. attorneys of the Department of Justice) was the plaintiff in about a sixth and the defendant in the remaining cases classified as "United States civil" in Table 7. Most such cases arise under particular federal statutes, although about 4300 were contract suits, 2200 were tort actions, and 1300 were suits over real property. Of the "private civil" cases in Table 7 over a third are diversity-of-citizenship cases, more than half raise "federal questions," and the remaining are "local" cases. In contrast to diversity jurisdiction (which requires that the national courts apply what they understand to be the public policy of the various states in regard to questions that are conceptualized, for substantive purpose, as being matters of "state law"), in "federal question" cases the federal courts are expected to provide the authoritative interpretation of the Constitution, statutes, administrative orders and regulations, and the judicial decisions that embody the policies of the national political system. Thus in deciding diversity cases, the United States district courts are supposed to follow the policy guidance of the state courts; but in deciding federal question cases, they are supposed to follow the policy guidance of the Supreme Court and of the courts of appeals for their own circuit. The third subcategory, "local" cases, arises exclusively in the national territories, and they consist (like the diversity cases) of policy questions that characteristically are decided otherwise by state courts.

The largest subcategory of the diversity category consists of tort cases, and the most frequent type of tort, about 7800 in 1972, was the "motor vehicle, personal injury" claim. The major subcategories of the federal question cases were prison officials, habeas corpus and other prisoner petitions, about 11,700; "marine, tort, personal injury," about 5900; civil rights, statutory claims, about 4450; "marine, contract," about 3600; labor litigation, about 2800; Federal Employers' Liability Act, about 1600; and antitrust, statutory claims, about 950. The state prisoner petitions had increased by over 1000 percent during the preceding decade, as a direct form of feedback to the Warren Court's policy of sympathy for claims to fair procedure, which did not become really firmly established until after Justice Felix Frankfurter retired in 1962.

There were over 4079 local cases in 1972, most of which arose in the District of Columbia. The largest subcategory of local cases—821—consisted of domestic relations cases. Second were about 794 "motor vehicle, personal injury" claims, and third were some 744 contract actions. These three together comprised over half of all local cases in the national courts.

Approximately 48,000 criminal cases were decided by the district courts in 1972, over half again as many as in 1968, but the latter had been *less* than in 1955. There had indeed been very little change in the annual number of criminal cases during the dozen years from the mid-fifties through the latter sixties, but there was a sharp rise in criminal cases under the Burger Court. Over two thirds of these cases were initiated after indictments by grand juries: this represented the culmination of a consistent increase over the period of the preceding eight years, at the beginning of which only about half of the cases were based upon grand jury indictment. As Figure 6 shows, over 80 percent of the total were classified under the following nine categories: immigration; narcotics; selective service; embezzlement and fraud; forgery and counterfeiting; larceny and theft; homicide, robbery, assault, and burglary; weapons and firearms; and auto theft. Juvenile delinquency proceedings had decreased by a quarter during the 1967 and 1968 fiscal years, due to a change in Justice Department policy, which now seeks to divert to trial in state and local jurisdictions juveniles charged with federal crimes; there was a similar continuing reduction to a total of less than 670 federal juvenile cases in 1972. But there were over 5100 prosecutions of draft violations in fiscal 1972; this was two-and-one-half times as many as only four years earlier in 1968, which in turn had been the largest number since World War II. There was also a sharp increase in the number of prosecutions for weapons and firearms offenses (from four hundred in 1968 to 2377 in 1972) and a smaller but still notable increase in escape charges (from 783 in 1968 to 1415 in 1972).

Of the almost fifty thousand federal criminal defendants in 1972, three fourths were convicted either of the offenses with which they were charged or of lesser offenses. The highest rates of conviction were for violations of the immigration and nationality laws (95 and 94 percent of 5873 and 31, respectively), the postal laws (95 percent of 1105), the motor carrier code (90 percent of 330), and for the white-collar crime of embezzlement (86 percent of 1922), followed by migratory bird laws (85 percent of 661) and liquor offenses at about 84 percent of 1853. The conviction rate for most major offense categories (including forgery and counterfeiting, narcotics, auto theft, burglary, larceny and general theft, and robbery) ranged from 77–83 percent. The lowest rates were for defendants in civil rights cases (21 percent of 115), for those prosecuted for securities and exchange (stock) fraud (54 percent of 97) followed by extortion and racketeering (59 percent of 796) and sex offenses (64 percent of 154). Of 37,220 persons who were sentenced, almost half received jail terms (averaging thirty-eight

FIGURE 6

Criminal Cases Commenced, by Offense, in United States District Courts

Fiscal Year 1972

TOTAL CRIMINAL CASES   47,043

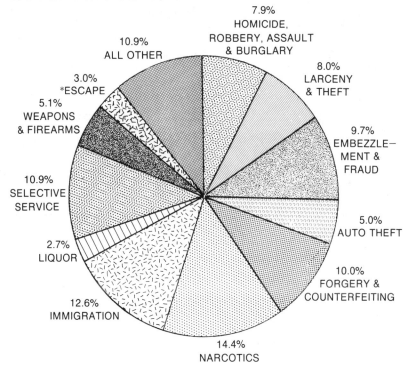

*Escape from custody, aiding or abetting an escape, failure to appear in court and bail jumping.

Source: Administrative Office of the United States Courts, 1972 *Annual Report of the Director*, p. 134.

months), and about 40 percent were placed on probation; the remaining 13 percent received fines or other punishment. But analyses of the types of sentence, in relation to the types of crime, suggest a consistent relationship between judicial leniency and the social status of the defendants: businessmen convicted of violations of economic regulatory legislation simply do not go to jail.[22] In 1968 none of the 103 businessmen sentenced for violation of the antitrust laws was imprisoned; twenty-two were put on probation,

[22]Vilhelm Aubert, "White Collar Crime and Social Structure," *American Journal of Sociology* 58 (1952), pp. 263–271.

and eighty-one were fined.[23] Similarly, none of the 532 business-men convicted of violations of the Motor Carrier Act in that year went to jail, although 90 percent were fined, 8 percent were put on probation, and 2 percent received "other" punishment. During fiscal year 1972, of 59 antitrust defendants—only a third of the total sentenced in the preceding year[24]—thirteen received only probation, forty-three were merely fined, while three received other punishment. Similarly, of 296 owner-operator defendants under the motor carrier acts (as compared to 772 the preceding year), none was imprisoned, twenty-two were put on probation, 256 were fined only, and eighteen received other punishment. And of eight employer defendants under the Fair Labor Standards Act, one was sentenced to a one-year maximum, while the other seven all were fined. Of the 810 bank robbers in 1968, however, 81 percent were sentenced to five or more years in jail, as were 100 percent of the sixteen convicted murderers; and 61 percent of the 953 violators of the narcotics acts (other than the Marihuana Tax Act and the border registration legislation) were sent to jail for five or more years. Similarly, 85 percent of the 1419 bank robbers and 80 percent of the twenty-five convicted murderers during 1972 went to the penitentiary for sentences of five years or longer, as did also 44 percent of the 763 "other" narcotics violators.

[23]See Lee Loevinger, "How to Succeed in Business Without Being Tried—The Potentiality of Antitrust Prosecution," *Arizona Law Review* 12 (1970), pp. 443–461.

[24]Such sharp changes in the numbers of cases docketed from year to year, in regard to both economic control and common-law felony categories of offenses, reflect considerations beyond that of who is robbing interstate commerce or local banks (as the case may be) from time to time. Such variation is a consequence also of national administrative policy, as the Director of the Administrative Office of United States Courts has candidly remarked:

"The federal criminal caseload is to a large extent a reflection of the priorities of the Justice Department in regards to active prosecution. The number and types of defendants proceeded against are not necessarily a realistic index of the occurrence of Federal crimes. The Federal criminal caseload is rather an indication of the amount of investigative and prosecution resources that can be committed, enforcement agency priori-ties, changes in the criminal law, and lastly, the extent to which certain criminal cases can be diverted to state or local criminal systems. The number of auto theft cases filed in the Federal courts (e.g.) has continued to decline and was 54 percent below the 1961 filing level. A major factor in this decrease is the policy of the Department of Justice to prosecute only those auto thefts linked with organized crime or multi-theft violations." Administrative Office of United States Courts, *1972 Annual Report of the Director* (Washington, D.C.: Government Printing Office, 1973 preliminary edition), p. II–46.

During the period 1963–1968, delay in reaching civil cases for trial increased by 20 percent. By 1971 the delay for jury trials was fourteen months, which was about one-and-a-half times as long as the delay for nonjury trials. The problem was most exacerbated in the large metropolitan districts (i.e., those with five or more judges), for which the delay in even nonjury trials was: New York, Southern (Manhattan), thirty-five months, and California, Northern (San Francisco), twenty-nine months; and the same was true of jury trials also with Pennsylvania, Western (Pittsburgh), thirty-five months, Pennsylvania, Eastern (Philadelphia), thirty-three months, California, Northern, thirty-two months, and New York, Southern, twenty-nine months. But in conspicuously rural areas, trial time was relatively short (Canal Zone, one month, and Alabama, Middle, two months, for nonjury trials, and both Texas, Western and Missouri, Eastern, three months for jury trials). A third of the civil cases had been pending for from one to three years, and an additional 10 percent for more than three years, in 1971. On the other hand, only slightly more than half the criminal cases were brought to trial within six months; and even after excluding cases involving fugitives, over an eighth of the total had not yet been tried after a year or more—such year-or-more-old pending cases were less than 6 percent of the total in the Ninth Circuit, but they constituted 24 percent for the federal district courts comprising the Second Circuit, and the rate for New York, Southern was 34 percent: a third of the criminal defendants in the federal district court in the country's largest city could not expect their cases to be tried in less than a year—and unless they could make bail, they would be spending that year in jail. At that, this constituted a considerable improvement over three years earlier, when the corresponding ratios were 47 percent (for the Second Circuit) and 57 percent (for the New York, Southern district).

Over half of all 18,780 trials in 1972 (including both civil and criminal, and both jury and nonjury) were completed in one day or less; but the volume of all trials had increased by 54 percent over six years earlier, and the volume of long trials (ten days or more) by 73 percent.

A QUALITATIVE ANALYSIS

In the most general sense, both the national and the state judicial systems have the function of resolving conflicts of interest between persons. The parties to cases decided by the courts range in numbers from the solitary individual who frequently is the *in forma pauperis* defendant in a criminal case, to a complex bureaucracy such as the Department of Justice which, in the name of an even more huge and diffuse and complex aggregate called "the United States," prosecutes him. But armies and policemen and psychiatrists also resolve conflicts; the peculiar and characteristic function of courts is to legitimize proposed solutions to conflicts so that acceptance is consensual among observers as well as among parties to judicial proceedings. In the latter sense, all of society is indirectly an "observer of the proceedings." As the next two chapters will show, a judicial system transforms a heterogeneous aggregate of demands and interests into a much more homogeneous and stereotyped set of responses. By a process that results in immense oversimplification, a court substitutes limited and feasible goals—cast as imperative modes of behavior—for the much more extreme (and sometimes unlimited) demands that the opposing parties have made upon each other. By thus reducing relative chaos to relative order, the most basic function of judicial systems is to extend the bounds of rationality in human behavior.

The federal judicial system has the particular function of legitimizing acts of the other subsystems of the national political system, and the Supreme Court has the additional function of legitimizing the acts of the lower courts in the national judicial subsystem. The Supreme Court's most difficult function, however, is to attempt to legitimize its own acts; this is why the robes and ritual, the formality of oral argument and opinion reading, the secrecy of discussion, and, especially, the writing and content of opinions are so important in the Court's decision-making process. Necessarily, the public image of the legitimacy of the Supreme Court is affected by the communications about the Court that are disseminated through the mass media.[25] Suggestions by some senators, that Justice William O. Douglas should be impeached because of his involvement with a foundation allegedly supported

[25]See Chester A. Newland, "Press Coverage of the United States Supreme Court," *Western Political Quarterly* 17 (1964), pp. 15–36; David L. Grey, "The Supreme Court as a Communicator," *Houston Law Review* 5 (1968), pp. 405–429, and also his *The Supreme Court and the News Media* (Evanston, Ill.: Northwestern University Press, 1968); and Walter F. Murphy and Joseph Tanenhaus, "Public Opinion and the United States Supreme Court: A Preliminary Mapping of Some Prerequisites for Court Legitimation of Regime Changes," *Law and Society Review* 2 (1968), pp. 357–384; Lionel S. Sobel, "News Coverage of the Supreme Court," *American Bar Association Journal,* 56 (1970), pp. 547–550; and Donald Gregory and Stephen L. Wasby, "How to Get an Idea from Here to There: The Court and Communication Overload," *Public Affairs Bulletin* (Research Bureau, Southern Illinois University at Carbondale) 3, No. 5 (November–December 1970).

by big-time Las Vegas gambling interests, have the effect—and are intended to have the effect—of impairing the Court's ability to legitimize what its critics perceive to be the undesirable policies that it has been sponsoring. The Supreme Court's own legitimacy, upon which hinges its capacity to legitimize the policies of the national political system, is therefore a question of fundamental political significance.

The structure of the American polity is such that even when the federal judicial subsystem has been brought into accord with the rest of the national political system, substantial disequilibrium can occur between the federal courts and state political systems because of the gross disjunction between the values of a majority of Supreme Court justices, on one hand, and, on the other, of the local majorities (present or past) who dominate state policies on such issues as racial equality or legislative apportionment. Here, too, there is lag, but with the substantial difference that the lag lies in the traditional values accepted by discrete local popular pluralities—not necessarily majorities—rather than in the Supreme Court. Moreover, the political structure of Congress and of the American political party system and the method of electing the President are such that, on issues such as racial equality and legislative reapportionment, national decision makers whose own acts are indirectly but frequently subject to the legitimizing popular audit of the electoral process cannot assume the initiative in national policy making. This does not mean that the presidency and congressional majorities, or the popular pluralities whom they represent, are opposed to the Court's policies regarding race relations and political representation; on the contrary, it means that the rest of the political system can perform the indispensable function of legitimizing the policies of the Supreme Court, when the Court is the only national decision maker in a position to assume the initiative in such policy making. When President Eisenhower sent the National Guard to Little Rock in 1957, when President Kennedy sent United States marshals into Mississippi in 1962, and when Congress enacted the Civil Rights Acts of 1957, 1960, and 1964—the first such national legislation since the days of Reconstruction—the rest of the political system was legitimizing the fundamental national policy of racial nondiscrimination in education that the Supreme Court had assumed the initiative to make for the nation. Also fundamental, in its implications, was the Court's policy in regard to political representation, for by insisting upon legislative reapportionment in the states and upon redistricting for Congress on the basis of substantial equality among district populations, the Court was so restructuring the national and state political systems that these systems (1) would be more likely to continue to legitimize the Court's policy making in other fields—to the extent, at least, that the Court itself continues to represent majoritarian values—and (2) even more importantly, would be in a better position themselves to assume the initiative in policy making and thereby tend to constrain the Court to its more usual function of legitimizing the decisions of other major actors in the American political system.

On the basis of our entire federal experience to date, however, it can be anticipated that there probably will continue to be policy problems that are national in scope but federal in their resolution, because of conflict between national and local majorities, which in turn frequently will lead to conflict between national and state political systems. We can expect that in such policy fields the Supreme Court will act in response to widespread political demands that the rest of the national political system is unable to satisfy.

We have said that the basic function of any court is to resolve conflicts, that a particular function of the federal courts is to legitimize the policies of the rest of the national political system, and that it is a particular function of the Supreme Court to illegitimize policies that are favored by local but opposed by national majorities. In the performance of all three of these mutually reinforcing functions, the federal courts make the many decisions that were quantitatively summarized in the preceding section of this chapter. In addition to their obvious impact on the immediate parties to cases, such decisions are, in effect, policy directives to other political actors. And even when the federal courts are legitimizing the policies of other actors, the judges charge a toll for their imprimatur: their price is the reformulation, sometimes in major respects and sometimes in detail, of the *others'* policies that *they* interpret.[26] The Supreme Court, for example, issues policy directives to Congress and to state legislatures; occasionally to the presidency or to governors but more often to national or to state administrative agencies; and frequently to local police officials (in regard to such issues as search and seizure and coerced confessions) and to local school boards (as in "released time" and school prayer as well as racial integration cases). The Court also issues policy directives to guide the behavior of lawyers in their handling of future cases at both trial and appellate levels within the judicial system. Evidently, too, the Court's decisions (on such issues as school nondiscrimination or Sunday closing) function as policy directives to the American public as well.[27]

[26]The converse of this proposition also holds true.
[27]See G. Theodore Mitau, *Decade of Decision: The Supreme Court and the Constitutional Revolution, 1954–1964* (New York: Charles Scribner's Sons, 1967); and Theodore L. Becker, ed., *The Impact of Supreme Court Decisions: Empirical Studies* (New York: Oxford University Press, 1969).

HOW THE SUPREME COURT SUPERVISES LOWER COURTS

Technically, all of the Supreme Court's decisions (except for the fraction of 1 percent decided in original jurisdiction)[28] take the form of orders to *lower courts*. The Court gives directions only indirectly, through the intervening action of lower courts, to administrators, legislators, school boards, and special interest groups. Even the Court's orders to the immediate parties to a given case are given indirectly through lower courts. Typically, the Supreme Court's policy directives to lower courts assume one of three forms. The first two of these are overtly legislative in function and apply only within the national system.

FORMAL RULE MAKING

The first category consists of rules of procedure, which are formulated largely by professional working groups of lower court judges, lawyers, and law professors and which are promulgated by the Supreme Court under statutory delegations of authority. These rules are intended to guide the process of decision making in the trial (district) courts, and they are clustered under such

---

[28]Cases decided by the Supreme Court under original jurisdiction typically involve conflicts of interest among and between state political systems and the national political system, and, although few in number, such cases often raise for decision major issues of public policy. See Lucius J. Barker, "The Offshore Oil Cases," Chapter 7 in *The Third Branch of Government: 8 Cases in Constitutional Politics,* ed. C. Herman Pritchett and Alan F. Westin (New York: Harcourt Brace Jovanovich, Inc., 1963). Since the Supreme Court has neither the time nor the facilities to conduct trials, it appoints so-called special masters to function as the equivalent of *ad hoc* United States district judges, in order to compile a record and to formulate tentative decisions in the form of what are termed "recommendations" to the Supreme Court. An example of such a policy dispute is the allocation of the waters of the Colorado River among the seven states with a primary interest (particularly California, now the most populous state in the union, which for a long time has been absolutely dependent upon imported Colorado River water for almost its entire supply). This dispute was actively under way for over two generations, and the most recent—by no means the initial—Supreme Court litigation began in 1952. In June 1963, the Supreme Court finally filed the 101-page report of what has since then proved to be its principal decision, together with various opinions pro and con the accommodation of interests acceptable to a majority of the Court. *Arizona v. California,* 373 U.S. 546 (1963). Subsequent decisions in the same case are reported at 376 U.S. 340 (1964), 377 U.S. 921 (1964), and 383 U.S. 268 (1966).

major substantive legal categories as "civil law," "criminal law," "bankruptcy law," and "maritime and admiralty law." Such rules are subject to interpretation by the lower courts and by the Supreme Court in the same manner as are acts of Congress or administrative regulations.[29] There are also the procedural rules, previously mentioned, that each federal court, including the Supreme Court, makes for itself under a statutory delegation of authority that began in the Judiciary Act of 1789.[30]

INFORMAL RULE MAKING

The second category arises from a much more recent practice of the Court, begun barely two decades ago,[31] of announcing procedural rules in the opinions of the Court's majorities. These rules are intended to regulate the F.B.I. and other national police in their treatment of criminal defendants during investigations of crimes. The sanction behind these procedural rules is the Court's directive to the district courts not to receive as evidence information obtained from defendants in violation of the rules. Thus the Court uses what are in effect direct orders to lower court judges in order to extend its policy control over national police agencies. The purported power base for such policy directives is the Supreme Court's claim to "inherent" supervisory authority over lower national courts. In order to attempt to accomplish similar policy control over state and local police,[32] the Supreme Court must infer

[29]See, for example, *Sacher* v. *United States,* 343 U.S. 1 (1952). In a statement protesting some amendments that accompanied the chief justice's report to Congress, early in 1963, of draft *Rules of Civil Procedure* for the United States district courts, Justices Black and Douglas argued that the Supreme Court's participation in the rule-making process is both unconstitutional and unwise (viz., dysfunctional): 374 U.S. 865–866, 870; and Douglas continued to argue the point a decade later.

[30] *Wayman* v. *Southard,* 10 Wheaton 1 (1825).

[31] *McNabb* v. *United States,* 318 U.S. 332 (1943); and see *Jencks* v. *United States,* 353 U.S. 657 (1957). The latter decision was the basis for what is called the "Jencks rule"—that the "right to confrontation" requires the government to produce for inspection by the defense confidential reports to the F.B.I. by government witnesses concerning the substance of their testimony in criminal trials. The alternative to production of the reports is dismissal of the action.

[32]For an excellent discussion, see Neal Milner, "Supreme Court Effectiveness and the Police Organization," *Law and Contemporary Problems* 36 (1971), pp. 467–487; and Stephen L. Wasby, "Police and the Law in Illinois: A First Look at the Communication of Supreme Court Decisions," *Public Affairs Bulletin* 5, No. 4 (September–October 1972).

analogous procedural norms to be a "requirement of the Constitution"—usually as a part of the revealed meaning of the Fourteenth Amendment's due process clause.[33]

DECISIONAL RULE MAKING

The third category of Supreme Court rule making consists of the *ad hoc* and discrete orders that accompany the disposition of particular cases. From what they perceive to be logically related sets of decisional "rules," judges and law professors infer principles of "decisional law." In a few instances, quite elaborate attempts have been made to specify the precise, internally consistent content of the "decisional rules" associated with particular (and presumably homogeneous) sets of decisions, of which the work done on the "right to counsel" cases affords an example.[34] These so-called principles of law are not to be confused with the orders that direct lower courts in the disposition of particular cases; the latter are the "mandates" of the Court.

[33]Cf. *Weeks* v. *United States,* 232 U.S. 383 (1914); *Wolf* v. *Colorado,* 338 U.S. 25 (1949); *Mapp* v. *Ohio,* 367 U.S. 643 (1961).
[34]See Fred Kort, "Content Analysis of Judicial Opinions and Rules of Law," Chapter 6 in *Judicial Decision-Making,* ed. Glendon Schubert, op. cit.; and Reed C. Lawlor, "What Computers Can Do: Analysis and Prediction of Judicial Decisions," *American Bar Association Journal* 49 (April 1963), pp. 337–344, and his "Foundations of Logical Legal Decision-Making," *Modern Uses of Logic in Law* 3, No. 4 (June 1963), pp. 98–114.

Decision-Making Procedures

Judicial decision-making procedure can be regarded as a continuum of behaviors. The series of successive decisions in a single case—the trial decision, the decision at the first stage of appellate review, the decision at the second stage of appellate review, etc.—are the "sections" of the continuum; within each such section, we can identify half a dozen "segments" that correspond to developmental stages in the process of decision making. The following concepts afford a generalized way of talking about all of the discrete behaviors within any particular segment of a section of the continuum: initiation, accommodation, persuasion, decision, implementation, reconsideration. This set of concepts is sufficiently general to subsume all of the legal categories—many of which are overlapping and logically inconsistent—with which we must deal. Lawyers use, with meanings similar to ours, some but not all of these concepts.

TRIALS

INITIATION

Cases are initiated for potential decision making by courts because of conflicts of interests among persons in the political society in the name of which the courts act. From a legal point of view, some persons "injure" others by committing or threatening to commit "wrongs," which are defined (tautologically) as violations of the "rights" of the person injured. The task of courts is to provide remedies—frequently in the form of mandated substitutions for irreparable losses—with the objective of "righting wrongs" or of preventing them, to the extent possible. Under this view, it is clear that the fundamental objective of courts is to maintain, or to restore, the *status quo ante delictum*, that is, the way things were before the wrong was committed. This goal is in close accord with the concept of homeostasis that usually is associated with systems theory and analysis, for the court is seeking to restore human relationships to the balance or harmony which existed before the event which disturbed their "normal" condition. It can be and is argued that the primary goal of the judicial system is to protect individual rights.[1] But it also can be and is argued that the primary goal is to settle disputes—to maintain order.[2] Empirically, both points of view tend to be represented, and in competition with each other, in functioning judicial systems. Liberals tend to stress the importance of protecting individual rights, while conservatives emphasize the importance of conflict resolution—of stability.

From a political point of view which perceives courts as instruments that can be used by protagonists and antagonists to aggrandize their own power and influence, both of these perspectives are too narrow. The judicial system can be seen as merely one among many alternative instrumentalities that may appropriately

[1]"In this country the judiciary was made independent because it has, I believe, the primary responsibility and duty of giving force and effect to constitutional liberties and limitations upon the executive and legislative branches. . . . Suggestions were . . . made in and out of Congress [during its initial session in 1789] that a Bill of Rights would be a futile gesture since there would be no way to enforce the safeguards for freedom it provided. Mr. Madison answered this argument in these words:
If they [the Bill of Rights amendments] are incorporated into the Constitution, independent tribunals of justice will consider themselves in a peculiar manner the guardians of those rights; they will be an impenetrable bulwark against any assumption of power in the legislative or executive; they will be naturally led to resist every encroachment upon rights expressly stipulated for in the Constitution by the Declaration of Rights. [1 Annals of Cong. 439.]
I fail to see how courts can escape this sacred trust." Justice Hugo Black, "The Bill of Rights," *New York University Law Review* 35 (1960), pp. 870, 880.
[2]"Stare decisis is usually the wise policy, because *in most matters it is more important that the applicable rule of law be settled than that it be settled right.*" Justice Louis Brandeis, dissenting in *Burnet* v. *Coronado Oil and Gas Co.*, 285 U.S. 393, 406 (1932). Emphasis added.

be invoked—singly, in sequence, or several simultaneously—in order to realize political ends. Under such a view, the moralistic overtones of both individual "right and wrong" and societal "good" become displaced by considerations of strategy and tactics for manipulating judicial systems.

The vocabulary used to describe court procedures was developed by lawyers, not by political scientists. Therefore, if we are to stay within a realm of discourse that encompasses practically all of the published work on this subject, we must use concepts that clearly presume the legal point of view, even though our own assumption is that the political perspective is at least equally relevant. From such a legal point of view, there is a basic distinction between civil and criminal cases. In civil cases, the conflict of interest is between or among individuals or groups of individuals, one or more of whom has a complaint against another or others. If the parties have made an agreement to act in concert in order to better accomplish some common and legal objective, then the failure of one party to carry out his part of the bargain is an offense against the rights of the other party or parties to the contract, and he or they may seek to have the offense redressed by filing a complaint in an appropriate court. Other injuries, which may lead to a judicial finding of private liability in the absence of a contractual relationship, are classified as torts.

Crimes are torts against society. Many local communities still rely upon the older system of private prosecution for many petty offenses. This requires some individual or individuals to assume the initiative in "bringing malefactors to justice" by appearing before a magistrate to swear out a complaint against the particular defendant or defendants who are accused of having committed designated wrongs, which are defined by law to be offenses against the interests of the state—as well as often being private torts against the injured individuals. Once the complaint has been filed, the remainder of the function of prosecuting the defendant is carried out by the government of which the court is a part. For most minor offenses and practically all major crimes, however, court action is initiated by the filing of complaints by police officers, with the result that both initiation and the subsequent steps in prosecution are made by employees of the government. Although in most states the title of criminal cases is "The People of the State of *X* versus John Doe," the parties whose immediate interests appear to be in conflict in most criminal cases are the police and prosecutor, on the one hand, and the defendant, on the other hand.

There are technical and historical differences between the initiation in civil procedure of complaints at law and at equity, but we shall note in subsequent discussion only such major differences as the use of juries and the form of verdicts. The party who initiates a case, in both civil and criminal procedure, is the *plaintiff;* the opposing party who is required to answer the complaint is the *defendant.* The initiation of criminal procedure is more complicated than the relatively simple filing of a complaint, which civil procedure requires. Closely associated with the criminal complaint are supporting administrative procedures. Usually the police investigate the alleged offense. In cases involving serious crimes the police, either alone or in cooperation with investigators working directly under the prosecuting attorney, undertake to apprehend, arrest, temporarily confine, and interrogate various suspects, often including the person who subsequently becomes the defendant in the case. The counterpart in civil procedure of these investigatory activities in criminal procedure consists of the consultation between the plaintiff and his counsel, and the latter's inquiry into the facts alleged by his client and also into the law (the policy norms) that he predicts most likely to be applied by the court or courts in which he might file a complaint on behalf of the plaintiff.

In criminal procedure, the functional equivalent of the civil complaint is the filing of an accusation with a court, charging with explicit offenses a named person (who thereby becomes a defendant). Such a charge must state both the law which allegedly has been violated and also, in a general way, the relevant facts—that is, the specific acts of the defendant that are presumed to constitute the stated violation of law. There are two principal ways in which such charges are filed. The most common method, used exclusively in about half of the states and for lesser offenses in the remaining states and in the federal judicial system, is for the prosecutor and his staff, without recourse to jury proceedings, to decide to file an initiating complaint called an *information.* The other common method, used in about half of the states and in the federal judicial system to bring charges against defendants accused of serious crimes, requires that a grand jury rather than the prosecutor make the formal decision whether to file a complaint against a suspect.

Depending on the state, the grand jury consists of from one to two dozen persons who are selected—presumably at random—from a list of qualified citizens maintained by the clerk of the court. There is a presumption that a grand jury represents a cross section of the dominant opinions in a community. This notion has long since been discredited as a legal fiction.[3] The universal practice is to exempt those classes of citizens who would be best qualified (by education, by awareness, and by involvement in the affairs of the community) to serve as jurors. The consequence, for both grand juries and also for the petit juries to be discussed below, is that jury panels are loaded with middle-aged housewives whose children are grown, with semi-professional jurors for whom the juror's fee provides an attractive day's wages, and with senior citizens who come out of retirement to serve as jurors. Far from constituting a sample representative of the community, such a grand jury appears (from a political point of view) to be a sample biased toward conservatism and dogmatism[4] relative to whatever would be average on these dimensions for a particular community. The prosecutor appears before such a group, which convenes in the courthouse in secret proceedings, and presents his charges and evidence. If the group votes (by a majority or some other requisite proportion or quantity of jurors) to accept the prosecutor's charges, then a suspect is indicted; otherwise, he is not charged with the crime. The *indictment* is technically the statement of charges that the grand jury directs to be filed in the court. Where the grand jury participates in the initiation of criminal cases, the prosecutor must share part of his decision-making authority with it, just as, when trial by jury is used, the judge must share part of his decision-making authority with the petit jury.

Another kind of complaint, known as the *presentment,* occasionally emanates from grand juries. Here the jury acts on the basis of information "of its own knowledge," which necessarily is acquired by having the jury itself supervise police investigatory activities. Instead of having the prosecutor select what part of his evidence he chooses to put before the grand jury, in support of charges that he has decided upon, the jury (at least in form) draws upon funds and personnel made available to it by the court and conducts its own investigation. The practical difference is that such investigations almost invariably are sallies into local politics as much as, or more than, they are inquisitions into local crime. This is evidenced by the kinds of complaints that are made to the court; often, a presentment will inform the court that gambling and vice are rampant in the community, and instead of charging specific

[3]See W. S. Robinson, "Bias, Probability, and Trial by Jury," *American Sociological Review* 15 (1950), pp. 73–78; Edwin S. Mills, "A Statistical Study of Occupations of Jurors in a U.S. District Court," *Maryland Law Review* 22 (1962), pp. 204–214; Michael O. Finkelstein, "The Application of Statistical Decision Theory to the Jury Discrimination Cases," *Harvard Law Review* 80 (1966), pp. 338–376; Charles A. Lindquist, "An Analysis of Juror Selection Procedure in the United States District Courts," *Temple Law Quarterly* 41 (1967), pp. 32–50, and Edwin S. Mills, "A Statistical Profile of Jurors in a United States District Court," *Law and Social Order* (1969), pp. 329–339.

[4]Herbert McClosky, "Conservatism and Personality," *American Political Science Review* 52 (1958), pp. 27–45; Milton Rokeach, *The Open and Closed Mind* (New York: Basic Books, Inc., 1960); Hans Eysenck, *The Psychology of Politics* (London: Routledge and Kegan Paul, 1954).

individuals with indictable offenses, the presentment will charge the community at large with "moral laxity" and with "responsibility" for the cited evils. Evidently, the objective is to influence public opinion and political behavior rather than to initiate criminal proceedings in court against any defendant in particular. Presentments are relatively rare in state judicial systems, and they are practically unknown in the federal judicial system.

ACCOMMODATION

In civil procedure at common law in Shakespeare's day, the issue that the court was asked to decide was precisely defined by a complex (and, as it eventually became, quite stereotyped) series of alternative motions filed by the parties. These motions constituted the *pleadings* in the case. Any error in the prescribed form of such statements could result in a motion by opposing counsel to have the judge "quash" (dismiss) the complaint. Today more importance is attached to the substance than to the form of civil complaints, and auxiliary procedures have been developed to explore the issue further than can be done through the pleadings. One such procedure is that of *discovery,* under which an attorney can ascertain, before the trial takes place, what sort of evidence opposing counsel has available for use; thus discovery is a procedure for developing consensus as to the facts of the case. Increasing use also is being made of pretrial *conference,* which brings opposing counsel and the judge together to discuss the *case*—that is, the evidence and the arguments—that each party expects to present; and the result is that greater consensus with regard to the legal issues develops among all of the principal actors in the impending trial. Another consequence of the conference is that the opposing counsel often will agree to *stipulate*—that is, to agree upon a statement, which becomes part of the record—concerning many of the "facts" that initially were in dispute. This reduces the costs of a trial, since most of the time at a trial is devoted to attempts to introduce, or to preclude the introduction of, evidence that is intended to support one set of inferences concerning "the facts" instead of various possible alternative versions. The general effect of these various pretrial procedures, plus such others as direct negotiation between the opposing counsel, is to bring about a compromise settlement, "out of court" (as the newspaper phrase goes), of most complaints. It will be remembered that almost 90 percent of the civil cases filed in the federal court system never go to trial.

Over 80 percent of criminal complaints also are accommodated without a trial. In many, the complaint is in effect dismissed by the prosecutor for any of a variety of undisclosed reasons: because he thinks that his evidence, community sentiment, or the attitudes of the judge are such that his own "record" would be impaired if the case went to trial, because of the improbability of securing a conviction; because he believes the defendant to be innocent; because of political influence brought to bear in behalf of the defendant; because he has thereby purchased the cooperation of an undercover agent to assist him in subsequent investigations of more important suspects; and so forth. Similarly, many defendants who are guilty decide or are advised by counsel that the probabilities of their being convicted are so great that their best bet is to "throw themselves on the mercy of the court" and hope for some leniency in punishment in exchange for having "saved the government the expense of a trial." Most other complaints that do not go to trial are compromised, usually as the result of negotiations between defendant's counsel and the prosecuting attorney: the defendant either pleads guilty to a reduced charge, or he pleads guilty with what he understands to be an informal commitment concerning his sentence.[5]

These accommodations are formalized at a hearing called an *arraignment,* which in the federal court system is held before a United States magistrate rather than before a judge. At the arraignment, the defendant pleads to the initial or substitute charges that have been filed against him, unless at this time the charges are withdrawn on motion of the prosecutor. Only those cases go to trial in which the defendant's plea is "not guilty" or in which such a plea is entered for him because he "stands mute" (refuses to respond to the charge).

Federal magistrates displaced the former United States commissioners (who formerly performed some similar functions) throughout the federal judicial system in the early 1970s, under a statute that was intended to pave the way for greater delegation of decision-making authority from the federal district judges. The year 1972 was the first full one of operations with the new procedures (which tended to vary considerably in different districts and circuits); by then there were ninety full-time and 453 part-time magistrates, plus sixteen persons with combined appointments as

---

[5]Abraham S. Blumberg, "The Practice of Law as a Confidence Game: Organizational Cooptation of a Profession," *Law and Society Review* 2 (1967), pp. 15–39, and also his *Criminal Justice* (Chicago: Quadrangle Books, Inc., 1967); and Donald J. Newman, "Pleading Guilty for Considerations: A Study of Bargain Justice," Ch. 10 in George F. Cole, ed., *Criminal Justice: Law and Politics* (Belmont, Calif.: Wadsworth Publishing Co., Inc., 1972); and John Kaplan, ed., *Criminal Justice: Introductory Cases and Materials* (Mineola, N.Y.: The Foundation Press, Inc., 1973), Ch. 8.

(for example) magistrate and clerk of the court. These magistrates made some 237,522 dispositions in that year, including the trial of some 72,082 minor (including petty) offenses such as traffic, theft, food and drug, immigration, and hunting, fishing, and camping violations. In more than two thirds of the districts, magistrates screened habeas corpus and other prisoner petitions; in more than half of the districts, magistrates conducted pretrial conferences and reviewed pretrial motions in both civil and criminal cases.

A system of federal public defenders also was begun in the early 1970s. The Public Defender Service for the District of Columbia, for instance, comprised 114 persons in 1972, including a director and his deputy, forty-four staff attorneys, sixteen investigators, thirteen social workers, fourteen persons to arrange the appointment of counsel, and some twenty-five clerks and secretaries. This office, which was supervised by the Administrative Office of United States Courts, represented defendants before both trial and appeals courts of both the District of Columbia government and the United States Circuit for the District of Columbia.[6]

PERSUASION

The trial of a case consists of a public hearing in a courtroom, at which a judge presides over argument between opposing counsel. In state judicial systems, most cases are decided by the judge alone, acting without a jury. In the federal courts, two thirds of the civil cases are decided without juries, and so also are a third of the criminal cases. The reason for the decreasing use of juries, in both civil and criminal trials and in both state and the federal judicial systems, is their high cost in both time and money. In direct reflection of the high costs of jury utilization and the frequently inefficient court use of jurors' time, considerable research and administrative management attention was focused beginning in the late 1960s upon jury use in both state and federal courts.[7] Many states turned to juries smaller than the traditional twelve persons for both civil and criminal trials;[8] and by 1972 six-man juries were

[6]Cf. Jonathan D. Casper, "Did You Have a Lawyer When You Went to Court? No, I Had a Public Defender," Ch. 13 in George F. Cole, *Criminal Justice: Law and Politics* (Belmont, Calif.: Wadsworth Publishing Co., Inc., 1972).

[7]See, e.g., Administrative Office of :he United States Courts, *1972 Juror Utilization in United States Courts* (Washington: Superintendent of Documents, 1972).

[8]The Supreme Court held that the federal Constitution did not require jury unanimity in the *state* courts even for felony convictions: *Johnson* v. *Louisiana,* 406 U.S. 356 (1972), and *Apodaca* v. *Oregon,* 406 U.S. 404 (1972).

in use for civil trials in well over half of the federal judicial districts—with the subsequent but explicit approval of the United States Supreme Court.[9] Moreover, a trial before a jury is substantively a quite different kind of proceeding than a trial before a judge alone. A petit jury of whatever size consists of lay persons whose average socioeconomic and educational status is at or below the level of mediocrity.

In some states, but not in the federal courts, special panels of "blue-ribbon" jurors are established, from which particular juries are selected from time to time for criminal cases deemed important by the prosecutor. Such juries are biased to be above average in education and socioeconomic status, since they are packed with upper-middle-class, white-collar, professional males. It is believed, and the available empirical evidence tends to confirm, that such juries will vote for conviction more frequently than will juries drawn from the ordinary lists in the same community.[10]

Even when an above-average group of citizens comprises the jury, they are put in that role precisely because they are laymen— that is, because they are generally inexperienced in and ignorant of trial procedure. As a consequence, lawyers must appeal primarily to the beliefs and values of the jurors, and the introduction of evidence is directed not so much to the transcendental notion of trying to establish what "the facts" are, but rather to the much more directly significant question of what the jury will believe the facts to be.[11] In most civil cases, whether either a simple or an extraordinary majority must agree in order for the jury to reach a decision, counsel can afford to ignore one or two jurors whose values are idiosyncratic and play instead for the majority sentiment; but in a federal criminal case, where unanimity is required for decision, the prosecutor must convince every juror of the defendant's guilt,

---

[9] *Colegrove* v. *Battin,* 41 *Law Week* 5025 (1973).

[10] John P. Reed, "Jury Deliberations, Voting, and Verdict Trends," *Southwestern Social Science Quarterly* 45 (1965), pp. 361–370; John H. Vanderzell, "The Jury As a Community Cross Section," *Western Political Quarterly* 19 (1966), pp. 136–149; Ronald C. Wolf, "Trial by Jury: A Sociological Analysis," *Wisconsin Law Review* 1956 (1966), pp. 820–830; and Daniel H. Swett, "Cultural Bias in the American Legal System," *Law and Society Review* 4 (1969), at pp. 96–97.

[11] Rita James Simon, *The Jury and the Defense of Insanity* (Boston: Little, Brown and Company, 1967); and Harold Garfinkel and Saul Mendlovitz, "Some Rules of Correct Decisions That Jurors Respect," Chapter 4 in Harold Garfinkel, *Studies in Ethnomethodology* (Englewood Cliffs: Prentice-Hall, Inc., 1967), pp. 104–115.

while the defense counsel has only to convince a single juror of his client's innocence.[12]

The petit jury has been used in Anglo-American criminal trial procedure for over eight centuries, but relatively little social scientific knowledge is available about jury behavior.[13] Both the defense and the prosecution may "challenge" prospective jurors after asking them questions, and we do know that experienced trial lawyers do their best to manipulate, within the relatively narrow limits where choice can roam, the value composition of juries by this blackballing procedure known as the examination of jurors *voir dire*. In the 1964 trial in Dallas of Jack Ruby for the murder of Lee Oswald—a murder which millions saw on TV—chief defense counsel Melvin Belli so maneuvered that considerably more time was devoted to the selection of the jury than to the trial itself.

Research in jury decision making is difficult to carry out because the secrecy of proceedings precludes direct observation of how real juries make decisions. Most work has been done either with simulated jury groups[14] or with anecdotal materials provided by the reminiscences of ex-jurors.[15] Recent experimental research suggests that when a pseudo-jury group is almost consensual on the initial ballot, the lone dissenter, in most instances, soon succumbs to social pressure to defer to what appears quite literally to be overwhelming majority opinion.[16]

---

[12]See the excellent study, using mathematical probability theory as a model, by David F. Walbert, "The Effect of Jury Size on the Probability of Conviction: An Evaluation of *Williams* v. *Florida,"Case Western Reserve Law Review* 22 (1971), pp. 529–554.

[13]See Charles Winick, "The Psychology of Juries," Chapter 5 in *Legal and Criminal Psychology,* ed. Hans Toch (New York: Holt, Rinehart and Winston, Inc., 1961), pp. 96–120; and Rita James Simon, ed., *The Sociology of Law: Interdisciplinary Readings* (San Francisco: Chandler, 1968), Part 4, Section 2, pp. 291–363.

[14]Fred L. Strodtbeck, "Social Process, the Law, and Jury Functioning," in *Law and Sociology: Exploratory Essays,* ed. William M. Evan (New York: The Free Press of Glencoe, 1962), pp. 144–164.

[15]Dale W. Broeder, "Plaintiff's Family Status as Affecting Juror Behavior: Some Tentative Insights," *Journal of Public Law* 14 (1965), pp. 131–141; Broeder, "Voir Dire Examinations: An Empirical Study," *Southern California Law Review* 38 (1965), pp. 503–528; and Broeder, "Previous Jury Trial Service Affecting Juror Behavior," *Insurance Law Journal,* 506 (1965), pp. 138–143.

[16]Theodore L. Becker, Donald C. Hildrun, and Keith Bateman, "The Influence of Jurors' Values on Their Verdicts: A Courts and Politics Experiment," *Southwestern Social Science Quarterly* 46 (1965), pp. 130–140;

In the realm of fiction, the public trial, which constitutes the most conspicuous ceremonial aspect of criminal procedure, is highlighted, and even casual viewers of television's Perry Mason show might well conclude that the innocence or guilt of most criminal defendants is determined by the histrionic artistry of opposing counsel.[17] A more realistic fictional view is that presented in the best-selling novel of the late 1950s, *The Anatomy of a Murder* by "Robert Traver" (former Michigan Supreme Court Justice John D. Voelker), in which the drama of a criminal trial is of central importance but most of the action takes place offstage.

There is very little scientific research on the extent to which trial judges are persuaded by the arguments of counsel to modify their attitudes toward the policy issues that are either explicit or implicit in trials.[18] Judges are continuously exposed to the arts of advocacy, and even after making due allowance for differences in personality types, it seems likely that experienced trial judges are influenced by the persuasion of counsel to the extent that the lawyers' arguments function as stimuli to activate responses that reflect the judges' underlying belief systems and accepted values. Of course, the actions that occur in the courtroom and that are directly observed by the trial judge also affect his perceptions of counsel, of witnesses, of parties, and therefore his attitude toward the policy issues with which these actors variously are identified.[19] Undoubtedly, too, the *interaction* between judges and counsel, both in and out of the courtroom, has an important effect upon the attitudes of judges *toward the lawyers* and therefore indirectly upon their judicial perceptions of the policy views advocated by the attorneys.[20] For example, social psychologists have shown that the *intensity* of interpersonal attitudes is positively correlated with, and probably is a direct function of, the *frequency* of interpersonal

and cf. Robert G. Lawson, "Order of Presentation as a Factor in Jury Persuasion," *Kentucky Law Journal* 56 (1967–1968), pp. 523–555.

[17]Cf. *The New York Times,* September 6, 1963, p. 59, col. 5.

[18]Richard Arens and Jackwell Susman, "Judges, Jury Charges and Insanity," *Howard Law Journal* 12 (1966), pp. 1–34.

[19]Louis Blom-Cooper and Judith Wegner, "Psychological Selectivity in the Courtroom," *Medical Science and Law* 8 (1968), pp. 31–37. For an example, see *Sacher* v. *United States,* 343 U.S. 1 (1952), especially the Appendix to the dissenting opinion of Mr. Justice Frankfurter, pp. 42–89.

[20]Charles Winick, Israel Gerver, and Abraham Blumberg, "The Psychology of Judges," Chapter 6 in *Legal and Criminal Psychology,* op. cit., pp. 121–145.

contacts.[21] From this general theoretical proposition, one ought logically to infer that the decisions of trial judges in criminal cases will be influenced most by the lawyers who appear most frequently before the court—in most criminal courts, the local prosecuting attorneys. This is the kind of hypothesis about judicial behavior that appears to have a high probability of being confirmed by empirical evidence, not only at all levels in the judicial system of the United States but in judicial systems throughout the world and in cultures that range from the most primitive to the most highly developed Western industrialized societies.[22] If such confirmation proved possible, notwithstanding the great diversity and vast cultural differences among the societies in which courts function,[23] it could only be because our hypothesis derives from a theoretical proposition that describes a very fundamental communality in human behavior—which applies to the relationship between judges and attorneys because they, too, despite their specialized sociopolitical roles, are human.

Of course, a judge influences a jury by his own demeanor, and lawyers are sensitive to the possibility of such influence.[24] (Even if the judge were capable of preventing the emission of any cues, he

[21]Dorwin Cartwright and Alvin Zander, eds., *Group Dynamics,* 2nd ed. (Evanston, Ill.: Harper & Row, Publishers, 1960); Robert F. Bales, *Personality and Interpersonal Behavior* (New York: Holt, Rinehart & Winston, Inc., 1970); and Bernard Berelson and Gary A. Steiner, *Human Behavior: An Inventory of Scientific Findings* (New York: Harcourt Brace Jovanovich, Inc., 1964), Chapter 8: "Face-to-Face Relations in Small Groups."

[22]See Laura Nader, ed., *Law in Culture and Society* (Chicago: Aldine, 1969).

[23]Stuart S. Nagel, "Cultural Patterns and Judicial Systems," *Vanderbilt Law Review* 16 (1962), pp. 147–157; Richard D. Schwartz and James C. Miller, "Legal Evolution and Societal Complexity," *American Journal of Sociology* 70 (1964), pp. 159–169; Glendon Schubert and David Danelski, eds., *Comparative Judicial Behavior: Cross-Cultural Studies of Political Decision-Making in the East and West* (New York: Oxford University Press, 1969); and Theodore L. Becker, *Comparative Judicial Politics: The Political Functionings of Courts* (Chicago: Rand McNally & Company, 1970).

[24]Leslie L. Conner, "The Trial Judge, His Facial Expressions, Gestures and General Demeanor—Their Effect on the Administration of Justice," *American Criminal Law Quarterly* 6 (1968), pp. 175–186; cf. Silvan S. Tomkins and Carroll E. Izard, eds., *Affect, Cognition, and Personality: Empirical Studies* (New York: Springer, 1965), Part Six: "Affect and Facial Responses," at pp. 295–350; and Charles E. Osgood, "Dimensionality of the Semantic Space for Communication via Facial Expressions," *Scandinavian Journal of Psychology* 7 (1966), pp. 1–30.

could not prevent individual jurors from imagining that he had revealed his own attitude by his tone or gesture—as perceived by the jurors.) However, there is a much more direct and "legitimate" procedure by which a judge can influence the jury. When both counsel have completed their introduction of evidence and their concluding speeches, in which they implore the jurors to vote in behalf of their respective clients, then the judge presents his "charge" to the jurors before they retire from the courtroom to begin their own task of persuading each other to agree. The judge's charge purports to summarize in "lay language" (viz., English) the legal jargon in which the relevant decision-making norms find expression as the "law."[25] The judge defines for the jury the issue or issues that they are to decide, and in so doing he may comment selectively on "the facts" as well as on "the law." Although some jurors may be persuaded while others are antagonized by the judge's remarks, it is inconceivable that juries generally are not influenced by the judges who charge them; indeed, it is part of their respective roles that the jury *should* be influenced by the judge's charge. Needless to say, the judge's influence is maximal when he "directs" (i.e., orders) the jury to report back to him a verdict which he specifies to them and thus (at least in effect) preempts to himself the function of jury as well as that of judge.

DECISION MAKING

The role of juries in judicial decision making cannot be ignored, but the right to trial by jury is usually waived by defendants in both civil and criminal cases. In the state judicial systems, there are many relatively less important cases for which no right to jury trial exists. In the federal system, juries are not used in civil cases tried under either equity procedure or by the three-judge district courts, and juries rarely are used in trials under the admiralty rules of procedure. When juries do share with judges the decision-making function, their role in the United States district courts is restricted to complex inferences concerning the probability of occurrence of events which are alleged to have transpired before the invocation of judicial proceedings: such events are conceptualized as *"facts,"* and the decision of a jury about facts is called a *"verdict."* The probability of a jury reaching an agreement concerning the facts is maximal when the decisional norm is simple

---

[25]Richard Arens, Dom David Granfield, and Jackwell Susman, "Jurors, Jury Charges and Insanity," *Catholic University of America Law Review* 14 (1965), pp. 1–28.

majority rule, but minimal when unanimity is required (as for the conviction of federal criminal defendants). The jury's view of the facts is not the only one, nor is it by any means even the only view to get into the official record of the case; and opposing counsel and the judge and witnesses (among others) no doubt adhere to their own views, notwithstanding the verdict of the jury. But the jury's view of the facts is usually the most important set of perceptions, since the procedures for decision making are so designed as to give the most weight to the jury's verdict.

Depending upon the demands of counsel and their disposition by the judge, a jury may be asked to bring in a general verdict or a set of special verdicts; that is, the questions that the jury is asked to decide may be cast in a relatively general or in specific form. The more general the issue that the jury is asked to decide, the greater its share in the decision. In many state judicial systems, juries are asked to assume a much larger share of the decision-making authority than are federal juries: some state juries are asked to decide the offense, its degree (in a legal sense), and the appropriate punishment if they agree that a defendant is guilty. However, the jury's verdict is subject not only to influence by the judge in all cases but also to his veto in at least some types of civil cases. If the trial judge's own perception of the facts is considerably at variance with that of the jury, he may usually do either or both of two things. In "discharging" (releasing) the jurors from their official roles, the judge may emphasize his disagreement by converting them into a captive audience who must suffer in silence (under threat of summary punishment for contempt of court) while he lectures them on their iniquities. (This kind of judicial behavior is intended, presumably, to deter future juries from pursuing a similar course of action, at least before this same judge; but it also has the incidental effect of getting into the record the *judge's* view of the facts, for whatever weight it may have if the case should be appealed to a higher court. It thus constitutes an invitation to the losing counsel to appeal the case.) An even stronger way in which the judge can manifest his disagreement is to substitute his own decision "n.o.v."—*non obstante verdictum,* notwithstanding the verdict—for that of the jury. This action differs from that of the directed verdict primarily in that here the jury is permitted to disagree and to assume the initiative in making the decision—and these are differences of some importance. The legal theory is that the "weight of the evidence" must so overwhelmingly support the judge's position, in the case of either directed verdicts or "n.o.v." judgments, that no rational (honest, unprejudiced, dispassionate, etc.) group of jurors could possibly disagree with him. Nevertheless, Supreme Court majorities not infrequently find themselves in agreement with juries rather than with trial judges. In regard, for example, to Federal Employers' Liability Act cases (where juries often vote that railroads must pay monetary compensation to injured railroad employees), the Supreme Court in 1956 reversed two affirmances, one by a United States court of appeals and the other by a state supreme court, of judgment for the defendant railroad, notwithstanding jury verdicts for the plaintiffs; and in the following term the Court reversed a state supreme court that had affirmed a state trial judge's directed verdict in favor of a railroad.[26]

The judge himself is supposed to decide questions of law—that is, he is supposed to rule upon disputed questions relating to the procedural norms that are presumed to guide the decision-making processes of the trial—and he also is supposed to decide the disputed questions of substantive policy which constitute the issues that purport to bring to a focus the underlying conflict of interests between the parties to the case.[27] The final decision of the trial judge upon the latter issue (or set of issues) constitutes the *"judgment"* in the case. In the three-judge United States district courts, of course, the judgment depends upon the agreement of at least two of the participating judges.

Together, the verdict and the judgment constitute what is usually and somewhat loosely called *"the decision of the court,"* although in a more technical legal sense, the court's decision takes the form of an order requiring that some specified action be taken by, or in regard to, one or both of the parties to the case. The most usual (and the classic) forms of a decision are these: (1) in civil cases "at law," the court orders one of the parties to return property belonging to another, to pay the monetary equivalent of the property, or to pay monetary compensation for personal injury; (2) in civil cases in equity, the court's decree orders one party to do—or more often, to refrain from doing—some specified act or set of actions affecting the interests of the other party; and (3) in criminal cases, the defendant is either released from the custody of the court or detained for sentencing, usually at a later time. In many civil cases, the judge, after he has announced his judgment, will

[26]Glendon Schubert, *Quantitative Analysis of Judicial Behavior* (New York: The Free Press of Glencoe, 1959), pp. 264–265.

[27]Thus, whether a defendant should be charged with second-degree murder or first-degree manslaughter is conceptualized as a question of substantive legal policy; whether a confession that he gave to the police may be admitted as evidence against him is considered to be a question of procedural law; while whether he is guilty of the offense with which he is charged is deemed a question of fact.

request opposing counsel to agree upon the draft of a decree. As a result, the opposing counsel usually participate in the preparation of the order which the judge signs to dispose of the case. The legal theory is that once he has "clarified" the relevant legal principles, then the mere application of those principles to the (by now) authoritatively determined facts of the case is only a clerical matter that reasonable men (such as the opposing counsel) who are officers of the court will perform almost mechanically, thus relieving the court of the burden of drafting the decree. More realistically, however, the right of counsel to formulate the specific terms of the settlement is important as an additional means for accommodating and compromising the conflicts of interest that remain after the decision in the case has been made.

Most decisions of trial courts are announced orally by judges who are talking to lawyers in open court. It is only in a small minority of the trials that written opinions are filed by the presiding judges. Moreover, by no means all of the written opinions of the United States district courts and courts of appeals are published: there is no official sponsorship of the printing of the written opinions of the district courts and courts of appeals, although the reports of the Supreme Court have been published by the government since 1882,[28] and there is official publication of the reports (opinions) of the Customs Court, the Court of Customs and Patent Appeals, the Court of Claims, and the Tax Court of the United States. However, a commercial law book company does publish (though selectively) many lower federal court reports—for the district courts in what is called the *Federal Supplement* series and for the courts of appeals in the *Federal Reporter, Second Series* (F.2d.).

IMPLEMENTATION

The implementation of the orders of trial courts is a function of the supporting administrative structures described in Chapter Three. The sanction behind orders for the transfer between the parties of money or property is the attachment by the United States marshal of the same or an equivalent amount of the property of the civil losing party, and if necessary the liquidation of the property through a distress sale. For civil decrees, in equity form, the sanction is the authority of the court summarily to punish dis-

[28]For a more comprehensive discussion, see "The Publication of Reports of the Supreme Court's Decisions," Appendix A in Glendon Schubert, *Constitutional Politics* (New York: Holt, Rinehart & Winston, Inc., 1960), pp. 703–706.

obedience of the order through an ancillary criminal proceeding, in which the judge is the prosecutor and the losing party is cast in the role of defendant against charges of contempt of the court. In criminal cases, convicted defendants are investigated by probation officers, upon whose report—together with whatever recommendations may have been made by the prosecuting attorney or by the petit jury—the judge places as much reliance as he chooses when deciding the sentence. The sentence may take the form of imprisonment, a monetary fine, probation, parole, or a combination of these. It will be recalled that district judges of the federal courts increasingly are being conditioned to utilize the indeterminate procedure for sentencing, which involves the allocation to presumably expert bureaucrats of a larger share, and to presumably inexpert (because they are generalists) judges a smaller share, in the decision-making function for implementing decisions in criminal cases.

Of course, what a United States district court can do to punish and/or rehabilitate a young man who drives a "hot" car across the George Washington Bridge from New York to Fort Lee, New Jersey, presents a very different kind of implementation problem than does a civil antitrust decree against a corporate giant (such as DuPont), ordering that it divest its dominating stock interest in another super corporation (such as General Motors). The complex interlocking relationships between two or more such corporations can well involve thousands—perhaps millions—of people over a period of more than forty or fifty years, while the casual theft of the car and its transportation in interstate commerce could be carried out, from inception near the New York end of the bridge to arrest upon arrival at the Jersey shore, by one individual in less than ten minutes. Typically, it takes from one to two *decades* from the early planning of a major antitrust case (such as the example above) through trial(s) and the exhaustion of appellate review to reach the point in the process—usually, the return to the district court of the Supreme Court's order requiring that one firm sell its stock in the other—at which time it is possible to start talking about implementation of the antitrust decree. When the district court finally confronts that problem, considerably more is involved than merely calling in the marshal or a probation officer. The "enforcement" of the court's decree will itself require many complicated decisions to be made by many people over an extended period of time. Implementation may involve not only the presidency, Congress, several divisions of the Department of Justice (including of course, the antitrust division), the Treasury Department, the Securities and Exchange Commission, and the Department of Commerce, but also many other agencies, state and private as well as national. The trial court of necessity retains a continuing supervisory role in the proceedings, in order to assure that the monopolistic relationship is not resumed and that the court's orders are carried out. Within five to ten years *after* the "final" decree is approved, by the trial court, for administrative enforcement, one can expect that there may have been some changes made in the structure of the corporate relationships and in the functioning of the competitive relationships of the major industries involved in the antitrust prosecution.[29]

RECONSIDERATION

We have discussed implementation before reconsideration because in most cases no appeal is made from the decisions of trial courts. The data in Table 7 indicate that only about 8 percent of the decisions of the district courts, in all of the major categories, are appealed. We might well, therefore, look upon reconsideration as an auxiliary subsystem of the federal judicial system, into which a few cases are diverted for specialized processing before they are fed back into the main channel of the system for final processing.

There are three principal types of reconsideration. The first is that in which the counsel for either or both parties—since most decisions constitute a compromise between their conflicting claims —ask the trial judge to change his decision, in whole or in part. Such requests, almost routine in some types of cases, are rejected with equally routine uniformity, and they rarely lead to any change in the court's order. The usual purpose in asking for this type of reconsideration is to "complete the record" by having it show that all possible "remedies" have been exhausted before an appeal is filed. Appeal is the second, and by far the most common, type of reconsideration. The filing of an appeal to a higher court in either a civil or a criminal case constitutes the first step in the initiation procedure for the higher court; thus, in effect, it amounts to a recycling, although in somewhat different form, of the stages in the process just described for the trial courts. The third type of reconsideration, habeas corpus, is available ordinarily only to persons who are confined against their will. In the national judicial system, it applies primarily to prisoners in penitentiaries or jails, to persons held in detention centers by the immigration authorities, and to inmates of mental hospitals.

Originating in common law, habeas corpus is a petition to a

[29]See Richard A. Posner, "A Statistical Study of Antitrust Enforcement," *Journal of Law and Economics* 13 (1970), pp. 365–419; and Lee Loevinger, "The Closed Mind Inquiry—Antitrust Reports is Raiders' Nadir," *The Antitrust Bulletin* 17 (1972), pp. 737–762.

judge, filed by the prisoner himself *(pro se)* or by his counsel or his "next friend" or a relative in his behalf, alleging that his detention is contrary to law and asking that the court inquire into the matter. If the judge is satisfied that the petition *prima facie* ("on its face") establishes grounds for reasonable doubt that the detention is legal, he directs the jailer to reply, and thus a suit is joined. As Chapter Three indicated, this procedure is used primarily by state prisoners who seek to upset ("attack collaterally" is the legal phrase) their convictions by asking United States district judges to review (in effect) the decisions of the state courts. Of course, the legal theory is that the federal judges are concerned not with the guilt or innocence of the petitioners but only with the "constitutional" question—usually whether the conviction is contrary to the Fourteenth Amendment's guarantee of due process. The inevitable effect of the use of this procedure is that some prisoners are released from state jails on orders of federal district judges because the policy norms accepted within the federal judicial system are more liberal than the equivalent norms within the respective state judicial systems.

The second largest category of habeas corpus petitioners are federal prisoners in the custody of the United States Bureau of Prisons. For several reasons, this is a smaller group. There are far fewer federal than state prisoners. Federal rules of criminal procedure are generally more liberal than the corresponding norms of most of the states in defining the legal rights of criminal defendants and the limitations upon the investigatory and prosecutory powers of the government. And actual practice seems to correspond more closely to the relevant norms in the federal courts than it does in most state criminal courts.

Habeas corpus petitions must be filed in the district courts that have territorial jurisdiction over the jailers. This means that the dozen or so federal district judges whose bailiwicks happen to include the major national penal institutions become highly specialized in interacting with the sponsors of such petitions. State prison petitioners, on the other hand, are dispersed throughout practically all of the federal judicial districts, and almost every United States district judge gets some petitions.

The prisoners of immigration and hospital authorities who invoke habeas corpus use what is for this purpose conceptualized as a "civil" rather than a "criminal" remedy, since the legal theory is that persons detained under these circumstances are not being punished. Most immigration suits are filed against district directors of the Immigration and Naturalization Service, by persons who seek judicial review of administrative deportation or exclusion. One notorious example involved a man who, though an alien, had resided in Buffalo, New York, for a quarter of a century; upon his return from a trip abroad for the ostensible purpose of visiting his dying mother, he was denied readmission. Since no other country would accept him, he remained in the then custodial facility on a small island in New York harbor, apparently under what amounted to a decree of life detention after his efforts to obtain his release through habeas corpus were rejected by the United States District Court for the Southern District of New York, the Court of Appeals for the Second Circuit, and (in 1953) the Supreme Court.[30] The use of habeas corpus to challenge the legality of detention in mental hospitals has been less common until recently. For defense counsel, a plea of not guilty by reason of insanity often functions as an alternative stratagem to an attempted defense on the merits of the charge. Widespread judicial recognition of this functional equivalence used to result, because of judicial refusal to accept pleas of insanity, in the execution of defendants who evidently were insane;[31] and it continues to result in the insistence, by trial judges, that mental hospitals be used as instruments for the punishment of criminals[32]—although in this latter case, too, habeas corpus can be used as the basis for obtaining reconsideration and appellate review of the trial court's decision.[33]

PRIMARY APPEALS

In this section, we shall summarize briefly only the major respects in which the procedure for deciding primary appeals differs from trial procedure. In the concluding part of this chapter, we shall discuss in somewhat greater detail the Supreme Court's procedure, which is concerned almost exclusively with secondary appeals.

In the federal court system, only two stages of appellate review of the decisions of trial courts are possible: (1) primary, from single-judge courts (such as the ordinary district court, or a division of the Customs Court or of the Tax Court) to the Courts of Appeals (or to the Court of Customs and Patent Appeals), and (2) secondary, from multi-judge courts (the courts of appeals, the three-judge district courts, and the Court of Claims) to the Supreme Court. There are only rare exceptions in which a case

---

[30]*Shaughnessy* v. *United States ex rel. Mezei,* 345 U.S. 206 (1953). But see *The New York Times,* Aug. 12, 1954, p. 10, col. 4.
[31]*Smith* v. *Baldi,* 344 U.S. 561 (1953).
[32]Richard Arens, "The Durham Rule in Action: Judicial Psychiatry and Psychiatric Justice," *Law and Society Review* 1 (1967), pp. 41–80.
[33]*Lynch* v. *Overholser,* 369 U.S. 705 (1962).

(such as one that comes into the Supreme Court via the Court of Appeals of the District of Columbia from the strictly municipal courts of the District) may pass through more than two stages of direct appellate court review. Many conservative judges (such as the late Justice Frankfurter) have argued that only one appeal should be provided, in an efficient judicial system, for the consideration of complaints about any trial court's decision. In Frankfurter's view, the purpose of a second level of appeal is to use cases as instruments for policy making for the entire system or as instruments for policing the consistency with which courts at the primary appellate level adhere to the Supreme Court's policies. It follows logically (and it was Frankfurter's view) that the Supreme Court should confine its activities exclusively to such functions—which it ought also to monopolize. This is a highly rationalistic model of the federal judicial system, and it presumes that efficiency is a primary value of the system. A pluralistic model affords recognition to the substantial influence upon policy making of judges at all levels in the system. This appears to be in much closer correspondence with the available empirical evidence. But liberal judges (such as Justice Douglas) argue that in addition to the Supreme Court's policy function, it is a proper function of review at the secondary level to be concerned with outcomes in individual cases despite the impossibility of the Court's "righting all wrongs" committed by lower courts and despite the intrusion of such a charitable function upon the time available for the policy function.

INITIATION

To petition a court of appeals to consider an appeal from a district court decision is to recycle the process of decision making. Accordingly, appellate procedures, also, may be analyzed in terms of the stages of initiation, accommodation, persuasion, decision, implementation, and reconsideration. But appellate operations tend to be more stereotyped than those of trial courts. Consequently, the description that follows applies to both criminal and civil cases and, among the latter, to both those in which the trial procedures are primarily legal and those in which they are primarily equitable.

Notwithstanding statutes of limitations and doctrines of laches (relating to delay in beginning suits), the plaintiff in a trial has considerably more room for maneuver, in terms of where and when he will commence his suit, than does the appellant (the party—either plaintiff or defendant—who seeks to upset the decision of a trial court). The appellant has no choice concerning the court of appeals in which he will file—there is only one with jurisdiction over his appeal—and the time during which he must file is strictly and narrowly defined by rule. Once an appeal has been initiated, the other party automatically is cast in the role of appellee, unless he chooses to file a cross-appeal of his own, so that both parties must play the dual role of appellant and appellee.

ACCOMMODATION

Accommodation is accomplished by the appellee's answer to the appellant's petition and by direct negotiation between their respective counsel. Often an appeal is taken by a relatively affluent litigant who does not expect to obtain a reversal of the trial court decision but who does hope to exhaust the litigative capacity of his opponent. The threat of continuing expenditures of both time and money in combination with the uncertainty that to some extent always characterizes the probable outcome of an appeal—for reasons developed below—induces some appellees to agree to compromise settlements "out of court." Thus large corporations, which maintain legal counsel as a cost of "doing business," can (and not infrequently do) maximize their economic power to attain legal advantage over private litigants of inferior socioeconomic status. The classic example is provided by the insurance company that uses litigation—including the extension of litigation beyond the trial—as a means to harass widows and orphans. The example (like the phrase that describes it) is both trite and true: see *Dick* v. *New York Life Insurance Co.*, 359 U.S. 437 (1959).

PERSUASION

Persuasion takes the form of the briefs on the merits filed, and the oral arguments presented, by opposing counsel. The audience for both written briefs and oral argument is a panel of three circuit judges. A *"brief"* is a statement in writing which is addressed to a court and which argues, with supporting citations to "legal authorities," the policy alternatives preferred by the party whose counsel submits the brief. Such alternatives are described as questions of "law" to be decided by the judge. Briefs sometimes are filed in the trial of certain kinds of civil cases (e.g., antitrust) but rarely in most trial proceedings; in appellate courts, however, the use of formal written briefs is an almost universal characteristic of persuasive tactics. Moreover, *"oral argument"* is not primarily fragmented and *ad hoc* as it is in trial proceedings; instead, it consists of prepared formal speeches, limited in duration and opportunity to a single appointed occasion. The content of oral argument tends to be more technical in appeals than in trials, in part because of the sharper focus (and the sublimation of dramatic context) afforded by both the administrative and the physical milieu in which arguments are delivered in primary appeals, and in part because there are no roles for laymen to play in the appellate courtroom. There are no jurors, and the proceedings are not sufficiently well publicized to attract the spectators who at least used to pass through the portals of the small auditorium in which the Supreme Court entertains oral argument. Consequently, the objective of counsel is to attract the voting support of at least two of the circuit judges, while at the same time losing the vote of no more than one (and preferably none) of them. This kind of game makes the vote of the most moderate judge (in relation to the value constellations of the other two) critical to the outcome of the appeal, and it tends to keep the style as well as the content of argumentation within narrower bounds, since an overly hyperbolic statement may boomerang and alienate the critical middleman.

DECISION MAKING

Since most courts of appeals (eight of the eleven) are composed of from seven to nine circuit judges each (and two of the others have thirteen and fifteen, respectively), many different panels of three judges can be established. From a population of seven circuit judges, for example, thirty-five different samples (i.e., panels) can be drawn; with a court of appeals composed of nine circuit judges, eighty-four different three-judge panels are possible; and with a court as large as the fifth (with fifteen circuit judges), 455 different panels could be established. Consequently, although we can assume that all possible combinations are unlikely to occur empirically, there is enough variation in panel composition in most courts of appeals that the outcome of any particular appeal may well depend more upon the "luck of the draw" than upon anything else. Assuming that the judges of a nine-man court—the average size of the courts of appeals—can be arrayed along a continuum according to their relative degrees of liberalism and conservatism, many cases might be decided by the "court" in opposite ways, depending upon whether the panel includes the court's three most liberal or most conservative members. Neither combination is likely to occur empirically, however; mixtures of conservatives and liberals with each other and with moderates will be the rule. Nevertheless, panels biased with either liberal or conservative majorities could form a fourth of the time, even on a chance basis—which underscores both the speculative and the manipulative propensities of the panel system.[34] The first circuit, with only three judges, is the only court of appeals with a fixed composition for the decision of all cases. The strategies of counsel, in contemplation of primary appeals, must be quite different in the first circuit than elsewhere in the national judicial system. The panel usually makes separate decisions on the questions of jurisdiction and of the merits of the issues at dispute. But sometimes the jurisdictional decision is "reserved pending consideration of the merits," which is a legalistic way of saying that judges occasionally choose to put the cart before the horse. Such action is not taken arbitrarily, at least in a psychological sense, since the judges usually have a strong identification with some policy issue in a case when they thus depart from the ordinary sequence of decision making. Both jurisdictional decisions and those on the merits are based upon initiating petitions and the opposing motions of appellees, plus the printed record of the trial; they differ in that negative jurisdictional decisions usually preclude counsel from having an opportunity to attempt to influence the court through further written and oral argumentation.

Unlike the decrees of trial courts, which characteristically take the form of orders from the judge directly to the parties, or indirectly to them through judicial agents (marshals, jailers, etc.), the orders of courts of appeals are directed to district courts. Appellate judges, in other words, make decisions in the form of orders to trial judges. Such orders have become quite stereotyped, and in most cases they consist of one or a combination of the following three words: affirmed, remanded, reversed. "Affirmed" means that the court of appeals accepts and approves—technically, to the extent that it was questioned—the trial court's decision; "remanded" means that the trial court is directed to reconsider its initial decision, usually in the light of somewhat ambiguous guidance which the court of appeals provides, either in the form of a statement of instructions or through the citation of particular legal sources; "reversed" means that the appellate court disagrees with the decision below. Some reversals have the effect of terminating the case, usually in favor of the appellant; but others result in reconsideration by the trial court, and a few require that the trial process be recycled and repeated from the initiation stage.

[34]For a more extended discussion, see Burton M. Atkins, "Some Theoretical Effects of the Decision-Making Rules on the United States Courts of Appeals," *Jurimetrics Journal* 11, pp. 13–22 (1970), and "Decision-Making Rules and Judicial Strategy on the United States Courts of Appeals," *Western Political Quarterly* 25 (1972), pp. 626–642.

IMPLEMENTATION AND RECONSIDERATION

In most instances, implementation of the decisions of courts of appeals occurs by the return of the case for further action by the district court (or, in cases that are appealed directly from the regulatory commissions, on the part of the administrative agency). Reconsideration by the courts of appeals, on motion of counsel for the losing party, takes place rarely; as in the trial courts, such motions are routinely filed and denied, in order to "perfect the record"—they have no chance of being granted, unless at least one of the judges on the panel is willing to change his mind. However, the very fact that panels are utilized results in a special procedure which, in a technical legal sense, is a form of reconsideration. This is the *en banc* procedure, previously mentioned in Chapter Three, under which, upon recommendation of a majority of the panel for the case or in response to a petition filed by counsel for the losing party, the entire court participates in what is in effect an appellate review of the panel's decision. The procedure for *en banc* decision making varies among the circuits. In some, the entire membership of the court is assembled to hear reargument, both orally by counsel and through the submission of revised briefs; in others, the membership simply is polled by the chief judge and a written ballot determines the outcome. Under either procedure, the judges who formed the decision-making panel for the case also participate in the decision *en banc*. The usual grounds for granting *en banc* consideration are that conflict exists between the decision of the present panel and that of another panel in some earlier but similar case.

In a small minority of cases, one or both of the parties chooses to continue the litigation by filing a petition with the Supreme Court, with the objective of recycling the process again by initiating proceedings there.

SECONDARY APPEALS: SUPREME COURT PROCEDURE

INITIATION

Most cases decided by the Supreme Court are appealed by use of the statutory writ of certiorari. Under this procedure, the petitioner and (usually) his opposing respondent both file jurisdictional briefs and either or both may subsequently file a brief on the substantive issues in dispute. In civil cases, and in criminal cases in which the petitioner can afford counsel and can meet such other substantial costs as the printing of the certiorari petition and brief and the record of the proceedings in the courts below, assignments are made to the docket by the Clerk of the Supreme Court. Under a special rule of the court, a petitioner who does not have money to pay the costs of preparing the elaborate papers normally required may file a simplified petition that he can prepare himself. These petitions *"in forma pauperis"* were assigned to a "Miscellaneous Docket," from 1945 until that special docket was consolidated with the former "appellate docket" at the beginning of the 1970 term. (The difference was not insignificant: by no means all of them but *only* Appellate Docket cases were scheduled for oral argument, providing [usually] that they survived jurisdictional screening.) At least 95 percent of the *in forma pauperis* certioraris are denied or dismissed; only the remainder are placed on the "discuss list," and many of these latter are decided summarily on the merits without any opportunity having been provided to influence the Court through oral argument. For a case to survive jurisdictional screening, at least four justices must vote to grant the petition (although with a minimal quorum of six, or with only seven participating justices, three favorable votes suffice). Apart from terminological differences, the procedures for processing statutory "appeals" are now substantially the same as those for certiorari cases.[35] In recognition of this fact, the study group appointed by Chief Justice Burger recommended that the distinction be abolished by eliminating all appeals.[36]

Two other processes for initiating appellate review by the Supreme Court are used infrequently. "Certification" is used when the judges of the court below are equally divided or when they wish to avoid making any decision upon what they consider to be an important question of (usually, constitutional) policy. Under such circumstances, a majority of the judges of the lower courts can vote to pass the buck to the Supreme Court by suspending their own proceedings and by transmitting a copy of the record for the case, together with a "certificate" in which they ask the Supreme Court to respond to several questions that raise the policy issues about which the lower court declares itself to be "uncertain." Usually such questions are so dichotomously framed that they imply a yes or no response. Certifications are always (so far as we are aware) accepted in the modern practice of the Supreme Court, and they are placed

---

[35]For a more extended discussion, see Schubert, *Constitutional Politics*, op. cit., pp. 89–114; the classic historical reference work is Felix Frankfurter and James M. Landis, *The Business of the Supreme Court* (New York: The Macmillan Company, 1928).

[36]*Report of the Study Group on the Caseload of the Supreme Court* (Washington, D.C.: Administrative Office of the United States Courts, December 1972), pp. 34–38.

on the docket for oral argument and decision on the merits. The parties to the case, it should be noted, have no direct control over the use of this appellate process, and its infrequent use suggests that its invocation by the courts of appeals must be discouraged by informal norms operating within the system.[37]

The remaining means of invoking appellate review by the Supreme Court is through the use of the extraordinary writs of mandamus, prohibition, habeas corpus, and certiorari; requests for habeas corpus and for certiorari—which is not to be confused with the *statutory* writ discussed above—are extremely rare. The Court grants only one out of each hundred requests for review by extraordinary writ, and heretofore less than a score have been granted over the course of a decade. Relics of the eighteenth-century jurisdiction of the court of King's Bench in England, their principal present use is to permit the Supreme Court to intervene directly in the decision-making process of trial courts; the requested writs take the form of orders to lower court judges, directing that they either do (mandamus) or refrain from doing (prohibition) specified acts which, presumably, are required or forbidden by their roles as defined by law.

ACCOMMODATION

Direct accommodation of disputes by negotiation between the parties occurs most frequently in the trial process and least often in cases that have been appealed to the Supreme Court. It seems evident that various factors, which have the effect of reinforcing the social distance between the parties to a case, would tend to have their greatest impact in cases that reach the stage of secondary appeals. For one thing, these are all cases that failed to be accommodated during earlier decision-making cycles. In addition, the investment of both parties in the outcome now is greater than at preceding stages, since the costs of extended litigations are decidedly cumulative. Third, at the conclusion of each earlier cycle, the number of surviving issues (i.e., those upon which it is possible, under the rules, to base an appeal) diminishes; as a consequence, the policy issues presented in appeals to the Supreme Court are very small subsets of the issues raised at the pretrial conference.

[37]For a celebrated example, see *Rathbun (Humphrey's Executor)* v. *United States* 295 U.S. 602 (1935). The Study Group on the Supreme Court's Caseload recommended in 1972 that the Court's certification jurisdiction also be abolished, and cited as the only example of a certification during the quarter of a century preceding their report *United States* v. *Barnett,* 376 U.S. 68 (1964).

Moreover, in granting certiorari or in noting probable jurisdiction in appeals, the Supreme Court very frequently limits the grant of jurisdiction to only one (or a few) of the larger number of issues about which the parties seek a decision. Occasionally the facts so change that the original conflict of interest between the parties no longer obtains by the time the Supreme Court is ready to decide the case. On a motion by counsel for one of the parties, such cases usually are dismissed as "moot": no matter what decision the Court might make (according to the legal theory), it could have no effect upon the resolution of the conflict in interests presented by the case. The other and more usual means of accommodation is for one of the parties to "confess error"—to concede, that is, that a decision below in his favor should be reversed. So far as we know, counsel for private parties may withdraw petitions or they may fail to contest those filed by opposing counsel, but they do not confess error. That action appears to be taken exclusively by the solicitor general, as a function of his administrative responsibility for the work, in lower courts, of the United States attorneys and of the attorneys employed in other divisions of the Department of Justice.[38] If the solicitor general decides, after a case has been docketed by the Supreme Court and as a consequence of either a change in Administration policy, conflict between that policy and what was done in the field, or the more complete knowledge about the case that his staff necessarily acquires in the process of preparing a brief and for oral argument, that he disagrees in some important respect with action previously taken by those who represented the government in the case, he indicates by confessing error his unwillingness to assume further responsibility for defending the case before the Supreme Court. The Court—although not bound by the solicitor general's concession—usually responds by summarily reversing the decision below in the case.

PERSUASION

The Supreme Court functions as a decision-making group for about nine months out of each twelve, beginning about the first week of October and continuing through the third or fourth week of the following June. During the early fall, the Court devotes

[38]William E. Brigman, "The Role of the Office of the Solicitor General of the United States in the Judicial Process," (Ph.D. dissertation in political science, University of North Carolina, Chapel Hill, 1967, University Microfilms 67-969).

relatively more time to jurisdictional decision making, since a considerable backlog of docketed cases accumulates during the summer vacation; during the late spring, more decisions on the merits are announced. From late November through early May, the usual routine is keyed to a two-week cycle, although this is now often interrupted by an intervening week or two of recess during the winter. On the first four days of alternate weeks the Court hears oral argument, with a conference on the following Friday for group discussion of the cases argued (among others); formerly the other Mondays were devoted to the ritual of announcing outcomes and reading opinions in cases that had been decided, and the remaining days of that week were reserved for research and writing.[39] Supposedly decisions have been since 1965 announced on various days throughout the workweek, primarily in order to facilitate their communication by the news media; in practice, Mondays continued to be preferred for the announcement of decisions 85 percent of the time during the remaining four terms of the Warren Court.[40]

On days when oral argument is scheduled, it is held for two hours before and two hours after lunch. In most cases, counsel for each party is allocated one-half hour, although in some cases it is less; and in a few cases that the Court has earmarked for major policy pronouncements, several days may be reserved. In such "landmark" cases—of which there will be only two or three in a decade—the Court may invite certain groups to participate in the oral argument as *amici curiae* ("friends of the court"); such invitations were extended to the states' attorneys general, for example, in the School Segregation cases and in the Tidelands Oil cases. When the Court does this, it is expanding the focus of the points of view bearing upon the pending decision in order better to inform itself of the probable consequences of the various decisional alternatives. Oral argument also may be presented by *volunteer* amici counsel,[41] provided that both parties agree, or with the consent of one party and that of the Court. Under these circumstances, an *amicus*

[39]David L. Grey, *The Supreme Court and the News Media* (Evanston: Northwestern University Press, 1968).

[40]Donald D. Gregory and Stephen L. Wasby, "How to Get an Idea from Here to There: The Court and Communication Overload," *Public Affairs Bulletin* (Research Bureau, Southern Illinois University at Carbondale) 3, No. 5 (November–December 1970), and especially the section entitled "Monday/Non-Monday."

[41]Samuel Krislov, "The Amicus Curiae Brief: From Friendship to Advocacy," *Yale Law Journal* 72 (1963), pp. 694–721.

counsel must share the time, assigned to counsel for the party whose position he supports, in contrast to the extra time the Court makes available to *invited* amici counsel.

Oral argument before the Supreme Court is, in considerable measure, direct interchange between the counsel and the justices. It is not quite group discussion since the communication links are bilateral, in the form of questions and comments directed by individual justices to the advocate, the advocate's replies, and the reading of his prepared statement. Some justices do not hesitate to "correct" counsel with whom they disagree; others feel free to offer advice and verbal support to counsel with whom they agree. Consequently, the persuasion that takes place is by no means a simple matter of the justices' becoming enlightened by the advocates' orations; the justices of the Supreme Court are the most influential participants in the controversies argued before them.[42] They refuse to play the role of dispassionate auditors (in which they are cast by the traditional view, perhaps because there is no systematic procedure for publishing the transcripts of oral argument[43] and little research based upon direct observation of the proceedings has been reported).[44] As a result, there is relatively little awareness of the extent to which oral argument—in reality, "with" rather than "before" the Supreme Court—is a highly political process of social interaction.

[42]Cf. Ralph K. Huitt, "The Congressional Committee: A Case Study," *American Political Science Review* 48 (1954), p. 364: "In the price control [hearings by the Senate Committee on Banking and Currency] the senators were not sitting as arbiters of the group struggle, but as participants; it flowed through them."

[43]Portions of the oral argument in what the editors consider to be the more important cases are published in the Supreme Court section of *United States Law Week* (Washington: Bureau of National Affairs), and the *New York Times* and other newspapers occasionally report parts of the oral argument in a case.

[44]For a professional journalist's report on one term (1962) of the work of the Supreme Court, based in part upon his direct observations of the justices in court, see James E. Clayton, *The Making of Justice* (New York: E. P. Dutton, 1964). There is also a study of Detroit traffic court judges, based upon direct observation of their courtroom behavior by political scientists Dean Jaros and Robert I. Mendelsohn, "The Judicial Role and Sentencing Behavior," *Midwest Journal of Political Science* 11 (1967), pp. 471–488; and similarly, there is a sociological report by Maureen Mileski, "Courtroom Encounters: An Observational Study of a Lower Criminal Court," *Law and Society Review* 5 (1971), pp. 473–538.

DECISION MAKING

The justices meet in conference (which by long-standing tradition has been on Fridays) with no one else present; the proceedings are confidential, and no record is kept of the discussion, although the chief justice does maintain a handwritten record of the outcome and voting division for each case. There are over ten times as many jurisdictional decisions as there are decisions on the merits; with a caseload approaching five thousand, it takes but simple arithmetic to determine how brief must be the time available for discussion of the average case. Assuming twenty conferences for the term—actually, there are usually less—the Court has two hundred and fifty cases to discuss and to vote upon at each conference. What happens is that a few cases receive a great deal of discussion, but most receive none at all. By the use of consent lists, prepared by the chief justice with the assistance of his clerks, jurisdiction is denied unless at least four justices vote in favor of granting it. In short, unless several members of the group really want to get at an issue through the instrumentality of a particular case, the case has no chance of being "appealed" to the Supreme Court.

When the chief justice calls a case for discussion, he states his own views first, and then the associate justices speak in the order of their seniority. For over a decade, extending from October 1953 almost to the end of June 1964, the first three to argue any case were Earl Warren, Hugo Black, and William Douglas—then the three most liberal members of the group.[45] Small-group theory tells us that this in itself gave an advantage to the liberals, since they could define the issues and exercise a dominant influence in setting the focus of the discussion.[46] These first three also probably

[45]Black's support of most liberal causes began a drastic backslide on the last day of the 1963 term; the specific issue on which he broke from Douglas and Warren was that of integration sit-ins by blacks in what theretofore by custom had been all-white segregated recreational and retail shopping facilities. For a discussion of Black's retreat, and of possible explanations for his sweeping change in attitude and behavior, see the latter part of Chapter 2 of Glendon Schubert, *The Constitutional Polity* (Boston: Boston University Press, 1970); and for an opposing view, see S. Sidney Ulmer, "The Longitudinal Behavior of Hugo Lafayette Black: Parabolic Support for Civil Liberties, 1937–1971," *Florida State University Law Review* 1 (1973), pp. 131–153. For his own explanation, see Hugo Lafayette Black, *A Constitutional Faith* (New York: Alfred A. Knopf, Inc., 1968).

[46]S. Sidney Ulmer, *Courts as Small and Not So Small Groups* (New York: General Learning Press, 1971).

preempted at least half, rather than their "fair share," a third, of the time available for discussion—or so, at least, do people tend to behave in other discussion groups of similar size about which we have direct observational knowledge. When the time for voting arrives, however, the sequence of participation is reversed; the most recently appointed "freshman" associate justice votes first, and the chief justice votes last. Again, this gives an advantage to the most senior members; for with a group this small, a bloc of three (and Warren, Black, and Douglas *did* then vote as a bloc most of the time) are in a position to wield the balance of power on the Court. From the point of view of game theory, the last three to vote can determine the outcome *either way,* provided they vote together and the remaining justices are divided. Of course, there will have been antecedent bilateral communication among the members of the group, so that probable votes are known more or less to all before the conference meets; and we do not intend, by the above remarks about the formal power advantages inherent in the discussion and voting sequences, to contradict what we shall state later concerning the primary importance of ideological differences as determinants of voting behavior. It is precisely because Warren, Black, and Douglas were highly and positively correlated in their belief systems that it was usually possible for them to vote as a bloc, but there are some issues on which it may be more important to decide cases with a show of unanimity than to win them with one-vote margins.[47] The purpose of the conference is for the justices to attempt to persuade each other, and it is not to be presumed that their attitudes are so dogmatically entertained that none of them ever changes his mind about how he is going to vote in a case as the result of his having participated in the group discussion. Consequently, we might well infer that the formal discussion and voting sequences are not very important to the outcome of most cases, but that it is precisely in the making of the most marginal decisions on the most controversial issues (regarding which moderate justices are apt to be swayed one way or another) that the order of participation, for discussion and for voting, is likely to be most significant.

Small-group theory also informs us that the positions at which people are seated at a table tends to have an important effect upon how they will interact: where self-selection of seats is possible, for example, research in jury behavior shows that the person most likely to be selected as foreman will choose a seat at either end of a rectangular table, where he can be most readily visible and can in

[47]For an excellent discussion and development of this subject, see David W. Rohde, "Policy Goals and Opinion Coalitions in the Supreme Court," *Midwest Journal of Political Science* 16 (1972), pp. 208–224.

turn maintain a direct face-to-face visual relationship with all other members of the group.[48] Evidently the chief justice has occupied such an end position, at least since the Court moved into its present conference room in what was then its new building in 1935, until Burger introduced a creative innovation (as described below) near the end of his third year in office. Apparently the pattern determining the positioning of the associate justices at the table has changed from time to time,[49] and Whitaker has reported[50] that in the first term of the Burger Court the seating arrangement was as Figure 7A indicates. Figure 7A shows a distinct pattern, with the senior associate (Black) and the associates to his left confronting the chief justice and the associates to *his* left: the two groups are divided, that is to say, by a diagonal drawn from the upper left to the lower right corner of the table. Moreover, the three associates to Black's left *are* arrayed in strict order of seniority, although those to Burger's left are not. This pattern is clearly one that magnifies and encourages the ideological division of the Court into liberal and conservative wings, by adding social reinforcement to both the structure and symbolization of the already substantial schisms that separate the justices on the issues of public policy that they are to decide, when they gather in the conference room to take their seats at the discussion table.

It was reported in the spring of 1972[51] that Chief Justice Burger had had the huge slab of Honduran mahogany sawed into three pieces and fitted together into the inverted "U" shape that Figure 7B portrays. Again, a pattern of confrontation is evident, with the three most liberal justices remaining in the same position

[48]Fred L. Strodtbeck and L. Harmon Hook, "The Social Dimensions of a Twelve-Man Jury Table," *Sociometry* 24 (1961), pp. 397–415.

[49]Ulmer reports the pattern of seating during the first (the 1953) term of the Warren Court and he remarks that neither strict seniority nor alternation by seniority was followed in conference room arrangements then, although convenience (viz., to permit the most recently appointed justice, who serves as doorkeeper, to occupy the seat nearest to the door) plays a major part in making changes. But when a vacancy occurs in the Court, the senior associate justice has first claim to the vacated chair. S. Sidney Ulmer, *Courts as Small and Not So Small Groups* (New York: General Learning Press, 1971), p. 11.

[50]Steve Whitaker, "A Role-Playing Simulation of the United States Supreme Court," a paper presented to Panel 14A at the Annual Meeting of the American Political Science Association (Chicago, Illinois: September 7, 1971), p. 2.

[51]John P. MacKenzie, in a news editorial on Chief Justice Warren Burger that was distributed nationally by the Washington Post Service in May 1972.

FIGURE 7

Seating Arrangements at Conference of the Burger Court

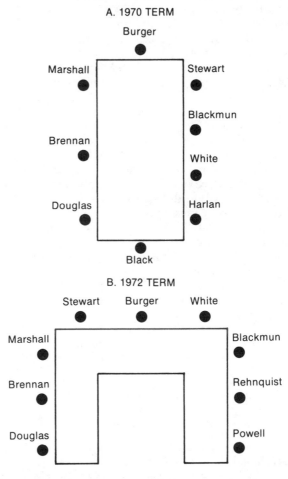

A. 1970 TERM

Burger

Marshall   Stewart

Blackmun

Brennan

White

Douglas   Harlan

Black

B. 1972 TERM

Stewart   Burger   White

Marshall   Blackmun

Brennan   Rehnquist

Douglas   Powell

and order as in Figure 7A, in direct opposition to the three most recent Nixon appointees; and with Stewart and White (the two senior conservative associates) alternating by seniority beside the chief justice. But one thing plainly had been accomplished: the second "end" of the table had been eliminated, and along with it had gone the possibility of legitimizing by special position the role of leadership of the liberal opposition to the chief justice.[52] In

[52]Cf. John N. Hazard, "Furniture Arrangement as a Symbol of Judicial Roles," *Etc.,* 19 (1962), pp. 181–188.

order to keep Douglas from taking over Black's seat opposite to the chief at the far end of the traditional rectangular table, Burger sawed the table up!

As the chairman of the conference, the chief justice also controls the agenda—that is, the sequence in which cases will be discussed. (There is probably a positive, but certainly a low, correlation among the sequence of cases on the docket, their calendar position, and the order of their discussion in conference.) It is also the chief justice who is primarily responsible for the content of the Court's opinions in the cases for which the decisions are reported in per curiam form, and it is he who assigns the writing of the Opinion of the Court except when he is on the losing side of the issue, in which event the senior associate voting with the majority makes the assignment.[53] Majority opinions are instruments for the articulation of the rationale for the decision that is acceptable to all members of the majority; hence, the larger the majority, the less the opinion of the Court can function as a vehicle for the expression of the unadulterated personal views of the individual "author" of that opinion. Justices who accept the majority decision but who reject, in whole or in part, the "official" rationale proffered in behalf of the majority can write separate (or joint, if two or more of them agree) concurring opinions; and one or more justices who disagree with the decision may (but will not necessarily)[54] dissent, with or without opinion, and if with opinion, either individually or collectively.

On opinion days the Court assembles for the ritual of pronouncing its formal decisions by means of the ancient device of oral delivery. It has long been the custom of the Court for justices to read their written opinions, but occasional nonconformists (such as Frankfurter) have preferred to give somewhat briefer—and frequently more colorful—oral, and to some extent extemporaneous, summaries of their prepared speeches (viz., written opinions). At the same time, printed copies of the written opinions are made available to the press and to anyone else who is present and interested.[55]

[53]For discussion see William P. McLaughlan, "Research Note: Ideology and Conflict in Supreme Court Opinion Assignment, 1946–62," *Western Political Quarterly* 25 (1972), pp. 16–27; and S. Sidney Ulmer, "The Use of Power in the Supreme Court: The Opinion Assignments of Earl Warren, 1953–1960," *Journal of Public Law* 19 (1970), pp. 49–67.
[54]See Alexander M. Bickel, *The Unpublished Opinions of Mr. Justice Brandeis* (Cambridge, Mass.: Belknap Press of Harvard University Press, 1957).
[55]David L. Grey, "The Supreme Court as a Communicator," *Houston Law Review* 5 (1968), pp. 405–429.

IMPLEMENTATION

As we found to be true for the courts of appeals, the decisions of the Supreme Court are in the form of orders to lower courts. In substantial degree, the question of the ultimate enforcement of Supreme Court decisions is the same as that of the enforcement of trial court decisions. It differs primarily to the extent that trial court judges may be more strongly motivated to enforce their own decisions (with which, presumably, they are more or less in continuing agreement, most of the time) than they are to enforce Supreme Court decisions, the frequent effect of which is to order the trial judge to do the *opposite* of what *he* initially had decided. Further, the Supreme Court tends to get more "faithful execution of the laws"—as it has decreed "the laws"—from federal than from state judges.[56] Similarly, the extent to which the Court can depend upon the presidency and Congress to assist in the enforcement of the Court's policies depends at least in part upon the degree of communality between the value preferences of the majority of the Court, of the key minorities of Congress, and of the President and whatever advisors he listens to on the issue.

RECONSIDERATION

The Supreme Court rarely grants a motion for rehearing and then changes an announced decision, although occasionally it does so; in order for this to happen, at least one justice must change his mind. A much more common form of reconsideration (of the issue rather than of the case) occurs when a minority bloc in a particular decision solicits business by asking in effect that some lawyer bring the same issue up again in a new case, by which time (because of anticipated personnel changes in the group) the minority may have become the majority. Even more common is the complicated case, relating frequently to governmental regulation of economic relationships, for which decision making by the administrative agency

[56]See Thomas Barth, "Perception and Acceptance of Supreme Court Decisions at the State and Local Level," *Journal of Public Law* 19 (1968), pp. 308–350; "Evasion of Supreme Court Mandates in Cases Remanded to State Courts Since 1941," *Harvard Law Review* 47 (1954), pp. 1251–1259; Walter F. Murphy, "Lower Court Checks on Supreme Court Power," *American Political Science Review* 53 (1959), pp. 1017–1031; Lucius J. Barker and Twiley W. Barker, Jr., *Freedoms, Courts, Politics: Studies in Civil Liberties* (Englewood Cliffs: Prentice-Hall, Inc., 1965), Chapter 5: "The Revolt of the Century: Racial Problems in the Balance"; and G. Theodore Mitau, *Decade of Decision: The Supreme Court and the Constitutional Revolution, 1954–1964* (New York: Charles Scribner's Sons, 1967).

and the trial court does not lead up to a single event (which can be appealed only once) but instead consists of a set of decisions over an extended period of time. This sort of reconsideration, both of cases and of issues, is particularly likely to occur when the policy position of the administrative agency conflicts with that of a Supreme Court majority, as illustrated by the tension between the New Deal and the Hughes Court over governmental regulation of stockyard markets. The statutory policy had been established twenty years earlier, and it was not until Franklin Roosevelt succeeded in "packing the Court" that it was possible for the Department of Agriculture effectively to carry out this part of the congressional policy and program. But the Supreme Court finally yielded. The Court had, in effect, forced a reconsideration of the underlying issue of public policy more than a dozen times. Thus the federal judicial system was able to delay the change for a generation, but it could not prevent it from taking place.

Policy-Making
Analysis

The preceding chapter examined the processes of judicial decision making through a description of the sequences of major actions. The discussion was almost entirely at the empirical level of observable events: who does what to whom and with what effects? In this chapter we shall employ an analytical rather than an empirical approach and shall undertake to interpret the process of judicial policy making in terms of an explicit theoretical model. Our focus, in other words, now shifts from the manifest to the latent aspects of decision making.

"Decision making" and "policy making" are by no means synonymous. Individual decisions of different courts have differing policy implications—even in the same case—and for any given court individual decisions may reflect a wide range of values in their policy significance. Indeed, judicial policy making does not necessarily utilize case decisions as an instrument for articulation; the Supreme Court's notorious admission of corporations to the constitutional status of "persons" under the Fourteenth Amendment (which protected them from public control through state regulation)—a policy-making act of considerable importance—took the form of an oral "concession" by the chief justice to a railroad lawyer that the point need not be argued further since the whole Court was willing to "admit" it.[1] Most of the time, however, judges make policies through their decisions in regard to issues raised in cases.

A SYSTEMIC MODEL OF JUDICIAL POLICY MAKING

Figure 8 presents a model of judicial policy-making processes. The model is "systemic" because it portrays certain functional interrelationships among stipulated structures; the relationships are ordered and are assumed to be relatively stable. The seven components denoted as "structures" are *STRESS, INPUTS, WITHINPUTS, CONVERSION, OUTPUTS, IMPACT,* and *FEEDBACK.* We shall describe several of these structures in considerably more detail in the remaining sections of this chapter. The six interaction processes, which correspond to the stages of decision making examined in the preceding chapter, link the structures. Thus, the process of *initiation* links environmental *STRESS* to judicial *INPUTS,* which in turn are linked to *CON-VERSION* by the processes of *accommodation* and *persuasion. Decision making* connects *CONVERSION* to *OUTPUTS,* and judicial *OUTPUTS* are linked to environmental *IMPACT* by the process of *implementation.* Judicial *OUTPUTS* also generate a *FEEDBACK* structure that becomes cycled back as an alternative source of judicial *INPUTS* by the process of *reconsideration. STRESS* and *IMPACT* are both environmental structures, and therefore they are beyond the boundaries of the judicial system per se; the four structures of the judicial system all are linked in a circular (linear) sequence by sociopsychological functions. The judicial system is a social system; but distinguishable from such a social system, and indispensable to its functioning, are the psychological systems of the discrete human beings who act as judges; and each such psychological system is contained—literally as well as figuratively—within an individual biological system. In order to direct attention to the importance of the interaction between the personality system and the physiological system of each individual

---

[1] *Santa Clara County* v. *Southern Pacific R.R.,* 118 U.S. 394 (1886); Walton H. Hamilton, "The Path of Due Process of Law," in *The Constitution Reconsidered,* ed. Conyers Read (New York: Columbia University Press, 1938), p. 181. The point had been argued but not decided during the preceding term in *San Mateo County* v. *Southern Pacific Railroad Co.,* 116 U.S. 138 (1885).

FIGURE 8

A Systemic Model of Judicial Policy Making

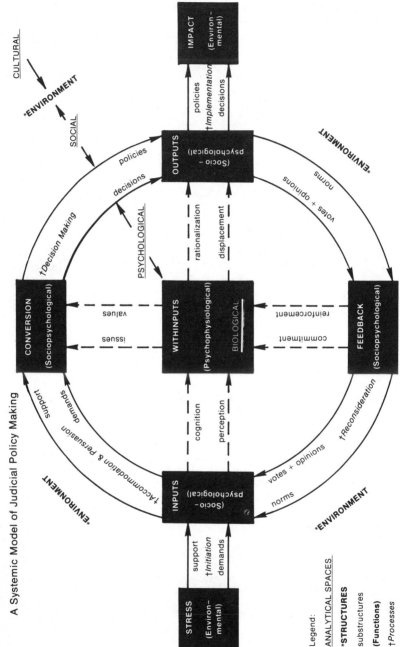

Legend:

ANALYTICAL SPACES

*STRUCTURES

substructures

(Functions)

†Processes

judicial actor, we denote also a structure of (following Easton[2]) *WITHINPUTS,* which are linked by psychophysiological processes to *FEEDBACK* and *INPUTS,* and to *CONVERSION* and *OUT-PUTS.* Evidently, *CONVERSION* refers to a structure of social interaction, while *WITHINPUTS* denotes a structure of psychophysiological interaction. Evidently, also, the social structures mediate between the individual and his environment; and furthermore, psychological processes mediate, for each judicial actor, between his biological system and the social system within which he interacts. Thus, Figure 8 specifies five types of space: the core BIOLOGICAL space,[3] the PSYCHOLOGICAL space that encompassed the core; the SOCIOPSYCHOLOGICAL space of the judicial system; the SOCIAL space that surrounds the judicial system; and the outermost CULTURAL space which, in combination with the SOCIAL space, defines the limits of the relevant socioeconomic and politico-legal environment.[4]

Pairs of substructures connect sequences of the larger structural components. Thus, support and demands connect *INPUTS* to both *STRESS* and *CONVERSION,* just as policies and decisions connect *OUTPUTS* to both *CONVERSION* and *IMPACT,* and norms and votes and opinions connect *FEEDBACK* to both *OUTPUTS* and *INPUTS.* Similarly, for each individual judge, cognition and perception connect *INPUTS* to *WITHINPUTS,* and commitment and reinforcement connect *FEEDBACK* to *WITH-INPUTS,* while issues and values connect *WITHINPUTS* to *CONVERSION,* and rationalization and displacement connect *WITHINPUTS* to *OUTPUTS.* In the broadest sense, the figure suggests that *STRESS* arising within the environment and outside the boundaries of the judicial system leads to the initiation of support for and demands upon the judicial system, which accepts

[2]David Easton, *A Framework for Political Analysis* (Englewood Cliffs: Prentice-Hall, Inc., 1965), pp. 114–115. For other applications of Eastonian theory to the analysis of judicial systems, see Jay Sigler, "A Cybernetic Model of the Judicial System," *Temple Law Quarterly* 58 (1968), pp. 398–428; and Sheldon Goldman and Thomas P. Jahnige, "Eastonian Systems Analysis and Legal Research," *Rutgers-Camden Law Journal* 2 (1970), pp. 285–300.

[3]See LeRoy L. Lamborn, "Social Control through the Reconstitution of Man," *University of Florida Law Review* 26 (1969), pp. 452–476; and Harry Cohen, "Confronting Myth in the American Legal Profession: A Territorial Perspective," *Alabama Law Review* 22 (1970), pp. 513–551.

[4]For a discussion of the relationship between judicial policy making and political cultures, see Joel B. Grossman and Austin Sarat, "Political Culture and Judicial Research," *Washington University Law Quarterly* (1971), pp. 177–207.

these supports and demands as *INPUTS*. As a result of their own cognitions and perceptions, individual judges redefine *INPUTS* as *WITHINPUTS* which, in the form of what they accept as the relevant issues and values, provide the psychological content to be converted. But at the same time that such psychological processes are taking place, so also are the *socio*psychological processes of accommodation and persuasion redefining the content of the social *INPUTS* that are accepted for *CONVERSION*. The structure of *CONVERSION* has as its counterpart the process of decision making, which results in a social content of policies and decisions (as well as a psychological content of rationalization and displacement); the policies and decisions are the *OUTPUTS* of the judicial system, and as the result of implementation they have an (of course, variable) *IMPACT* upon the environment (including an impact upon the parties to the litigation). But *OUTPUTS* also have an effect within the judicial system; and norms as well as votes and opinions constitute the structural subcomponents of *FEEDBACK*, which becomes recycled (in effect) as a source of further *INPUTS* for the judicial system, and which also provides commitment and reinforcement (leading to both cognitive and affective responses) for the individual judicial actor.[5]

For conceptual purposes we can distinguish between "issues" and "values." Issues denominate the questions of policy to which the judge purports to respond in his decision making, while values are the internalized beliefs of the judge. The judge, however, can take cognizance of issues in a case only through the intermediation of his own beliefs and expectations concerning the empirical events to which issues of public policy relate; that is, issues can be perceived by a judge only through his own personal system of

[5]For discussion of an alternative model of judicial systems (based upon set theory), and for further discussion of many of the concepts used in the present model, see Glendon Schubert, "Behavioral Jurisprudence," *Law and Society Review* 2 (1968), pp. 407–428; and for other alternative models, see Daryl R. Fair, "A Framework for Analyzing the Elements of Stability in Judicial Policy-Making," *Rutgers-Camden Law Journal* 3 (1972), pp. 395–409; Sheldon Goldman, "Behavioral Approaches to Judicial Decision-Making: Toward a Theory of Judicial Voting Behavior," *Jurimetrics Journal* 11 (1971), pp. 142–164; and Charles H. Sheldon, "Structuring a Model of the Judicial Process," *Georgetown Law Journal* 58 (1970), pp. 1153–1184. For a critique of judicial systems models, see Sheldon Goldman and Thomas P. Jahnige, "Systems Analysis and Judicial Systems: Potential and Limitations," *Polity* 3 (1971), pp. 334–359; and Jay A. Sigler, "A Cybernetic Model of the Judicial System," *Temple Law Quarterly* 41 (1968), pp. 398–428, which discusses explicitly the model described in the text above.

values. Hence, the issue is the manifest policy question to be decided; the values of the judge are the latent parameters that determine how he will define and respond to the issue. There is also a close relationship between "norms" and "decisions." Decisions, as we know, are the orders of judges that provide directions for other actors in a particular case. Norms are probability statements about how judges can be expected to behave in making future decisions. Thus decisions are, from this point of view, descriptions of particular sets of empirical events, while norms are inferences—based upon such descriptions—about the likelihood that future judicial action will be consistent with past judicial action.

According to the traditional theory of the judicial process, consistency is to be sought in logical interrelationships among norms; conventional theory looks for consistency in the observable patterns of interaction between judges and other actors; behavioral theory focuses upon consistency in the *patterning* of individual sets of values, consistency *between* individual sets of values, and consistency *among* an individual's inputs, his values, and his outputs. Both traditional and conventional theory tend to deemphasize the significance of the *CONVERSION* structure; traditional theory ignores the *INPUT* structure as well, while perhaps overemphasizing *FEEDBACK*. Conventional theory postulates a deterministic cause-and-effect relationship between inputs and outputs: judges are viewed as though the inputs define a tree from which a block of judicial wood is cut (as one kind of output), and the other outputs—such as policy decisions—are just chips off the old block. Quite to the contrary, behavioral theory generally, and our model in particular, assumes that the *CONVERSION* and *WITHINPUT* structures (which consist of judges and other persons who comprise the personnel of courts) are critical and independent variables in the judicial policy-making process. To summarize, we can distinguish among the three theoretical approaches in the following way: traditional theory deals with bivariate *OUTPUT-FEEDBACK* relationships; conventional theory with an extended linear sequence of *STRESS-INPUT-OUTPUT-IMPACT* relationships; while behavioral theory deals with much more complex multivariate relationships that involve those four structures plus *CONVERSION, WITHINPUTS,* and *FEEDBACK.*

At the psychological level of analysis, we can distinguish the demands that other actors make upon the values of individual judicial decision makers. These demands may be thought of as stimuli which, after having been perceived by the judge, induce from him responses in the form of decisional acts (such as voting or writing an opinion). This results either in direct feedback to the parties, in the form of satisfying or rejecting demands, or it leads to a new demand upon another (usually a higher) court as the process recycles. At the social level of analysis, we can conceptualize support (which may be either affirmative, absent, or negative) as a patterning of individual acts of demand. Support tends to reinforce or to contravene particular degrees of acceptance or rejection of public policy issues, and public policy issues are collective value perceptions—in the sense of intercorrelated individuals rather than of simple aggregations. Norms (which we have defined as predictions concerning the positions that one or a group of judges will take in regard to a given issue) are transmitted as feedback through channels of social communication and thereby condition the scope, direction, and intensity of supportive acts. Figure 8 postulates an outer, or social, limit and an inner, or psychological, limit for processes of interaction that affect policy making in the model. But the system of interaction, between these limits, is sociopsychological—interaction among individuals in small groups and in face-to-face relationships. The postulated processes, far from being independent, are (like the corresponding components in the several structures) highly interdependent.

This model is very general. Certainly it is applicable to the American federal judicial system with which we are concerned here, as well as to state judicial systems; and probably it can also be used to analyze the judicial systems of other countries. Of course, with such a degree of abstraction this model cannot entirely distinguish the differences among even seemingly quite different systems, but the model can be used to guide empirical observations on the basis of which further distinctions can be made. Here we shall use the model to help analyze empirical data relating to the Supreme Court, although it could be used just as well to analyze the policy-making process of any other court in the federal judicial system for which adequate empirical data were available.[6]

POLICY INPUTS

We can readily distinguish several major classes of inputs for the Supreme Court. In the most direct and literal sense, demands emanate from litigants, although such demands usually are translated into the legal idiom before being presented to the Court by

[6]Cf. the pioneering analysis of policy making in federal district courts by Kenneth M. Dolbeare, "The Federal District Courts and Urban Policy: An Exploratory Study (1960–1967)," Chapter 12 in *Frontiers of Judicial Research,* ed. Joel Grossman and Joseph Tanenhaus (New York: John Wiley & Sons, Inc., 1969), pp. 373–404.

counsel who are specialists in translating lay interests (and empirical events) into legal language (and other forms of legal behavior). Some litigants—many large corporations, for example—hire such specialists as part of their staff; for such litigants, supporting issues in and making demands upon the Supreme Court is a part of (as well as a part of the cost of) doing business. We may properly speak of "litigation management"[7] as constituting one method of accommodation by means of which such an organization can conduct its relationships with the government, other organizations, its clientele, etc. The National Association for the Advancement of Colored People (NAACP) is an example of a litigant organization that specialized, with extraordinary success during the late 1940s through the mid-1960s, in making demands upon and providing support for the Supreme Court.[8] Indeed, the NAACP was so successful that Thurgood Marshall, the lawyer who personally had presented, in oral argument of cases, most of its demands upon the Court and who had won twenty-nine of thirty-two cases that he had argued before the Court, himself was appointed to the United States Court of Appeals for the Second Circuit early in the Kennedy administration. The time was out of joint, or, rather, not yet sufficiently "in joint," for President Kennedy to have been willing to pay the political costs that might have been entailed by acceding to the NAACP's suggestion—whether made directly or through other groups—that Marshall, the son of a Pullman porter and the great-grandson of a slave, be appointed at that time to a Supreme Court vacancy; but the black revolution was progressing so rapidly that only half a dozen years later Lyndon Johnson was glad to be able to put Marshall on the Court. Kennedy did, however, accede to what was doubtless a similar suggestion from the AFL-CIO in appointing its general counsel, Arthur Goldberg,[9] to such a vacancy, with a delay en route as Secretary of Labor. Only thirty years ago, it was just as "impossible" to appoint a union lawyer to the Court as it has been until recently to appoint a

[7]See Nathan Hakman, "The Supreme Court's Political Environment: The Processing of Noncommercial Litigation," Chapter 7 in ibid., pp. 199–253.
[8]See Richard C. Cortner, "Strategies and Tactics of Litigants in Constitutional Cases," *Journal of Public Law* 17 (1968), pp. 287–307; and Clement E. Vose, "Litigation as a Form of Pressure Group Activity," *Annals of the American Academy of Political and Social Science* 319 (September 1958), pp. 22, 24–25; Vose, *Caucasians Only: The Supreme Court, The NAACP, and the Restrictive Covenant Cases* (Berkeley and Los Angeles: University of California Press, 1959).
[9]On Goldberg's brief performance in the Warren Court, see Ira H. Carmen, "One Civil Libertarian Among Many: The Case of Mr. Justice Goldberg," *Michigan Law Review* 65 (1966), pp. 301–336.

black—or as it remained, at least until 1973, to appoint a female, irrespective of her "race, color, or previous condition of servitude" (to quote the Fifteenth Amendment).[10]

The explicit assumption of our model is that the Supreme Court perceives demands not as "objective content" but as functions of the litigants who make them. Let us assume that the National Association of Manufacturers and the AFL-CIO each is party to a different case, in which they make equivalent demands upon the Court in regard to the extension of the jurisdiction of the National Labor Relations Board. Even if the demands were "objectively" the same, the Court would evaluate them as different because of the difference in the Court's expectations concerning the orientation, toward such a policy issue, of the employer's organization and the labor organization.[11]

The status and competence of the counsel who present demands to the Court also are differentially perceived. We already have discussed the situational bias in favor of the solicitor general, which we construed to be a function of his more frequent, more intensive, and more extensive interaction with the justices, in comparison with other counsel.[12] Similarly (but to a lesser extent), lawyers of great reputation (such as Thurman Arnold, the late John W. Davis, Edward Bennett Williams, or Frederick Bernays Wiener) can communicate with the Court much more effectively than can a lawyer from (say) South Dakota who has been specially admitted to the Supreme Court bar to make his first appearance

---

[10]Nixon did attempt to appoint Mildred Lillie, a California state judge, in the fall of 1971; but the ABA committee had disapproved her, supposedly on professional grounds, by an overwhelmingly negative eleven-to-one majority. *Time* 98, No. 18 (November 1, 1971), p. 16. But barely a year later it was expected that he would try again: see Ilene Barth, "If a Seat Opens—Will Nixon Choose a Woman for the Supreme Court?" *Parade* (The Sunday Newspaper Magazine), January 7, 1973, pp. 8, 10. There have been a few lower federal court female judges: see Maurine Howard Abernathy, "Woman Judges in United States Courts," *Women Lawyers Journal* 55 (1969), pp. 57–58.

[11]On the general subject of differences among judicial perceptions of litigant status, see Jessie Bernard, "Dimensions and Axes of Supreme Court Decisions," *Social Forces* 34 (1955), pp. 19–27; Stuart S. Nagel and Lenore J. Weitzman, "Women as Litigants," *Hastings Law Journal* 23 (1971), pp. 171–198; and S. Sidney Ulmer, "Support for Negro Claimants in the Warren Court: The Case of the Chief Justice" *Jurimetrics Journal* 11 (1971), pp. 178–188.

[12]See the article, "Government Litigation in the Supreme Court: The Roles of the Solicitor General," *Yale Law Journal* 78 (1969), pp. 1442–1481.

before the Court.[13] This is not to say that all of the justices will respond more favorably to arguments because they have been presented by renowned advocates; to the contrary, the *direction* of judicial responses to "leading counsel" will vary with both the justice and the lawyer. But whatever the direction of judicial response, it is likely to be more intense when the stimulus (in the sense of argument about the issue) has been reinforced by the advocacy of a recognized personality who is experienced in interacting with the justices.

Lower courts are by no means equally prestigious in the eyes of Supreme Court justices. Of course, a few courts have the reputation of being outstanding, while a few others have the opposite reputation.[14] Not all justices would rank the lower courts in the same order, even when perception is consensual, and some justices tend more than others to weigh as important the prestige of a particular lower court. Moreover, a lower court's prestige may vary with the issue. For example, the Court of Appeals for the Fifth Circuit has been imputed to entertain a pronounced antilabor bias,[15] while the Court of Appeals for the Second Circuit (like the New York State Court of Appeals) received (especially from connoisseur Frankfurter) what frequently amounted to adulation as the champions of the American judicial league. Sometimes the Supreme Court has been able to take distinct advantage of lower-court prestige, as did Chief Justice Vinson in a politically conservative opinion supporting a decision approving conspiracy convictions of the leaders of the American Communist party, in a trial before Judge Medina.[16] Vinson attempted to advertise the position of the majority of the Court (for whom he spoke) as being really not illiberal, since the Supreme Court (as he pointed out) merely was approving the decision and supporting rationale that had been adopted in this very case by the Court of Appeals for the Second Circuit. That court had spoken, in turn, through no less august a personage than the great Learned Hand, author of *The Bill of Rights* and (both off and on the bench) of other reputedly liberal writings, and a federal judge whom most lawyers considered to be

[13]Cf. John P. Frank, *The Marble Palace* (New York: Alfred A. Knopf, Inc., 1958), pp. 84–94.
[14]Rodney L. Mott, "Judicial Influence," *American Political Science Review* 30 (1936), pp. 295–315; Stuart S. Nagel, "Sociometric Relations among American Courts," *Southwestern Social Science Quarterly* 43 (1962), pp. 136–142.
[15]See Jack W. Peltason, *Federal Courts in the Political Process* (New York: Random House, Inc., 1955), p. 16.
[16]*Dennis* v. *United States,* 341 U.S. 494, 510 (1951).

of much greater ability than all but a handful of the justices who have sat on the Supreme Court during the twentieth century.

We have spoken so far of the human actors whose roles in proceedings before the Supreme Court are such that they function as inputs. A second general source of inputs is the record of the case itself and the briefs and oral argument presented to the Court. As the previous chapter pointed out, lawyers tend to distinguish between "facts" and "law" in analyzing cases. Facts, in turn, can be divided into those *in* the case and those *of* the case. The former consist of descriptive statements about empirical events that relate to the conflict of interest between the parties. The Supreme Court is several steps removed from those events. One output of the trial is a particular version of the pretrial events, reflecting a multiplicity of decisions of the trial judge or of the trial judge and the petit jury. Circuit judges may or may not agree with the trial court's determinations of the facts in the case, but usually the court of appeals can change only a few of the many fact decisions made by the trial court; under the applicable procedural norms, most factual determinations of the trial are foreclosed from effective appellate review.

Not only are there these authoritative suppositions about what happened before the trial began, but from the point of view of the Supreme Court, the events that transpired in the decision-making processes of the trial court and of the court of appeals also constitute a set of facts: these are the facts *of* the case. Both of these two kinds of facts are in effect hypotheses, for which the associated levels of probability are unspecified, about the likelihood that a particular version of past human actions is valid. Such versions necessarily have widely varying ranges of validity; they are but images of reality. They function for the Supreme Court as stimuli that interrelate with issues.

The issues in a case are the judges' perceptions of what lawyers call "questions of law" and what many political scientists consider to be "questions of policy." Legal questions relate to normative propositions—assertions that persons ought to act in one way or another. In traditional theory, the task of judicial decision makers is to examine the degree of correspondence between facts (statements about how people actually have behaved) and laws (statements about how people should behave). An alternative conceptualization of the relationship between factual and legal inputs will be described below as policy conversion, in Figure 8.

There is a third general source of inputs, the critics of the Court. Law schools provide the most important forum for professional criticism of all the federal courts, including the Supreme Court. Justices frequently speak at major law schools, and such affairs provide an occasion for informal intermingling of the justice with the faculty and students of a law school. Most of the justices select their administrative assistants from favored law schools; for over forty years, Justice Felix Frankfurter, who was appointed to the Court directly from the Harvard law faculty, served as either sender or recipient of such assistants. During the 1920s and 1930s, Frankfurter dispatched from Harvard to Washington a succession of young men (whom some called the "happy hot dogs") to work as law clerks for various justices, but Holmes and Brandeis in particular; and then during the 1940s and 1950s, his faculty friends at Harvard continued the custom, by sending to him two of the honor graduates from each year's class.

The pervasive effect of the "old school tie" is very well illustrated by Jack W. Peltason, who offers many examples of the extent to which members of the Harvard law faculty supported Frankfurter but attacked Justice William O. Douglas, a former professor of the Yale law faculty, while the Yale law faculty reciprocated.[17] But although one's initial tendency is to smile at such genteel and old-fashioned academic antics and to discount such influence as arising primarily from the rivalry between the two universities, supporting behavior by the respective colleagues of Frankfurter and of Douglas can be understood at the psychological as well as at the sociological level of analysis. The reinforcing effects—and affects—due to the affiliation of the two justices with distinctive friendship groups are obvious enough, but a more fundamental explanation for the dichotomization of the supporting groups for the two justices may be found in the difference in the value orientation of both the justices and their supporters. Douglas has been the most liberal member of the Court during the past generation, while Frankfurter proved to be one of the most conservative (especially on economic issues).[18] Douglas and Frankfurter each spoke and wrote vociferously, both on and off the Court, so there could be little doubt concerning their respective ideological positions and differences. Their faculty acolytes could not support the justices without also supporting the values with which they were identified; and since law professors generally are sophisticated men, they doubtless were well aware that a Harvard "vote" for Frankfurter was a vote for economic conservatism, just as a Yale "vote" for Douglas was a vote for liberalism on the Supreme Court.

The law schools also publish law reviews, which are edited by

[17]Peltason, *Federal Courts,* op. cit., p. 72n.20.
[18]J. A. C. Grant, "Felix Frankfurter: A Dissenting Opinion," *UCLA Law Review* 10 (1965), pp. 1013–1042.

students and written partly by them and partly by law professors and lawyers. Members of the Supreme Court rely upon the law reviews to provide them with supporting arguments and rationales which they then can and do cite in their opinions in support of their decisions. The rationale for the Court's recent major decision on state legislative reapportionment, in *Baker* v. *Carr,* was taken directly from the brief submitted by Solicitor General Cox, which in turn relied heavily upon a then recent article in the *Harvard Law Review* written by the newspaperman who covered the Supreme Court for *The New York Times.*[19] The articles and case commentaries in the reviews also function as a nationwide set of "listening posts" that aid the justices in gauging audience reaction to their own performance.

The influence of the law reviews upon judicial decision making has not escaped congressional notice. Representative Wright Patman of Texas, for example, some years ago delivered a speech entitled "Effect of Lobbyists' Propaganda upon Our Supreme Court"; the congressman was particularly disturbed about several articles in the *Harvard Law Review,* on national antitrust policy.[20] The law reviews do take sides, but within certain limits of concern for objectivity and with at least seeming dispassion; and collectively they articulate arguments both pro and con most public policy issues.[21] Popular periodicals and newspapers are less subject to such restraint; in such major issues as legislative reapportionment and public school prayers, both so-called news coverage of the Court's decisions and what ostensibly was editorial commentary spanned a spectrum of behaviors ranging from strong support to hysterical opposition.[22] News coverage necessarily was biased by

[19]Anthony Lewis, "Legislative Apportionment and the Federal Courts," *Harvard Law Review* 71 (1958), pp. 1057–1098. (Most of Lewis' article, Cox's brief, and the Supreme Court's decision and opinions are reprinted in Glendon Schubert, *Reapportionment* [New York: Charles Scribner's Sons, 1965], Part 2.)

[20]*Congressional Record* 85th Cong., 1st Sess., Vol. 103, Part 12, pp. 16159–16169, especially pp. 16160–16161.

[21]Cf. Chester A. Newland, "Legal Periodicals and the United States Supreme Court," *Midwest Journal of Political Science* 3 (1959), pp. 58–74; and also his "The Supreme Court and Legal Writing: Learned Journals as Vehicles of an Anti-Trust Lobby?" *Georgetown Law Journal* 48 (1959), pp. 105–143.

[22]Chester A. Newland, "Press Coverage of the United States Supreme Court," *Western Political Quarterly* 17 (1964), pp. 15–36; Stuart S. Nagel and Robert Erikson, "Editorial Reaction to Supreme Court Decisions on Church and State," *Public Opinion Quarterly* 30 (1966–1967), pp. 647–655; and Richard M. Johnson, *The Dynamics of Compliance* (Evanston: Northwestern University Press, 1967), pp. 69–90.

the fact that many more public speakers attacked than defended the Warren Court.[23] The overwhelming majority of editorial commentators did favor the reapportionment decision, but an even more lopsided majority opposed the public school prayer decision. Generally, according to Professor Newland, wire service reporting of the Court's activities "reveals two serious faults . . . : choosing sensational material over more significant cases for reports and blowing up of stories to sensational dimensions."[24] By and large, the Supreme Court had a "bad press" during the 1950s and 1960s—reflecting also, no doubt, the extent to which the relatively liberal national policies of the Court's majorities then were repugnant to most American newspaper publishers.

POLICY CONVERSION

According to our model (Figure 8), the *WITHINPUTS* and *CONVERSION* structures are central in the judicial policy-making process. Withinputs are the product of a function of complex interactions between both somatic (physical) and psychological subsystems of each individual decision maker, and they embody both affective (emotional) and cognitive (rational) content; conversion is the subprocess by means of which issues are recognized and decided as a result of group interaction and the integration of the values of the individual justices. The conversion structure consists of the patterning of support and demands of litigants and their counsel (and others who intervene in the case to support or oppose them), and of the issues—the shared perceptions of the individual justices concerning the policy and factual questions raised by cases before them for a decision. In a formal sense, decision making as a process occurs when individual justices cast their votes on the disposition of a case at the group conference; and strictly speaking, the subsequent announcement both of the voting division of the Court, and of the opinions of the Court and of individual justices, are among the *OUTPUTS* of the decision-making process. Conversion relates, therefore, to both psychological and social processes. When each judge decides how he will vote, that is a psychological process; but when he announces his vote, in a fixed order of articulation, as a contributor to a group decision that depends upon an integration of the preferences of the individual participants, that is a social process. Analysis of the interrelation between individual decisions and the group decision in a case involves us in sociopsychological study.

[23]Clifford M. Lytle, *The Warren Court and Its Critics* (Tucson: University of Arizona Press, 1968).
[24]Newland, op. cit., p. 33.

Both values and issues are of course dynamic rather than static. From a functional point of view, issues and values are a major source of withinputs for the decision; both issues and values become in part transformed into the outputs of the policy-making process. However, a justice's values are relatively stable in comparison to the external sources of inputs discussed in the preceding section; they change but slowly, while the support and demand inputs fluctuate widely from case to case, over a range of several thousand cases each year. Moreover, the support and demand inputs are more consensually shared by all the justices.

Although the values and issues are also shared, the means by which each justice acquires his values is a very individual matter. An individual's values are a product of socialization, and his socialization experience results from a combination of chance considerations operating within the political culture in which he has been reared. Supreme Court justices acquire their values in part as a consequence of having been born into a particular family at a particular place and time: nationality, race, family, and early as well as later education all have some influence in building the political character of each justice, as do marriage, law school training, and subsequent professional experience. Table 8 presents a summary of three classes of judicial attributes (experience, appointing President, and partisan affiliation) and two classes of judicial values. Of course, it is not to be assumed that a mature man can be completely described by a handful of labels designated as "attribute" or "attitudinal" variables. His values, like his attributes, have been molded by a lifetime of experience. Nevertheless, it is quite possible that when we ask why he votes as he does in a particular case or series of cases (raising, for him, the same policy issue), a small number of variables may approximate *what is most relevant about him* closely enough to be useful in analyzing decision making. If such a focusing of attention, for analytical purposes, were not possible, then we could say nothing of scientific value about the causes of the behavior of judges (or of any other complex living organisms, for that matter).

Table 8 illustrates some of the kinds of relationships that characteristically have been investigated in studies of the effect of socialization upon judicial policy making. This table implies a set of hypotheses about the relationship among the attribute variables (i.e., appointing President and partisan affiliation), or between an attribute variable and one or both of the attitudinal variables. The sample of data presented in this table, which relates only to the justices incumbent during the 1972 term, is too small for any statistically significant relationships to be apparent; but studies of larger samples of judges indicate that there are some meaningful

TABLE 8

Status, Selected Attributes, and Attitudinal Orientations of Supreme Court
Justices (1972 Term)

Seniority status	Name	Major legal and/or political experience*	Appointed by	Political party affiliation	Attitudinal orientation	
					Political	Economic
1	Burger	P, NA, NJ (asst. U.S. attorney general; U.S. circuit judge for 13 years)	Nixon	Rep.	Conservative	Conservative
2	Douglas	P, NA (law professor; chairman of S.E.C.)	Roosevelt	Dem.	Liberal	Liberal
3	Brennan	SJ (state judge)	Eisenhower	Dem.	Moderate	Liberal
4	Stewart	P, NJ (corporation lawyer; U.S. circuit judge for 2 years)	Eisenhower	Rep.	Moderate	Moderate
5	White	NA (U.S. deputy attorney general)	Kennedy	Dem.	Moderate	Moderate
6	Marshall	P, NJ, NA (NAACP lawyer for 25 years; U.S. circuit judge for 4 years; U.S. solicitor general)	Johnson	Dem.	Liberal	Moderate
7	Blackmun	P, NJ (U.S. circuit judge for 11 years)	Nixon	Rep.	Conservative	Conservative
8	Powell	P (president of ABA and other bar organizations)	Nixon	Dem.	Conservative	Conservative
9	Rehnquist	NJ, NA (clerk to Justice Robert Jackson; asst. U.S. attorney general)	Nixon	Rep.	Conservative	Conservative

*Key to abbreviations for experience categories

P = private   S = state   J = judicial
N = national   A = administrative   L = legislative

and important correlations among these (and similar) attribute variables and these (and other) attitudinal variables.[25]

ATTRIBUTES

Supreme Court justices invariably have been males, whose age (at the time of appointment) has ranged from thirty-two to sixty-nine years; the average age of the nine justices incumbent in 1973 was sixty-three years. Nine out of ten (85 percent) have been of British ethnic origin, and of the others only three (Cardozo, Iberian; Goldberg, Slavic; Marshall, African) were not descended from emigrants from northwestern Europe. No Asians (or even Italians) ever have been appointed to the Supreme Court. Nine out of ten (89 percent) have been Protestant: during the first century of the Court's existence, only one Catholic (Taney) was appointed out of a total of fifty justices, and although one Jew was offered a nomination to the Court, none was appointed prior to 1916; among the forty-nine appointees since 1890 there have been five more Catholics and five Jews. Among the eighty-seven Protestants, about eight out of ten were affiliated with high social-status denominations (Episcopalian, Presbyterian, Unitarian, Congregational). During the first few decades after the establishment of the Court, most justices came from the landed aristocracy; since then, they have been drawn primarily from the professional upper-middle classes. As a group, they have been exceptionally well educated (in relation to the standards of the period in which they served), even in terms of nonlegal education: five sixths of them either attended a law school of high standing or studied as an apprentice under a prominent lawyer or judge. Moreover, they were born into politically active families, as a consequence of which the justices, as young men, were both encouraged and aided in their quests for political careers.[26]

Almost all of the justices had experience—frequently, quite extensive experience—in other public offices prior to their selec-

[25]See Don Ramsey Bowen, *The Explanation of Judicial Voting Behavior from Sociological Characteristics of Judges* (Ph.D. dissertation in political science, Yale University, 1965; University Microfilms No. 65–15,014); Sheldon Goldman, *Politics, Judges, and the Administration of Justice: The Backgrounds, Recruitment, and Decisional Tendencies of the Judges on the United States Courts of Appeals, 1961–1964* (Ph.D. dissertation in political science, Harvard University, 1965; University Microfilms No. 65–9924); and S. Sidney Ulmer, "Dissent Behavior and the Social Background of Supreme Court Justices," *Journal of Politics,* 32 (1970), pp. 580–598.

[26]John R. Schmidhauser, "The Justices of the Supreme Court: A Collective Portrait," *Midwest Journal of Political Science* 3 (1959), pp. 22–23.

tion for the Supreme Court. Although Republicans Eisenhower and Nixon showed a preference for corporation lawyers and the promotion of incumbent federal circuit judges, three recent Democratic Presidents (Roosevelt, Truman, and Kennedy) tended to prefer men from their own cabinets; thus had three of the justices incumbent in 1973 been promoted to the Court from earlier Democratic administrations. A much larger than usual majority of six also then had had some prior judicial experience, and for Burger and Brennan and Blackmun this had been extensive. Eisenhower had given both Harlan and Stewart a year or two of "seasoning" as federal circuit judges before he promoted them; and Marshall had almost four years on the court of appeals in the second circuit before he became solicitor general. But a majority of even the justices listed in Table 8 had no more than a couple of years of previous judicial experience, and four had had none at all. Such a situation, however, has been normal for the Court throughout its history. It has been assumed by many who have speculated on the subject that judges with prior judicial experience would tend to "follow precedent" more than those without such experience, but the only scholarly analysis of empirical data has failed to confirm that hypothesis. On the contrary, there has been a slight (though not statistically significant) tendency for justices with prior judicial experience to vote to overrule precedents to a greater extent than do justices without such experience.[27] The same study reported that the relatively few justices (nine) who came from families in the lower socioeconomic classes dissented much more often than did the much larger group of justices (sixty-two) who came from aristocratic or upper-middle-class families. The former group were always a small minority on the Court, but if there had been important differences between their own values and those of the court's upper-class majority, we should expect them to signify such differences by dissenting.

Table 8 shows that two of the incumbent justices (Brennan and Powell) were affiliated with a political party different from that of the Presidents who appointed them. Only one out of eight is the usual proportion of "nonpartisan" appointees. There have been eleven other instances, and during the half century spanned by the Taft through Eisenhower administrations, every President except Coolidge crossed party lines in at least one of his appointments to the Court. But the universal practice has been to recognize that Supreme Court positions are among the most important sources of

[27]John R. Schmidhauser, *"Stare Decisis,* Dissent, and the Background of the Justices of the Supreme Court of the United States," *University of Toronto Law Journal* 14 (1962), p. 202.

patronage available to an administration. Presidents expect to advance preferred policy goals in making such appointments, and a record of political party or administrative (and, as Schmidhauser has argued, of prior judicial[28]—which may explain Nixon's initial devotion to "nonpolitical" Supreme Court appointments) service provides what are assumed to be important clues to the ideological orientation of appointees. Nagel has demonstrated that, in general, Republican justices have supported the use of judicial review of national statutes when the effect has been to advance economic conservatism, while Democratic justices have supported judicial review when the effect has been to further political liberalism.[29] Moreover, many of the justices have remained so intensely involved in the liberal-conservative ideological struggle that they have not hesitated to attempt to influence Presidents who were in the process of selecting new colleagues for them—as exemplified by Burger's campaigning for Haynsworth and for Blackmun. Indeed, for a justice to behave otherwise is politically irrational.[30]

During the Court's first century, geographical considerations were much more important than they are today. At a time when Supreme Court justices still rode circuit and participated in the decision making of the circuit courts, there was a stronger functional reason why men should be picked from among the various subcultural regions of the country. Presumably such men would be more familiar with the variations in public policy that were preferred within their regions, more sympathetic to the cultural peculiarities of their regions, and hence more acceptable to the politically active denizens. Moreover, at a time when national politics was regionally organized, the ability of a justice to function as a regional political representative was important. Today, however, regional "balance" in the Court seems to be no more important a consideration than it is in the selection of a presidential cabinet. When Hoover appointed Cardozo in 1932, for example, a clear majority of the Court—three New Yorkers plus one justice each from Pennsylvania (Philadelphia) and Massachusetts (Boston)—came from a fairly short strip of the Atlantic seacoast. On the other hand, Nixon's strenuous efforts to put a deep southerner on

[28]Schmidhauser, "The Justices of the Supreme Court," op. cit., pp. 41–44, 47.
[29]Stuart S. Nagel, "Political Parties and Judicial Review in American History," *Journal of Public Law* 11 (1963), p. 340.
[30]William Howard Taft, for example, is well known both for the great importance that he as President attached to the many appointments that he made to the Court (six in four years) and also for the conspicuous manner in which, as chief justice during the 1920s, he beleaguered (in turn) Harding , Coolidge, and Hoover with his advice concerning the men who ought to be appointed to the courts. See p. 14, footnote 10, above.

the Supreme Court met with conspicuous failure—although the Senate's rejections were just as much a function of regional bias as were the nominations. The geographic distribution of the home residences of the incumbent justices listed in Table 8 is as follows: two from the Northeast; three from the Middle West; one from the South; two from the Rocky Mountain region; and one from the Far West. But the Supreme Court reshaped by Richard Nixon evinced less regional bias than usual (during recent decades),[31] with a majority from west of the banks of the Mississippi River for the first time in history, including one (Douglas) from beyond the Rocky Mountains. It is quite possible, of course, to have a Court that appears to be regionally well balanced even though it has been selected primarily for quite other reasons.

INTERACTION AND LEADERSHIP

There is consensus among many scholars using different methods of analysis that the justices of the Supreme Court, at least during the past four decades (upon which research thus far has tended to focus), have been divided consistently into subsets of relatively liberal and relatively conservative justices, with one or more moderate justices who have given consistent support to neither of the more extreme groups of ideological partisans.[32]

[31]For discussion of earlier biases in regional representation, see Cortez A. M. Ewing, *The Judges of the Supreme Court, 1789–1937* (Minneapolis: University of Minnesota Press, 1938), Chapter 3; Felix Frankfurter and James M. Landis, *The Business of the Supreme Court* (New York: The Macmillan Company, 1928); and John R. Schmidhauser, "Judicial Behavior and the Sectional Crisis of 1837–1860," *Journal of Politics* 23 (1961), pp. 615–638.

[32]C. Herman Pritchett, "Division of Opinion among Justices of the United States Supreme Court, 1939–1941," *American Political Science Review* 35 (1941), pp. 890–898; Pritchett, *The Roosevelt Court: A Study in Judicial Politics and Values, 1937–1947* (New York: The Macmillan Company, 1948; Louis L. Thurstone and James W. Degan, "A Factorial Study of the Supreme Court," *Proceedings of the National Academy of Science* 37 (1951), pp. 628–635; Jessie Bernard, "Dimensions and Axes of Supreme Court Decisions: A Study in the Sociology of Conflict," *Social Forces* 34 (1955), pp. 19–27; Eloise C. Snyder, "The Supreme Court as a Small Group," *Social Forces* 36 (1958), pp. 232–238; Glendon Schubert, *Quantitative Analysis of Judicial Behavior* (New York: The Free Press of Glencoe, 1959), pp. 77–172; S. Sidney Ulmer, "The Analysis of Behavior Patterns on the United States Supreme Court," *Journal of Politics* 22 (1960), pp. 629–653; Glendon Schubert, *The Judicial Mind: The Attitudes and Ideologies of Supreme Court Justices, 1946–1963* (Evanston: Northwestern University Press, 1965); and Glendon Schubert, *The Judicial Mind Revisited* (New York: Oxford University Press, 1974).

During the middle 1930s, for example, there was a liberal sub-group consisting of Brandeis, Cardozo, and Stone; a conservative subgroup consisting of Butler, McReynolds, Sutherland, and Van Devanter; and two justices, Hughes and Roberts, who gave somewhat greater support to the conservative bloc *before,* and to the liberal bloc *after,* President Roosevelt's attack on the Court in February 1937. During the 1940s, the liberal bloc consisted of Black, Douglas, Murphy, and Rutledge; the conservatives included Vinson, Burton, and Reed; while the other two justices, Frankfurter and Jackson, were even more conservative than the Vinson group on economic issues but more liberal than the Vinson group on issues of civil liberty. As Table 8 indicates, the 1973 Court contained only one consistent liberal (Douglas), but four consistent conservatives (Burger, Blackmun, Powell, and Rehnquist). Of the other four incumbent justices, Stewart and White are moderate on both issues, while Marshall is liberal on civil liberty issues but moderate on economic issues, and Brennan is moderate on civil liberties but economically liberal.

A study of the Taney Court (1837–1860)[33] indicates that it, too, was divided between liberal and conservative justices and in regard to political, economic, and social issues. The issues examined were state regulation of slavery, corporations, and interstate commerce—at the time, of course, there was little or no national governmental regulation of any of these. In terms of equivalent contemporary policy issues, the politically liberal (pro-civil liberty) position was to favor the abolition of slavery, and the economically liberal position was to uphold state control over business corporations. Somewhat surprisingly, the important cleavage was not between northerners and southerners. Instead, it was between Jacksonian Democrats (on these issues, politically conservative and economically liberal) and Whigs (politically liberal but economically conservative).

As previously suggested, certain aspects of the role of chief justice thrust him into a position of formal leadership.[34] Among the most important of his formal functions that facilitate his leadership of the group is his assignment of the opinion of the Court when he votes with the majority. The assignment to speak for the Court can be used to stake out a relatively extreme policy position, as when Burger has Rehnquist write in an anti-civil liberty

[33]Schmidhauser, op. cit.
[34]Particularly in regard to ceremonial and some administrative functions, such as presiding over oral argument and when decisions are announced; the preparation of the consent lists; and the preparation of the per curiam opinions.

decision; but when such a decision is five to four, the opinion is likely to be assigned to the moderate judge (such as, in regard to civil liberties, Stewart) who is the marginal member of the majority, because to do otherwise might result in losing the majority and hence control over the decision.

Some research indicates that it is useful to distinguish between two kinds of group leadership: "task" and "social."[35] In leading the justices through the decision making of the weekly conference, for example, one essential function is to get decisions made, so that the Court will not fall so far behind in its docket that criticism from outside will be attracted. To get decisions made, group discussion must be focused and to some extent limited, and this requires task leadership. But the discussion involves nine men—a relatively large "small group"—all of whom are quite independent of each other due to their life tenure and among whom there are complex patterns of relationships of ideological affinity and conflict, depending upon the issue under discussion. Their attitudes toward public policy issues tend to be reinforced by their attitudes toward each other: some are close personal friends, while others are involved in what at times have been notorious "feuds." In other words, social leadership is necessary to control the level of emotional relationships in the discussions if decision making is to proceed in an efficient manner.[36]

Some chief justices, such as Hughes, have been outstanding in both leadership roles. Others have done well in one role and poorly in the other. Taft, for example, was a good social leader, but he depended upon Van Devanter to function as the effective foreman in constructing the Court's majorities for decision making. Stone, on the other hand, was so much a democrat that he was not an effective task leader and so much an ideological partisan that he was also ineffective in the social leadership role. An analysis of the level of consensus in the Court's decision making under all seven of the chief justices between 1888 and 1958 has demonstrated that the justices were more deeply and variously divided in their voting under Stone than at any other time during the seven decades. Efficiency in getting decisions made, however, is not the only relevant standard of effective leadership, nor is it necessarily the best criterion. It has been argued that in comparison with Hughes'

[35]David J. Danelski, "The Influence of the Chief Justice in the Decisional Process," in *Courts, Judges and Politics,* ed. Walter F. Murphy and C. Herman Pritchett (New York: Random House, Inc., 1961), pp. 497–508.
[36]S. Sidney Ulmer, "Homeostatic Tendencies in the United States Supreme Court," in *Introductory Readings in Political Behavior,* ed. S. Ulmer (Chicago: Rand McNally & Company, 1961), pp. 167–188.

autocratic management, Stone encouraged full and open discussion of the issues. If a major aspect of the Supreme Court's role is to educate its audience, then open articulation of value and policy disagreements among the justices is preferable to their being smothered under a spurious mantle of togetherness and contrived consensus.[37]

ATTITUDES

Sociometric analysis of interagreement in voting behavior, which focused upon a pool of all of the votes of all of the justices, in cases decided on the merits during a stipulated period, showed (as reported above) that the Court characteristically divided into a liberal bloc and a conservative bloc. But bloc analysis also showed that there were usually some justices who did not seem to affiliate with either bloc, and there seemed to be a considerable amount of inconsistent voting, even among the bloc members—inconsistent, that is, in the sense that in some decisions one or more justices would vote with members of the "opposing" bloc rather than with members of their own bloc. The latter findings were perplexing, and it was not until the introduction of more powerful research tools that they were understood. At first through linear cumulative scaling and subsequently through factor analysis and multidimensional scaling, studies of the voting behavior of Supreme Court justices have shown that there are three major attitudinal components of judicial liberalism and conservatism. In order better to distinguish among them, we shall henceforth refer to the three components as *attitudes,* and we shall designate as *ideologies* the more general concepts of liberalism and conservatism.

The three major attitudes are (1) *political* liberalism and conservatism; (2) *social* liberalism and conservatism; and (3) *economic* liberalism and conservatism.[38] We shall exemplify and define in greater detail each of these attitudes in the concluding section of

[37]Glendon Schubert, *Constitutional Politics* (New York: Holt, Rinehart & Winston, Inc., 1960), pp. 123–125; John P. Frank, "Harlan Fiske Stone: An Estimate," *Stanford Law Review* 9 (1957), p. 629n.

[38]S. Sidney Ulmer, "A Note on Attitudinal Consistency in the United States Supreme Court," *Indian Journal of Political Science* 22 (1961), pp. 195–204 (the political scale); Harold J. Spaeth, "Warren Court Attitudes Toward Business: The 'B' Scale," in *Judicial Decision-Making,* ed. Glendon Schubert (New York: The Free Press of Glencoe, 1963), pp. 79–108, especially pp. 79–84 (the economic scale); Glendon Schubert, "The 1960 Term of the Supreme Court: A Psychological Analysis," *American Political Science Review* 56 (1962), pp. 90–107, especially 97–101 (both the political scale and the economic scale).

this chapter. Here it is sufficient to say that political liberalism is the belief in and the support of civil rights and liberties; political conservatism is the upholding of law and order and the defense of the status quo—no matter what may be the pattern of accepted values that the status quo happens to represent. Social liberalism advocates egalitarianism in regard to political representation, citizenship, and ethnic status; social conservatism opposes equality of access to the polity, to the economy, and to society. Economic liberalism is the belief in and the support of a more equal distribution of wealth, goods, and services; the economic conservative defends private enterprise, vested interests, and broad differentials in wealth and income between laborers and the owners of property. It is easy to see, however, that it is quite possible for a judge to feel that he is being consistent in his ideology if he favors political liberalism and economic conservatism, for this combination of attitudes means to uphold both the personal and the property rights of the individual. Similarly, a justice who consistently upholds the necessarily collectivized interests represented by the government will be politically conservative and economically liberal in his attitudes.

Let us assume that the attitude of social liberalism defines a position that is modal in a broader range of attitudes extending from political liberalism through economic liberalism, which together span the range of the liberal ideology (see Figure 9). Similarly, we can define an opposing conservative ideology. The range from economic conservatism to political liberalism defines the ideology of individualism; the opposite range defines collectivism.

FIGURE 9

A Paradigm of the Relationship Between Judicial Types and Output Norms

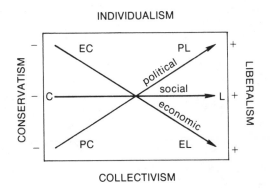

Over an extended period of time we can find Supreme Court justices in all four categories of ideological type: some are liberals, some are conservatives, some are individualists, some are collectivists. The Burger Court had not yet completed a full term in which the four Nixon appointees interacted together, however, as this is written; and although certain matters already were clear, the ideological patterning of the Burger Court was not yet distinctly apparent. It was quite clear, for example, that all four Nixon appointees were most conservative judges, in regard to issues of both political and economic policy. It was also clear that they were voting much more conservatively, during the 1972 term, than they had done in the previous term. The 1971 term had been the freshman year for both Powell and Rehnquist, and they had joined the Court in the middle of the term after many jurisdictional decisions already had been determined. But by the spring of 1973 Richard Nixon's apocalyptic vision was becoming more apparent to all, as his Four Horsemen began to take the bit and run with it.[39]

By that time the scale reflecting the response pattern of the judges of the Burger Court toward issues of political policy was very similar to that of the scale for economic policy, as Figure 10 shows, although there were very great differences among the justices. Ranging from most to least sympathetic on civil liberties issues, we find Douglas voting in support of political liberalism sixty-two times out of his sixty-four participations in split decisions during the 1971 term and the first half of the 1972 term;[40] Rehnquist, at the other end of the scale, voted against every one of the fifty-two civil liberties claims that he considered. The economic scale, although it subsumes fewer cases, is very similar, the principal difference being that Marshall, who favored civil liberties slightly more often than Brennan, is substantially less sympathetic than Brennan to claims of economic liberalism, in regard to which Marshall voted (consistently, since his appointment to the Warren Court) as a moderate. Douglas is also most supportive on the economic scale, with thirty-nine pro votes out of forty-one; and again Rehnquist is least supportive, although here there was a single case in which he did vote liberally (for a labor union). Marshall's moderation on the economic scale is positive in orientation; Stewart and White are moderates whose balance of support lies negatively on both scales, although there are certain subordinate issues on which Powell tended to be *more* politically liberal

[39]See Glendon Schubert, *The Future of the Nixon Court* (Honolulu: University of Hawaii Foundation, 1972).

[40]See Frank H. Way, Jr., "The Study of Judicial Attitudes: The Case of Mr. Justice Douglas," *Western Political Quarterly* 24 (1971), pp. 12–23.

FIGURE 10

Scales of Political and Economic Liberalism for the Burger Court

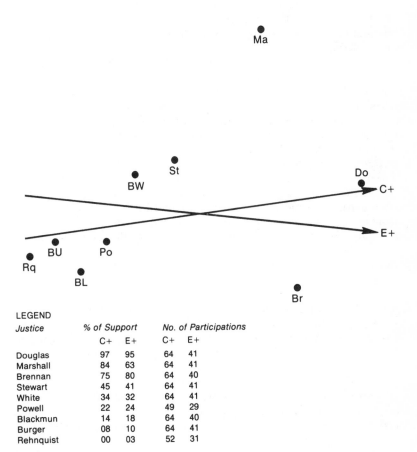

LEGEND

Justice	% of Support		No. of Participations	
	C+	E+	C+	E+
Douglas	97	95	64	41
Marshall	84	63	64	41
Brennan	75	80	64	40
Stewart	45	41	64	41
White	34	32	64	41
Powell	22	24	49	29
Blackmun	14	18	64	40
Burger	08	10	64	41
Rehnquist	00	03	52	31

than White, just as there were also certain subissues in regard to which Powell tended to be *less* economically liberal than Blackmun. But the overall, predominant patterns seem clearly to be those portrayed in Figure 10.

The attitudinal issues to which the justices respond are not necessarily manifest in either their opinions or the records of the cases. *Prima facie,* for example, no question of law is raised for decision by the Court when it reviews the decisions of lower courts (state or national) in Federal Employers' Liability Act evidentiary cases. The statutory law, presumably, is clear, or at least, to the extent that it is not, it was clarified long ago by interpretative decisions of the Supreme Court. The question at issue always is whether, given the unique set of facts that have been "found" by the trial court in the particular case, the evidence of employer negligence is sufficient to support a jury verdict of damages in favor of the injured railroad worker.

Conservative critics castigated the Warren Court throughout the 1960s for wasting its time in hearing such appeals; the precious time of the Court, the critics insisted, should be reserved for the decision of more important policy issues. (As Frankfurter again and again reminded his colleagues, it is not their role to play God; they cannot note the fall of every sparrow and attempt to correct all the mistakes in judgment of lower courts—if, indeed, they be mistakes.) But the issue is not exclusively "what really happened when the employee was injured?" The latent policy issue is: who should bear the economic costs of industrial accidents when the system for allocation consists of a right to a lawsuit instead of a workmen's compensation schedule? Should the economic as well as the physical injury be borne exclusively by the worker (or his bereaved family), or should the economic cost be collectively shared? Of course, the Supreme Court has no "legal right" to decide the latter question, since the Congress presumably answered it (primarily in the negative) when it enacted the statute more than half a century ago. Consequently, the opinions of the justices tend to be confined to ostensibly legal questions of "contributory negligence" and the "weight of the evidence." Nevertheless, the latent question, which taps the justices' attitudes and to which they respond in their voting, is where do your basic sympathies lie—with economic underdogs or with their employers? In case after case, no matter what the variation in the "facts," economic liberals vote to uphold the claims of workers, and economic conservatives vote against them.[41]

PREDICTION

In analyzing the prediction of judicial decision making, it is possible to work with various classes of variables. The broadest and most diffuse class consists of the kinds of cultural factors discussed in Chapter One as the political environment. The cultural variables define the range of variation for attribute variables, which include

---

[41]Glendon Schubert, "Policy Without Law: An Extension of the Certiorari Game," *Stanford Law Review* 14 (1962), pp. 284–327; and for a related decision that exemplifies the FELA type of issue, see *Michalic* v. *Cleveland Tankers,* 367 U.S. 325 (1960).

the kinds of personal background factors discussed above. Attributes, in turn affect attitudes, which determine decisions. We expect, therefore, that prediction will be most likely to succeed between adjacent classes of variables: between cultural and attribute variables; between attribute and either cultural or attitudinal variables; between attitudinal and either attribute or decisional variables; and between decisional and attitudinal variables. This implies that the prediction of judicial decision-making behavior will be most successful if it is based upon the observation and measurement of judicial attitudes.

In their search for rationality in decision making, lawyers have sought to find it in the patterns of policy norms, in the decisions and opinions that are the outputs of the conversion process.[42] One of the problems that they have encountered is that the norms appear to be continuously in flux, no doubt reflecting changes both in the composition of the Court and in the socioeconomic bases of the issues presented to it. There is a high degree of rationality in judicial decision making, but it consists primarily of the *psychological* rationality of consistency in the structuring of attitudes in the minds of individual judges, rather than of the *logical* rationality of consistency in the structuring of the rationalizations for outcomes found in their written opinions.[43] If judges did decide present cases in particular ways *because* their predecessors had so decided similar cases, then the principle of *stare decisis* would explain the conversion process. We should not then need to be concerned about judges' personal beliefs and individual attitudes, which would, in any event, be irrelevant to the outcomes of decisions and therefore to the outputs of courts. If this were true, *stare decisis* ought to operate, of course, only in phase with a "natural" chronology—that is, judges ought to decide present cases on the basis of past precedents; we should not expect to find them deciding cases, at some time in the past, on the basis of future "precedent" decisions that have not yet been established! Nevertheless, the recent work of a scholar who was seeking to validate— to prove that judges really do follow—the principle of *stare decisis* shows that in several different policy areas and with different courts it was possible for him to predict the outcomes of decisions just as well (and in some instances, better) working *backward* rather than

[42]See Karl N. Llewellyn, *The Common-Law Tradition: Deciding Appeals* (Boston: Little, Brown and Company, 1960); Richard A. Wasserstrom, *The Judicial Decision: Toward a Theory of Legal Justification* (Stanford: Stanford University Press, 1961).
[43]See Table III in Glendon Schubert, "Behavioral Jurisprudence," *Law and Society Review* 2 (1968), pp. 407–428, at 417.

forward through time.[44] In short, the "legal precedents" could be predicted just as well from the "future decisions" as the latter from the former. What this suggests, of course, is that the underlying consistency was very high but that this consistency was in the attitudes of the judicial decision makers toward the policy issues, not in cause-and-effect relationships among either the decisions or the output norms that the decisions are presumed to imply.

Attempts to improve the accuracy with which outcomes can be predicted have constituted an important research activity in recent years. Naturally, this is a question of considerable interest to, and with important practical consequences for, practicing lawyers. The usual approach to prediction of outcomes, which is highly qualitative and intensely personal and subjective, is well illustrated by the success with which a Yale law professor predicted the outcome in the Supreme Court's first major reapportionment decision, *Baker* v. *Carr*.[45] With this should be compared, however, the equally successful prediction, by a practicing lawyer who made his forecast using Boolean algebra and a computer, of one of the Court's major decisions on fair procedure for indigent criminal defendants.[46] The important difference between these two types of prediction is that the latter represents a technique that is communicable and transferable to other researchers and that can be replicated by them; the former does not. In the same research, the computer analyst found it necessary to distinguish among what he designated as three different types of *stare decisis:* traditional, local, and personal. By traditional *stare decisis* he meant the obligation of a lower court to follow the policy norms output by a higher court, or the obligation of the Supreme Court to follow its own precedents; by local *stare decisis* he meant the obligation of one panel of a court of appeals to follow the precedents established by other panels of the same court; and by personal *stare decisis* he meant the consistency of the individual justices with their own earlier voting behavior on similar issues.[47] Evidently, in his analysis of personal *stare decisis* he was measuring the consistency of the attitudes of individual justices toward the defined subissue of political liberal-

[44]Fred Kort, "Content Analysis of Judicial Opinions and Rules of Law," in *Judicial Decision-Making*, op. cit., pp. 133–197, especially pp. 177–178.

[45]Fred Rodell, "For Every Justice, Judicial Deference Is a Sometime Thing," *Georgetown Law Journal* 50 (1962), pp. 707–708.

[46]Reed C. Lawlor, "What Computers Can Do: Analysis and Prediction of Judicial Decisions," *American Bar Association Journal* 49 (1963), pp. 337–344, especially 343–344. The decision was *Gideon* v. *Wainwright,* 372 U.S. 335 (1963).

[47]Reed C. Lawlor, "Personal Stare Decisis," *Southern California Law Review* 41 (1967), pp. 73–118.

ism. His attempt to predict the Supreme Court's decision in *Gideon* v. *Wainwright* (discussed below) on the basis of traditional *stare decisis* was unsuccessful; but when he programmed his computer in terms of the personal attitudes of the then incumbent justices of the Supreme Court, he did very well indeed.

The research on outcomes focuses upon the particular decisions in individual cases; a different but at least as important recent emphasis has been upon statistical prediction—that is, upon sets of aggregate outcomes, which characterize the Court's decision-making behavior in broader but more comprehensive terms than does the prediction of individual case outcomes.[48] Several studies have analyzed the Supreme Court's jurisdictional decision making in order to specify the attributes of cases that the Court is most likely to accept for decision making on the merits.[49] The most fruitful and probably the most fundamental work done to date, however, has been the prediction of pattern relationships in voting behavior on the basis of the assumption of stability in individual attitudes. The rank-order relationships of the justices, on scales of political and economic liberalism, are highly stable from term to term.[50] As techniques for the analysis of the content of issue inputs become more refined,[51] it may be possible to predict both the

[48]Stuart S. Nagel, "Predicting Court Cases Quantitatively," *Michigan Law Review* 65 (1965), pp. 1411–1422; S. Sidney Ulmer, "Mathematical Models for Predicting Judicial Behavior," Chapter 4 in *Mathematical Applications in Political Science*, III, ed. Joseph L. Bernd (Charlottesville: University of Virginia Press, 1967), pp. 67–95, and Fred Kort, "Regression Analysis and Discriminant Analysis: An Application of R. A. Fisher's Theorem to Data in Political Science," *American Political Science Review* 67 (1973), pp. 555–559.

[49]Joseph Tanenhaus, Marvin Schick, Matthew Muraskin, and Daniel Rosen, "The Supreme Court's Certiorari Jurisdiction: Cue Theory," in Schubert, *Judicial Decision-Making*, op. cit., pp. 111–132; S. Sidney Ulmer, William Hintze, and Louise Kirklosky, "The Decision to Grant or Deny Certiorari: Further Consideration of Cue Theory," *Law and Society Review* 6 (1972), pp. 637–643; and S. Sidney Ulmer, "The Decision to Grant Certiorari as an Indicator to Decision 'On the Merits'," *Polity* 4 (1972), pp. 429–447.

[50]Ulmer, "A Note on Attitudinal Consistency," op. cit.; Schubert, *The Judicial Mind* and *The Judicial Mind Revisited*, op. cit.

[51]See Werner Grunbaum, *St. Louis Supreme Court Dictionary* (St. Louis: Washington University, and the University of Missouri, St. Louis, First Edition, August 1969); and Alan M. Sager, "From Brief to Decision: A Computer Simulation of the 1963 Supreme Court Term," (paper presented at the 65th Annual Meeting of the American Political Science Association; New York, September 2, 1969) for examples of contemporary content analysis techniques.

outcomes and other aspects of the decision-making behavior of the Supreme Court (and of other courts as well) on a systematic basis and with considerable accuracy. Prediction would thus serve to validate the construction of theory about judicial behavior, which in turn might have important implications for understanding the behavior of persons other than judges.

POLICY OUTPUTS

One way to conceptualize the Supreme Court's output is in terms of the policy norms that are associated with the decisions in cases. According to our theory, such policy norms are analogues of the major attitudinal components in terms of which we measure ideological differences among the justices. Inferences about the attitudes of individual justices and about the policy norms associated with decisions are both based upon scaling (rank-order) measurement of sets of judicial votes. We shall discuss below the major subcomponents of the Court's outputs as functions of the attitudinal variables considered above.

There are three important sets of subcomponent norms: political, social, and economic. The political norms are the output counterpart of the political liberalism attitudinal component; similarly, the economic norms are equivalent to positions on the economic attitudinal variable. The social norms correspond to an attitudinal position midway between political and economic liberalism. In other words, the social norms correspond to a continuum representing the attitudinal position (see Figure 9) of justices who are consistently either liberal or conservative on both political and economic issues; stated otherwise, the social policy norms constitute the heart of the ideological differences that separate liberals and conservatives.[52] Social norms define the policy area in which the Court's decisions have had the greatest impact upon the American polity during the past two decades. Political norms have been of secondary importance, while economic norms have been relegated to last place. It is worth noting that only four decades ago it would have been necessary to reverse the order of importance; at that time, the Court's economic norms were its most important output, then political norms, and last social norms. No doubt, this reversal is both an index and a result of the shift in the ideological control over the Court that has occurred during the past thirty years. The Hughes Court of the middle 1930s was dominated by conservatives; the Warren Court of the middle 1960s was dominated by liberals, and the Burger Court of the 1970s finds a

[52]See Schubert, *The Judicial Mind*, op. cit., Chapter 6.

conservative majority dominant again. Their defense of the status quo in the 1930s did not require the "Nine Old Men" of the New Deal era to consider directly the issues involved in social norms, but the Supreme Court's most conspicuous effect upon the federal polity during the 1950s and 1960s was to force the consideration of social issues by other decision makers.

SOCIAL NORMS

There can be little question that the Supreme Court's most important decisions since the end of World War II have been in regard to the issues traditionally denominated as "civil rights" issues—racial equality, representational equality, and citizenship equality, all of which constitute varying facets of the norm of equal rights of American citizenship. Typical of the Warren Court's extension of its policy of racial equality is a five-to-four decision (with Stewart, Clark, Harlan, and Black dissenting) upholding a black sit-in in a segregated rural Louisiana public library;[53] equally typical, however, is another five-to-four decision (with Brennan, Warren, Douglas, and Fortas dissenting) upholding the convictions of a group of black defendants who had insisted on parading on Good Friday and Easter Sunday, contrary to the temporary injunction issued by an Alabama circuit court judge.[54] The Court followed up *Baker* v. *Carr* with several more recent decisions that have extended to congressional and to local elections its policy requiring representational equality in state legislatures.[55] The changes that have occurred as a result of the Court's racial equality and legislative apportionment decisions are so conspicuous that we all are familiar with them. Somewhat less well publicized have been

[53]*Brown* v. *Louisiana,* 383 U.S. 131 (1966). For a similarly marginal decision upholding racial desegregation of rural public schools in Virginia by a five-to-four vote, with all four Nixon appointees in dissent, see *Wright* v. *Council of City of Emporia,* 407 U.S. 451 (1972). On the development of racial equality policy by the Warren Court, see Harold J. Spaeth, "Race Relations and the Warren Court," *University of Detroit Law Journal* 43 (1965), pp. 255–272; and Joel Grossman, "A Model for Judicial Policy Analysis: The Supreme Court and the Sit-In Cases," Chapter 13 in Grossman and Tanenhaus, op. cit., pp. 405–459.
[54]*Walker* v. *City of Birmingham,* 388 U.S. 307 (1967).
[55]See: (1) state legislatures, *Reynolds* v. *Sims,* 377 U.S. 533 (1964), (Harlan dissenting); (2) congressional districts, *Wesberry* v. *Sanders,* 376 U.S. 1 (1964), (Clark, Stewart, and Harlan dissenting), and *Kirkpatrick* v. *Preisler,* 394 U.S. 526 (1969), and *Wells* v. *Rockefeller,* 394 U.S. 542 (1969), (White, Stewart, and Harlan dissenting); and (3) local councils, *Avery* v. *Midland County,* 390 U.S. 474 (1968), (Fortas, Stewart, and Harlan dissenting).

the Court's decisions in regard to equal citizenship status and rights for Americans abroad—or seeking to go abroad.[56] In fact, this was the only policy basis upon which the Supreme Court declared acts of Congress to be unconstitutional during the decade 1955–1964, and there were no less than eleven such decisions.[57] (It has not been necessary for the Court to declare acts of *Congress* unconstitutional[58] in order to establish its policies regarding racial equality and legislative reapportionment, because in these latter areas it has been almost exclusively state legislation at issue. The Court has not hesitated, however, to declare such state statutes unconstitutional, generally on the rationale that they are in conflict with the equal protection clause of the Fourteenth Amendment.) Judging from the outputs reported in Figure 3, civic equality is the value that ranked highest in the beliefs of a majority of the justices of the Warren Court.

POLITICAL NORMS

There are four major subcomponents of political policy norms. All four are concerned with what traditionally have been called "civil liberties": personal privacy, fair procedure, religious freedom, and political freedom. Some justices apparently have perceived the issues of personal privacy and religious freedom to be sufficiently different, both from each other and from fair procedure and political freedom, that it is questionable whether—for these justices, at least—the four ought to be associated together

---

[56]John P. Roche, "The Expatriation Decisions: A Study in Constitutional Improvisation and the Uses of History," *American Political Science Review* 58 (1964), pp. 72–80; and Glendon Schubert, "Civilian Control and Stare Decisis in the Warren Court," Chapter 3 in Schubert, *Judicial Decision-Making*, op. cit., pp. 55–77.

[57]See the list of cases that comprises the legend for Figure 3, on p. 75, which shows that in 1965 the Court shifted its focus for the next couple of years to political equality for individual members of the Communist party (whose civil rights as a minority group had been illegitimized by legislation beginning in the McCarthy era); and that in 1968 there was a further shift in emphasis to fair procedure, which provided the base for the invalidation of several federal statutes in the last two terms of the Warren Court. Since then there has not only been a sharp drop in the volume of decisions adverse to the constitutionality of federal legislation, but also the focus has shifted away from the gut to the more exotic fringe issues of civil liberty—as we ought to expect should happen under a more conservative Court.

[58]Cf. *Hurd* v. *Hodge*, 334 U.S. 24 (1948); the only apparent exception is *Bolling* v. *Sharpe*, 347 U.S. 497 (1954).

in a common category.[59] Since the end of World War II, however, there has been consensual agreement among the justices that fair procedure is attitudinally isomorphic with political freedom, and a majority at least would associate the other two issues as well. By "attitudinally isomorphic" we mean that when the justices differ in their voting behavior in deciding cases that raise the issues of either fair procedure or political freedom, they do so in the same rank order. This does not mean that the direction of the policy outputs has been the same for these two issues. Until Warren's retirement, the Court's policies had been relatively most liberal in regard to personal privacy and fair procedure; they were relatively more conservative in regard to political freedom; and they were generally (but not consistently) liberal in regard to religious freedom. Under Burger the Court's mood has been one of deepening conservatism; and although the momentum of certain policy developments during the sixties impelled some conspicuously libertarian decisions (such as the ban on capital punishment) during the early years of the Burger regime, the general trend and prospects for the future were clearly in the opposite direction.[60]

Personal privacy. The legal questions subsumed in this issue are those of searches and seizures (in relation to the Fourth and Fourteenth Amendments) and involuntary confessions (in relation to the Fifth and Fourteenth Amendments). From a behavioral point of view, questions of both physiological and psychological privacy are relevant. In the 1960 Term, the Court overruled the conservative precedent that had been established in 1949, when the Court was dominated by Truman appointees, and established the policy that evidence obtained as the result of police invasions of personal privacy would not be admitted in either a state or a federal court.[61] In short, the trial courts of the nation were directed by the Court to punish illegal police behaviors by ignoring what often would be the most relevant "facts" necessary to convict criminals. And with only Black dissenting, the Warren Court overruled a forty-year-old precedent of the Taft Court by extending the constitutional right to privacy to preclude "bugging" and other forms of electronic eavesdropping.[62] Throughout his third of a century on the Court, Justice Black had been much more conservative in his attitude toward the issue of personal privacy than toward the issues of fair procedure and political freedom,

---

[59]Schubert, *The Judicial Mind,* op. cit., Chapter 6.
[60]Schubert, *The Future of the Nixon Court* (Honolulu: University of Hawaii Foundation, 1972).
[61]*Mapp* v. *Ohio,* 367 U.S. 643 (1961).
[62]*Katz* v. *United States,* 389 U.S. 347 (1967).

until the mid-1960s when his conservatism extended to all aspects of political freedom except traditional free speech.[63] A different aspect of the issue was presented by a challenge to the Connecticut statute that proscribed birth control clinics: this is a question that is complicated by religious and correlated ethnic interest divisions, but a majority of the justices voted to invalidate the statute as an invasion of the right to marital privacy; and subsequently the Burger Court upheld the right to abortion, invalidating restrictive legislation by Texas and Georgia.[64] Otherwise, however, the Court continued to show less regard for *physiological* than for psychological or economic privacy—the latter being its traditional focus of concern.[65] In a five-to-four decision that the usual Warren majority lost because Fortas voted conservatively, the Court reaffirmed its policy of approval for sterile blood-letting, by rejecting the claim that the use of a compulsory blood sample, to prove intoxication, constituted a violation of privacy.[66]

Fair procedure. This issue concerns the rights of accused defendants to a fair hearing and/or trial in proceedings before national or state courts, administrative agencies, and legislative committees. Term in and term out, the Supreme Court has in recent years decided more cases relating to this issue than to any other, and in general the decisions have been increasingly liberal. A crucial change came with several decisions of the 1962 Term. In *Gideon* v. *Wainwright*[67] the justices unanimously postulated the new policy norm that indigent criminal defendants in state trial courts must be provided counsel at public expense; this had been the Court's requirement for the national courts since 1938. The Court thus overruled a twenty-year-old precedent that had established the policy only for defendants charged with capital offenses—viz., the same policy that had applied in the national courts from 1790 until 1938. (But *Betts* v. *Brady* had been a relatively liberal policy pronouncement in 1942; previously there had been *no* national policy regarding the right to counsel in state courts.) This right of the indigent to counsel in the trial courts was then buttressed by a series of decisions establishing the new policy that, state law to the

---

[63]See Glendon Schubert, *The Constitutional Polity* (Boston: Boston University Press, 1970), Chapter 2.

[64]*Griswold* v. *Connecticut,* 381 U.S. 479 (1965), and cf. *Eisenstadt* v. *Baird,* 405 U.S. 438 (1972); *Rowe* v. *Wade* and *Doe* v. *Bolton,* 93 S. Ct. 705, 739 (1973).

[65]See Schubert, *Constitutional Politics,* op. cit., Chapter 12.

[66]*Schmerber* v. *California,* 384 U.S. 757 (1966).

[67]372 U.S. 335 (1963). For an excellent discussion see Anthony Lewis, *Gideon's Trumpet* (New York: Random House, Inc., 1964).

contrary notwithstanding, the majority of impecunious as well as the minority of affluent criminal defendants must be permitted to appeal their convictions to appellate state courts.[68] Subsequent developments include such widely publicized decisions as *Escobedo* and *Miranda*,[69] and *Gault*,[70] upholding (respectively) the right to counsel during police interrogation, the inadmissability of confessions induced under only *psychologically* coercive circumstances, and the legal right of juveniles to be tried like adults. The Court moved closer to the abolition of capital punishment, by positing, one after another, unattainable prerequisites to its valid imposition,[71] until a general ban—subject to the possibility of its resurrection by explicit state or federal legislative action—was announced on the final day of the 1972 term, in a five-to-four decision with all four Nixon appointees in dissent.[72] The Court even declared, in Warren's last term, that state courts must respect the generally tougher standards of the federal guarantee against double jeopardy, as an aspect of due process.[73] Thus, at long last it overruled the cornerstone precedent for its conservative Frankfurterweisian "sociological jurisprudence" of fair procedure during the 1940s and 1950s, which survived as long as it did at least in part because the revered Benjamin Cardozo had fathered the precedent. In a series of half a dozen cases beginning in the 1965 Term, the Warren Court also declared unconstitutional a series of federal statutes, for the first time in over two decades on fair procedure grounds (relating to statutory presumptions or requirements of self-incrimination).[74] Unanimously the Warren Court declared unconstitutional a provision of the Marihuana Tax Act, on behalf of the notorious Dr. Timothy Leary who claimed that the marihuana found on him and his accompanying teen-age children (as he was northward bound through U.S. customs on the bridge from Nuevo Laredo to Laredo, Texas) was not Mexican but rather was a New York product that he had taken with him to Mexico and was

---

[68]*Douglas* v. *California*, 372 U.S. 353 (1963); *Lane* v. *Brown*, 372 U.S. 477 (1963); *Draper* v. *Washington*, 372 U.S. 487 (1963).
[69]*Escobedo* v. *Illinois*, 378 U.S. 478 (1964); and *Miranda* v. *Arizona*, 384 U.S. 436 (1966).
[70]*In re Gault*, 387 U.S. 1 (1967).
[71]*Witherspoon* v. *Illinois*, 391 U.S. 510 (1968).
[72]*Furman* v. *Georgia*, 408 U.S. 238 (1972).
[73]*Palko* v. *Connecticut*, 302 U.S. 319 (1937), overruled in *Benton* v. *Maryland*, 395 U.S. 784 (1969); and see also *North Carolina* v. *Pearce*, 395 U.S. 711 (1969).
[74]See Nos. 19, 22–25, and 27 (from Romano through Leary) in the legend to Figure 3, p. 75.

now bringing back into the United States; the Court stated that the statutory presumption of unlawful possession violated Dr. Leary's right to fair procedure.[75]

Religious freedom. Lawyers distinguish between questions of "freedom of religion" and "the separation of church and state" because of the grammatical disjunction in the language of the First Amendment (which employs, incidentally, neither of the quoted phrases); but the justices themselves do not appear to make such a distinction in their attitudes and voting behavior, so neither shall we. In the early 1960s, the Warren Court was quite active in this area, and the result has been to engender more public controversy and discussion than has been provoked over any other of the issues that we discuss except racial equality.[76] A majority of the Court's conservative critics have attacked the generally libertarian policies of religious freedom, supported by a majority of the justices, as being "atheistic" and "communist inspired," as when the justices unanimously declared unconstitutional as a test oath a Maryland state constitutional provision that required notaries public to declare their belief in God.[77] In the Sunday Closing cases, however, preponderant majorities of the justices upheld the right of Christian popular majorities to compel Jews (and other Sabbatarians) to observe the Christian Sabbath in their entrepreneurial and employment practices. To the extent that this resulted in economic hardship for many Jews (who, unlike Christians, thus were compelled by a combination of conscience and the Christian law to close their shops two days a week), they could be comforted by Chief Justice Warren's implication that this was a small sacrifice for a Jewish minority to make so that Christians could enjoy the peace and quiet of family picnics and other leisure activities "customary" on the day of rest. Clearly, this was not a very liberal policy. But whatever goodwill the Court might have attracted from the Christian majority by its conservative policy on Sunday closing was dissipated by its decisions of the next two terms, to the effect that there should be no recitation of the Lord's Prayer or reading from the Bible in public schools.[78] In subsequent decisions the Warren

---

[75] *Leary* v. *United States,* 395 U.S. 6 (1969).
[76] Richard E. Morgan, *The Politics of Religious Conflict: Church and State in America* (New York: Pegasus, 1968).
[77] *Torcaso* v. *Watkins,* 367 U.S. 488 (1961).
[78] *Engel* v. *Vitale,* 370 U.S. 421 (1962); *School District of Abington Township, Pennsylvania* v. *Schempp,* 374 U.S. 203 (1963); *Murray* v. *Curlett,* 374 U.S. 203 (1963). For discussion, see Richard M. Johnson, *The Dynamics of Compliance* (Evanston: Northwestern University Press, 1967); William K. Muir, Jr., *Prayer in the Public Schools: Law and Attitude Change* (Chicago:

Court approved (over three dissents) a New York statute that authorizes the provision of free textbooks, at public expense, to Roman Catholic parochial and other private schools;[79] but it unanimously declared unconstitutional an Arkansas "anti-evolution" statute as a state law attempt at the establishment of a (viz., the Christian) religion,[80] and subsequently the Burger Court struck down a section of a federal statute that permitted buildings constructed with federal fiscal support to revert to general religious purposes after a twenty-year delay.[81]

Political freedom. Throughout the 1950s the two major questions of political freedom with which the Supreme Court dealt were: (1) the suppression of the Communist party and its satellite organizations; and (2) the censorship of books, magazines, and motion pictures. In short, the issues were the extent to which there should be communication of what were for the times relatively extremist ideas in matters of politics and sex. The Court vacillated on the communist issue throughout the 1950s, and in a series of decisions in the 1960 Term, a majority of the justices in effect upheld the authority of both national and state legislative investigative committees to punish witnesses who had engaged in earlier public criticism of the committees[82] and also upheld what some libertarians thought amounted (in the language of the eighteenth century) to "bills of attainder" against the Communist party[83] and its members.[84] (In this same term, a five-to-four majority upheld a lower court decision, the effect of which seemed to be that a person who took seriously the Declaration of Independence could not become a lawyer in Illinois.[85]) After Goldberg replaced Frankfurter, however, the Warren Court was able to muster a majority that was willing to reconsider its position on the issue of political freedom for communists; and the result was a series of libertarian decisions, all declaring acts of Congress to be unconstitutional: the

University of Chicago Press, 1967); Harrell R. Rodgers, Jr., *Community Conflict, Public Opinion and the Law: The Amish Dispute in Iowa* (Columbus: Charles E. Merrill, 1969); and Frank H. Way, Jr., "Survey Research on Judicial Decisions: The Prayer and Bible Reading Cases," *Western Political Quarterly* 21 (1968), pp. 189–205.

[79] *Board of Education* v. *Allen,* 392 U.S. 236 (1968).

[80] *Epperson* v. *Arkansas,* 393 U.S. 97 (1968).

[81] *Tilton* v. *Richardson,* 403 U.S. 672 (1971).

[82] *Wilkinson* v. *United States,* 365 U.S. 399 (1961); *Braden* v. *United States,* 365 U.S. 431 (1961); *Uphaus* v. *Wyman,* 364 U.S. 388 (1960).

[83] *Communist Party* v. *Subversive Activities Control Board,* 367 U.S. 1 (1961).

[84] *Scales* v. *United States,* 367 U.S. 203 (1961).

[85] *In re Anastaplo,* 366 U.S. 82 (1961).

censorship of procommunist mail was found to be a denial of a free press;[86] the denial of office in labor unions to communists was declared to constitute a bill of attainder;[87] after fifteen years of continuous litigation, the Court decided finally that to require the Communist party to register with the Subversive Activities Control Board would be to require its members to incriminate themselves;[88] and then the Court announced that it is unconstitutional for Congress to proscribe the employment of communists in United States defense industrial facilities, because to do so violates the "right of association."[89] Clearly, the Court's policy line on communism had taken an abrupt turn to the left.

But throughout the 1960s the Court remained generally liberal in its policy making in regard to the censorship of artistic expression.[90] In sharp contrast even to the years of World War II, during the past two decades there occurred a wholesale loosening of the puritanical ties by which the mass media had been confined. As a direct consequence of the libertarian policies of the Supreme Court, for example, what might be called the proletarian response to the Court's liberalism has taken the form of the proliferation of much bad art accompanying the more open communication of ideas about sex.[91] *Fanny Hill,*[92] *Tom Jones,* and *Evergreen* are in; *Playboy* has taken the place of the *Saturday Evening Post* as a national family magazine; and one of the Court's former beneficiaries, characterized at the time as purveying the "smoking room type of humor," has by now become a rather stuffily conventional fashion

[86]*Lamont* v. *Postmaster General,* 381 U.S. 301 (1965).
[87]*United States* v. *Brown,* 381 U.S. 437 (1965).
[88]*Albertson* v. *Subversive Activities Control Board,* 382 U.S. 70 (1965).
[89]*United States* v. *Robel,* 389 U.S. 258 (1967).
[90]See Martin Shapiro, "Obscenity Law: A Public Policy Analysis," *Journal of Public Law* 20 (1971), pp. 503–521.
[91]Thomas Barth, "Perception and Acceptance of Supreme Court Decisions at the State and Local Level," *Journal of Public Law* 17 (1968), pp. 308–350; Ira H. Carmen, *Movies, Censorship, and Law* (Ann Arbor: University of Michigan Press, 1967); James P. Levine, "An Empirical Approach to Civil Liberties: The Bookseller and Obscenity Law," *Wisconsin Law Review* 1969 (1969), pp. 153–169; Stephen L. Wasby, "Public Law, Politics, and the Local Courts: Obscene Literature in Portland," *Journal of Public Law* 14 (1965), pp. 105–130, and also his "The Pure and the Prurient: The Supreme Court, Obscenity, and Oregon Policy," in *The Supreme Court as Policy-Maker,* ed. David Everson (Carbondale: Southern Illinois University, 1968), pp. 82–116.
[92]*A Book Named "John Cleland's Memoirs of a Woman of Pleasure"* v. *Attorney General of Massachusetts,* 383 U.S. 413 (1966).

magazine.[93] But the Court has stuck by its principles and denied overt access to the federal mails for what (little) it has recognized as constituting hard-core pornography (which the Court has described as "titillating"),[94] and it also has purported to distinguish between juvenile and adult consumers of pornography.[95] But while the justices from time to time continue to tilt with these windmills of (largely) their own invention, a host of newly developed facets of free political expression lend an aura of quaint otherworldliness to the Court's continuing preoccupation with what its Roman Catholic justice, Brennan, likes to call "prurience."

One of these newer issues has been the persistent and widespread focus of concern upon the expression of a variety of forms of political protest, ranging from the wearing of mourning armbands by school children,[96] the presentation of street skits,[97] and the divulgence of official secrets by the publication of the Pentagon Papers,[98] to an audacious attempt to lobby with the Congress on its home grounds,[99] all with the intent of halting American participation in the Vietnam War. But the Burger Court took a much harder line on some of the more traditional issues of political freedom: it returned, for example, to the precedents of the McCarthy era and broke sharply with the policy line that had been established by the Warren Court during the 1960s, rushing through a four-to-three decision upholding the Massachusetts loyalty oath for public employees,[100] and incidentally advertising to the nation the change that was taking place in the judicial climate of opinion in the Marble Palace.

---

[93] *Hannegan* v. *Esquire,* 327 U.S. 146 (1946).
[94] *Ginzburg* v. *United States,* 383 U.S. 463 (1966).
[95] *Ginsberg* v. *New York,* 390 U.S. 629 (1968).
[96] *Tinker* v. *Des Moines Independent Community School District,* 393 U.S. 503 (1969). This decision, coming in the last term of the Warren Court, was PF+ (pro political freedom) by a seven-to-two vote, with Black and Harlan in dissent.
[97] *Schacht* v. *United States,* 398 U.S. 58 (1970), was unanimously PF+. (Cf. Figure 3, p. 75.)
[98] *New York Times Co.* v. *United States,* 403 U.S. 713 (1971), was PF+ by a six-to-three margin, with Chief Justice Burger, Blackmun, and Harlan dissenting.
[99] *Capitol Police* v. *Jeannette Rankin Brigade,* 409 U.S. 972 (1972), was a unanimous per curiam affirmance, without opinion, of a decision of the United States Court of Appeals for the District of Columbia, declaring unconstitutional a federal statute which forbade such demonstrations.
[100] *Cole* v. *Richardson,* 405 U.S. 676 (1972).

ECONOMIC NORMS

Our analysis of the workload of the lower national courts indicated that most cases raised questions of conflicting property interests rather than of civil rights or liberties. Although there is variance from term to term, in the period from World War II through the 1962 Term, and again since Burger became Chief Justice in 1969, the Supreme Court decided on the merits almost precisely the same number of cases raising economic issues as it did cases raising social or political issues; only during the last half-dozen terms of the Warren Court did the ratio shift to about two-to-one in favor of civil liberties over economic issues. But with the single exception of the claims of injured workers under the Federal Employers' Liability Act and related statutes (and at that, only during the Warren Court era),[101] the Court generally has not taken a policy position in conflict with that of Congress, the administration, or most state legislatures.[102] To the contrary, the Supreme Court has played a supporting role, adjusting legislative policies (through statutory interpretation) but not opposing them as the Hughes Court did so conspicuously thirty years ago.[103] Generally, therefore, the economic policies supported by the majority of the justices have been relatively liberal. The Warren Court tended to be prounion, progovernmental regulation of business, antimonopoly, and supportive of state taxation (which businessmen claim has violated various provisions of the national Constitution).[104] The liberal majority, however, construed economic liberalism to require the upholding of unions, even though doing so had the effect of forcing individual members to support (through union dues) a political party or candidates other than those preferred by such members,[105] and even when unions

---

[101]For a typical Warren Court FELA decision, see *Grunenthal* v. *Long Island Rail Road Co.*, 393 U.S. 156 (1968).

[102]A recent exception is the Court's declaration that a District of Columbia residency requirement for welfare assistance, like the similar provisions of two state statutes considered at the same time, denied equal protection to indigent migrants. See *Washington* v. *Legrant*, 394 U.S. 618 (1969). This was, of course, a pro-economic-underdog outcome, and therefore an economically libertarian decision. It is also the only instance since 1937 in which the Court has declared an act of Congress to be unconstitutional on economic grounds.

[103]See Arthur S. Miller, *The Supreme Court and American Capitalism* (New York: The Free Press of Glencoe, 1968).

[104]Martin Shapiro, *Law and Politics in the Supreme Court* (New York: The Free Press of Glencoe, 1964), Chapters 3, 4, and 6.

[105]*Machinists* v. *Street*, 367 U.S. 740 (1961).

discriminated against some of their own members.[106] Other typical prolabor decisions of the Warren Court upheld the imposition of union fines upon scabbing members who had crossed the picket lines of their own local to work during a strike;[107] and the upholding of Arkansas "full-crew" railroad legislation (adopted over half a century earlier) without regard to its featherbedding effects under contemporary operating conditions.[108] Characteristic of the Warren Court's decisions upholding governmental regulation of business is *United States* v. *Parke Davis,*[109] an antitrust case in which the majority upheld action by the Department of Justice to stop a major drug producer from rigging retail prices at artificially high levels; and *Seagram* v. *Hostetter, Chairman, New York State Liquor Authority,*[110] unanimously upholding state maximum liquor price legislation. A majority of seven justices joined in a pro-economic-underdog decision invalidating Wisconsin's wage-garnishment statute because it violated "fundamental principles of procedural due process"; and only Hugo Black—who by June 1969 had backslid on economic as well as on civil liberties issues—was sufficiently conservative to dissent.[111] An example of the Warren Court's typical response to claims that state taxation[112] is unconstitutionally in conflict with the commerce or equal protection clauses of the national Constitution is *Alaska* v. *Arctic Maid,*[113] in which an eight-man majority upheld a 4 percent tax on salmon freezer ships;

[106]*Local 357, Teamsters* v. *National Labor Relations Board,* 365 U.S. 667 (1961).

[107]*National Labor Relations Board* v. *Allis-Chalmers Manufacturing Co.,* 388 U.S. 175 (1967).

[108]*Brotherhood of Locomotive Firemen & Enginemen* v. *Chicago, Rock Island & Pacific Railroad Co.,* 393 U.S. 129 (1968).

[109]362 U.S. 29 (1960).

[110]384 U.S. 35 (1966).

[111]*Sniadach* v. *Family Finance Corp.,* 395 U.S. 337 (1969). According to Black, "the Court is today overruling a number of its own decisions and abandoning the legal customs and practices in this country with reference to attachments and garnishments wholly on the ground that the garnishment laws of this kind are based on unwise policies of government. . . . " Ibid., at p. 350. For discussion of wage garnishment and consumer bankruptcy in Wisconsin, see Herbert Jacob, "Judicial and Political Efficacy of Litigants: A Preliminary Analysis," Chapter 8 in *Frontiers of Judicial Research,* ed. Joel Grossman and Joseph Tanenhaus (New York: John Wiley & Sons, Inc., 1969), pp. 255–271.

[112]It should be noted that questions of *national* taxation relate to a different attitudinal variable, which is largely independent of the issues of liberalism and conservatism considered in this chapter.

[113]366 U.S. 199 (1961).

only Harlan was sufficiently conservative in his economic attitude to dissent in favor of the freedom of "interstate commerce" (viz., business enterprise) from state regulation.

The displacement of the Warren Court by the Burger Court entailed a reversal in what had been the thirty-five-year trend in the direction of increasing economic liberalism in the decisions of the Supreme Court. The change was to some extent arrested or delayed by such events as Nixon's bumbling in the quest for a suitable replacement for Fortas (which left a vacancy for almost an entire term), and the two empty seats on the Court throughout the autumn of 1971. It was therefore still possible as late as June 1972 to observe an occasional marginal (if minority) liberal outcome, as in the Court's decision declaring unconstitutional the replevin statutes of Florida and Pennsylvania (and, by implication, of most other states as well), which permitted installment lenders to repossess property in the possession of consumer purchasers without notice or hearing; but this result hardly reflected what was by then the ideological composition of the Burger Court.[114] The vote was four-to-three, with White joining Blackmun and the Chief Justice in dissent, and with neither Powell nor Rehnquist participating because argument had been held in November prior to their appointments. As Figure 10 suggests, because White voted to uphold the state replevin statutes, then so should Powell and Rehnquist also have voted (if they were consistent with their modal positions). Evidently the participation of Powell and Rehnquist would have resulted in an opposite policy outcome; and it is economically conservative policy results like the latter that we can anticipate increasingly from now on. Indeed, such results had begun to appear in that same term, in decisions in which the full court participated, and in the very next term as exemplified by the Court's five-to-four rejection of the claim that the ad valorem property tax, as it operates as the basis for local financing of public schools in Texas (as most other American states), produces unconstitutional discrimination against the possibility of equal educational opportunity for the children of the poor.[115]

It soon became quite clear, therefore, that things were going to be different with the Burger Court. The early 1970s were the first time in over three decades that it was possible to muster Supreme Court majorities manifestly hostile to the economic and social egalitarianism that has characterized much of the past forty years of American national political life. Proof of this assertion is found

[114]*Fuentes* v. *Shevin* and *Parham* v. *Cortese*, 407 U.S. 067 (1972).
[115]*San Antonio Independent School District* v. *Rodriguez*, 93 S.Ct. 1278 (March 21, 1973).

both in the direction of decisions and in the tenor of the language accompanying them. An excellent barometer of economic liberalism and conservatism has been, throughout the twentieth century, the Federal Employers' Liability Act-type cases mentioned above; and this was the policy sector in which conservative backsliding came most quickly and sharply. Burger hardly had taken his seat before the Court reversed an en banc decision of the entire United States Court of Appeals for the Fourth Circuit, with the consequence that an injured longshoreman's claim was ultimately rejected, provoking Douglas to remark (for himself and Black and Brennan) that "It is incongruous to us that in an accident on a pier over navigable waters, coverage of the [federal statute] depends on where the body falls after the accident has happened."[116] Actually Marshall could have switched the outcome, because an equal division would have upheld the result below; and two or three years earlier any of three incumbents then—Warren or Clark or Fortas—would have done so. So this was a policy opposite to what the Warren Court would have produced—or, indeed, apparently *did* produce: the case was initially argued in March, and then was reargued in October; evidently, the initial decision was a five-to-four vote for affirmance and in behalf of the injured claimant, but when Fortas resigned in May, the vote then became a four-to-four deadlock; and with Warren's retirement only another month away from becoming effective, the decision to reargue—in effect, a motion for reconsideration—was made. Then Warren did resign and Burger took his place; and thus a five-to-four economically liberal decision was metamorphosed into a three-to-five conservative one.

The Burger Court's conservative policy toward injured workers was confirmed by the full Court of the 1970 Term, this time by a four-to-five vote and in regard to a seaman injured by a crane (when the shoreside operator dropped the sling on the seaman's head); and Douglas responded by again complaining that "Changes in membership do change decisions; and those changes are expected at the level of constitutional law. But when private rights not rooted in the Constitution are at issue, it is surprising to find new law made by new judges taking the place of law made by prior judges."[117] Of course, candor compels the admission that the views of the elder Douglas stand in sharp contrast to the expressions of his opinion during his early years on the Court, when he thought it not only seemly but essential that he join with Murphy and Black and Rutledge who, with the customary assistance of

[116]*Nacirema Operating Co.* v. *Johnson,* 396 U.S. 212, 225 (1969).
[117]*Usner* v. *Luckenback,* 400 U.S. 494 (1971).

Frankfurter (back in those days) were busily formulating new marching orders for federal district judges, for the trial of F.E.L.A. and Longshoremen's and Harbor Workers' Act evidentiary cases, in explicit substitution for the proemployer reversals that had been the unbroken bill of fare provided by the Taft and Hughes Courts.

Another sector of economic policy in which the Burger Court took a consistently conservative stance was in regard to problems of environmental control and pollution of the biosphere. The Burger Court found time to give its explicit imprimatur to the mundane details involved in—and I'm going to use the precise legal term here—the escheating of widows' mites and of orphans' tuppences,[118] but the same Court did not think it appropriate that it should devote its time and attention to a case, concededly among the few that fall squarely within its own original jurisdiction, involving international as well as interstate relations, and concerned with the present and future effects upon American life of the death by poisoning of what had once been a great inland sea: in what surely is a strictly political and most mistaken decision, eight members of the Burger Court (all except Douglas) ducked the issue, leaving to the Ohio state courts the task of wrestling with the pollution and pollutors of Lake Erie.[119] Then in the spring of 1972 the same Court, in like vein, left it up to Hawaii and seventeen other states individually to attempt to bring the five largest (and of course, nationally organized) automakers, to account for their culpability in the pollution of the highways and byways alike of all of the states.[120] (The Nixon Department of Justice had long since compromised its suit in behalf of the nation; so, with General Motors as with Union Carbide and Chemical, it is now every state for itself, leaving open the question: how long will it be before it becomes every man for himself?)[121]

Also in the 1971 Term came several decisions which were direct rebuffs of what now tends to be called "public interest" litigation, including the rejection of the State of Hawaii's civil antitrust suit against the Standard Oil Corporation, for damages inflicted upon the state economy,[122] and the dismissal of a stockholder's suit

---

[118] *United States* v. *Mitchell,* 403 U.S. 190, 205 (1971).

[119] *Ohio* v. *Wyandotte Chemical Co.,* 401 U.S. 493 (1971).

[120] *State of Washington* v. *General Motors,* 406 U.S. 109 (1972).

[121] Cf. James L. Hildebrand, "Soviet International Law: An Exemplar for Optimal Decision Theory Analysis," *Case Western Reserve Law Review* 20 (1968), pp. 141–250, especially pp. 221–229 "On Aggression and the Territorial Imperative," at p. 227 n. 337.

[122] *State of Hawaii* v. *Standard Oil Company of California,* 405 U.S. 251 (1972).

intended to force Dow Chemical to publicize its sale of napalm as war materiel;[123] but at the same time the Court upheld unanimously an Ohio procedure whereby debtors can contract away their constitutional right to due process of law.[124] Similarly, the Court rejected the claim that an injured worker, otherwise eligible to receive social security benefits and workmen's compensation, could accept both at the same time;[125] and it upheld the eviction of tenants, who had withheld rent pending repairs that a slum landlord refused to make, from tenements that the Portland (Oregon) Bureau of Buildings had declared unfit for human habitation in the absence of such repairs.[126] Later in the same term the Burger Court announced that the Sierra Club—a group of California outdoor enthusiasts—had no standing to challenge the plans of Walt Disney enterprises, in collaboration with the U.S. Forest Service, to build a massive resort complex in the heart of Sequoia National Forest; supporting the public interest wasn't good enough—the club needed to show how (and how much) its members individually would be injured.[127] The Burger Court majority appears to have based its economic philosophy squarely upon the classical foundations laid, some two-and-a-half centuries ago, by Bernard Mandeville in his *Fable of the Bees,* a most economically conservative book which is subtitled *Private Vices, Publick Benefits.*[128]

---

[123]*Securities and Exchange Commission* v. *Medical Committee for Human Rights,* 404 U.S. 403 (1972).
[124]*Overmyer* v. *Frick,* 405 U.S. 174 (1972).
[125]*Richardson* v. *Belcher,* 404 U.S. 78 (1971).
[126]*Lindsey* v. *Normet,* 405 U.S. 56 (1972).
[127]*Sierra Club* v. *Morton,* 405 U.S. 727 (1972). The discussion in the preceding four paragraphs, of the economic policy decisions of the Burger Court, is taken with only minor changes from my *The Future of the Nixon Court* (Honolulu, Hawaii: University of Hawaii Foundation, 1972), at pp. 23–24, 26–27.
[128]Originally published incrementally over the period 1705–1728, the most convenient complete modern version of *The Fable* is the two-volume edition published by Oxford University Press in 1924, and reprinted in 1957, under the editorship of F. B. Kaye.

Political Ideology
and
Judicial Activism

The Constitution of the United States was a by-product of a physical revolution that took the form of a successful civil war; it was also the product of a revolutionary ideological movement[1]—an uprising of aristocrats and men of property in the face of what they perceived to be a crisis created by the democratic excesses of the war and postwar periods (roughly, 1775–1788). Ever since then, a basic ambivalence of political attitudes toward judicial review has persisted. Conservatives have looked upon the courts as a bulwark to safeguard property rights generally and privilege and preferred status in all forms,[2] while liberals have expected courts to protect individual liberty and civil rights. By and large, the strongly conservative orientation of the legal profession has in fact resulted in the courts functioning much more in accord with the conservative than with the liberal ideal.

The reasons for the conservatism of the legal profession have

[1]See Alpheus Thomas Mason, "To Be More Safe: America's Continuing Dilemma," *The Virginia Quarterly Review* 45 (1969), pp. 545–562.
[2]Charles Grove Haines, *The Role of the Supreme Court in American Government and Politics, 1789–1835* (Berkeley and Los Angeles: University of California Press, 1944), p. 29 and cf. Chapter 3, especially pp. 78–82.

often been adduced. The common law tradition looks backward to the problems of the past and to the accommodations for those problems that were contrived by judges of an earlier day. With very few exceptions, commentators upon and teachers of law have looked upon it as a great stabilizing force, the purpose of which is to improve the predictability of future outcomes of present human decisions, rather than as an instrument for helping to bring about social, economic, and political change. In practice, lawyers typically associate with—and find their own economic interests to be aligned with—the business sector of the community. Throughout American history, the lawyer who has risen to a position of national preeminence has generally done so on the basis of his demonstrated ability to defend and represent with exceptional ability and unusual success the interests of whatever form of wealth was dominant at the time. Thus the great lawyers have utilized their skills to bring the law into congruence with demands for special advantage: in the nineteenth century, of the land companies, plantation owners, railroad magnates, cattle barons, and lumber kings; and in the twentieth century, of the great "trusts," industrial combinations including big oil, coal, steel, shipping, automobiles, air transport, hydroelectric power, and now big labor. In the near future, we can expect to find great lawyers identifying their careers with the complex of industries that has emerged in relation to the development of atomic power and space exploration, and that will emerge soon in regard to environmental pollution control. As the most distinguished elite group of the legal profession, judges have tended to include predominantly those lawyers who, because of their background and experience, were in the most conservative wing of the profession. Thus it is not surprising that most judges, in their decisions, have identified with conservative rather than liberal ideals.

STRUCTURAL THEORIES OF JUDICIAL REVIEW

THE SEPARATION OF POWERS

The relative influence of conservative and liberal ideas[3] in the decision making of the United States Supreme Court can be traced

[3]Although radical ideas are a predominant aspect of the American political culture in the seventies, they have been unrepresented on the United States Supreme Court (except by William O. Douglas); and it seems unlikely that radical justices or judges will be appointed by the Nixon-Agnew administration. Our discussion here, of empirical trends to date, is necessarily confined to the points of view that the Supreme Court actually has espoused.

by examining the major trends in the Court's use of judicial review and the patterns of constitutional norms that the Court has preferred. Usually, judicial review is defined in normative terms as a function of judicial activism and restraint, concepts which are themselves derived from the structural constitutional principles of the separation of powers and of federalism. (We shall discuss at a later point in this chapter a functional theory of judicial activism and restraint.) Thus it is argued that the separation of powers demands that the Court ought (or ought not) to exercise restraint by deferring to the decision making of Congress and/or the President, who are directly elected by the people and hence are politically responsible while the justices themselves are said to be politically irresponsible. Thus liberalism sometimes is equated with judicial restraint and conservatism with judicial activism.

As examples of constitutional interpretation based upon such an approach, we might consider Marshall's decision in *Marbury* v. *Madison,* which often is cited as both the initial and a most extreme instance of an activist attempt by the justices to extend their power over legislative and executive policy making. A more recent instance is *Panama Refining Co.* v. *Ryan,* in which the Hughes Court declared unconstitutional part of the National Industrial Recovery Act of the New Deal era. It happens, of course, that in both these instances there had been a recent major shift in party control over the presidency and the Congress;[4] and holdover justices, who had been appointed by conservative (Federalist and Republican) administrations that recently had been repudiated at the polls, used judicial review to attempt to check political changes initiated by the newly installed liberal (Democratic-Republican and Democratic) administrations of Thomas Jefferson and Franklin Roosevelt. Therefore, in both examples, the orthodox conception of judicial review (as an institutional instrument for defending conservative values) is compatible with the outcomes of the Court's decisions. The consensus is that, in terms of the substantive content of the public policy issues at stake in these cases, the Court upheld the conservative position.

But the concept no longer is compatible with the impact of the Court's decisions once judicial review is used to check conservative policies of Congress and the President. (Suppose, for example, that Marshall's Court *had* struck down the Alien and Sedition Acts, or, similarly, suppose the Chase Court had declared unconstitutional the Reconstruction Acts.) It is, in fact, only beginning with the recent period of modern liberalism that we find a majority of the

[4]Wallace Mendelson, "Judicial Review and Party Politics," *Vanderbilt Law Review* 12 (1959), pp. 447–457.

Supreme Court taking a more liberal position on public policy issues than Congress and the President, but it is now clear that judicial review is by no means restricted to serving as a conservative check on liberal policies.[5] Therefore this structural theory of judicial review, which presumes that judicial review necessarily is a conservative weapon, is no longer supported by the available empirical evidence.

FEDERALISM

A second structural theory of judicial review is based upon the constitutional principle of federalism. According to this theory, the Court ought (or ought not) to defer to state policy making—to uphold "states' rights" (in legal terminology). Liberalism generally has been identified with judicial restraint in the review of state action, while conservatism has been equated with activist judicial decisions that declare state action to be unconstitutional. Hamilton and Jefferson were in diametric opposition on the desirability of expanding the authority of the new national government, and the Marshall Court did implement the Federalist point of view in many decisions, such as in *McCulloch* v. *Maryland* and *Gibbons* v. *Ogden*. But who would characterize the states' rights decision of the Taney Court in *Dred Scott* v. *Sanford* as a liberal decision? Obviously, the tenability of the association of judicial activism with conservatism depended upon the validity of the assumption that state governments were "closer to the people" and more responsive to their electorates than was the national government. Certainly, such an assumption is most dubious today. The focusing of attention upon reapportionment during the 1960s demonstrated conclusively that there is no more distortion of representation in the national House of Representatives than in many of the states; and the Senate, though constitutionally malapportioned (if judged by the "one man, one vote" principle), is chosen from such relatively large constituencies that on most contemporary issues it takes a more liberal position than does the House. The Holmes-Brandeis notion of the states functioning as "laboratories for social and economic experiments," however meritorious it may have been fifty years ago, no longer fits the most patent facts of political life. As a rough generalization, it is true that the states tended to be both more politically responsive and more liberal in policy making than the

[5]See Glendon Schubert, *The Constitutional Polity* (Boston: Boston University Press, 1970), Chapter 1.

national government during the latter nineteenth century and the first three decades of the twentieth; but the nation and the states have reversed roles since the advent of the Great Depression and the New Deal. Consequently, continued judicial deference to state policy making no longer has the general effect of upholding liberal values.

The difficulty with both of the structural theories of judicial review is that they were developed to explain a set of relationships that no longer obtains in regard to congressional-presidential policy making, vis-à-vis either the Court or the states. In normative terms, the values relied upon to justify judicial review in the earlier period function instead to justify judicial restraint in the contemporary period. In short, the judicial liberal no longer can have his cake and eat it too. This explains the dilemma that has troubled many of those who seek to resolve today's problems on the basis of the judicial "philosophies" of Holmes and Brandeis, for whom it was possible to advocate judicial restraint toward the review of state legislation establishing, for instance, a minimum wage law for female laborers, with the effect of upholding both principles—state experimentation in social policy and the furtherance of liberal social policies. But when a state today enacts an antiunion statute, a purported disciple of Holmes and Brandeis (such as the late Justice Frankfurter) must choose between liberalism defined as legislative deference and liberalism defined as support for organized labor. The former congruence between institutional and substantive values has been displaced by what is today often a conflict between them.

TABLE 9

Supreme Court Policies toward Political and Economic
Liberalism, 1790–1973

Period	Dates	Political Liberalism	Economic Liberalism
1. Federalist/Marshall	1790–1835	–	–
2. Taney/Miller	1836–1890	–	+
3. Modern Conservatism	1890–1937	–	–
4. Modern Liberalism	1937–1969	+	+
5. Contemporary Conservatism	1970–	–	–

TRENDS IN SUPREME COURT POLICY MAKING

A more satisfactory explanation of the role of ideology in Supreme Court decision making than that offered by the two structural theories can be based upon an examination of the substantive values that the Court has tended to prefer at different periods of time. If we further distinguish between the Court's policies in regard to civil liberties and economic issues, four basic periods can be denoted. Table 9 shows that the Court has favored

TABLE 10

Attitudes of Supreme Court Justices toward Civil Liberties and Economic Policy, 1790–1973

Period	Dates	Political		Economic	
		Liberalism	Conservatism	Liberalism	Conservatism
1. Federalist/ Marshall	1790– 1835			Iredell Johnson	Jay J. Marshall Story
2. Taney/Miller	1836– 1890	Harlan (Sr.)		Daniel Campbell Miller Waite	Story Field
3. Modern Conservatism	1890– 1937	Harlan (Sr.) Holmes Brandeis	Brown Moody Taft Sanford	Holmes Brandeis	Fuller Peckham Van Devanter McReynolds Taft
4. Modern Liberalism	1937– 1969	Murphy Rutledge Black Douglas Warren Brennan Goldberg Fortas T. Marshall	Reed Minton Vinson Clark B. White	Black Douglas Murphy Rutledge Warren	Frankfurter Jackson Harlan (Jr.) Stewart
5. Contemporary Conservatism	1970–	Douglas T. Marshall	Rehnquist Burger Blackmun Powell	Douglas Brennan	Rehnquist Burger Blackmun Powell

civil liberties only during the contemporary period, while it has alternated between long periods of economic conservatism and of economic liberalism.

In Table 10, the justices are classified according to the major periods and in terms of those who have been most extreme in their support of economic and political liberalism and conservatism. There were relatively few civil liberties decisions made by the Court before the Civil War; during the period 1837–1860, for example, there were only five nonunanimous decisions in which slavery was the major issue.[6] The data, or at least the studies that have been made thus far, are not adequate to support a valid and reliable classification of the attitudes of the justices toward civil liberties during the antebellum era. Otherwise, the justices listed are notable for the typicality of their representation, in both their voting and opinion behavior, of the liberal and conservative points of view in regard to the characteristic forms in which issues of economic and political policy arose at different times in the history of the Court.

In the discussion that follows, we shall supplement both Tables 9 and 10 with references to the dominant legal norms which the Court invoked to support its decisions (as summarized in Table 11) and also to some of the decisions typical of the three earlier periods.

THE FEDERALIST/MARSHALL ERA

As Table 11 shows, the primary legal norms with which the Court worked during the Federalist/Marshall period were the contract and commerce clauses and an extraconstitutional "higher-law" theory of vested rights.[7] During the first decade of the Court's existence, few questions of constitutional interpretation were decided, although the political conservatism of the justices was amply demonstrated by their efforts to establish federal crimes on a "common law" (in lieu of a statutory) basis and by their active participation on circuit in the prosecution (under the Sedition Act) of the supporters of Jefferson.[8] The most important decision

[6]John R. Schmidhauser, "Judicial Behavior and the Sectional Crisis of 1837–1860," *Journal of Politics* 23 (1961), p. 628.
[7]Edward S. Corwin, "The 'Higher-Law' Background of American Constitutional Law," *Harvard Law Review* 42 (1928–1929), pp. 149, 365; Charles G. Haines, *The Revival of Natural Law Concepts* (Cambridge, Mass.: Harvard University Press, 1930); J. A. C. Grant, "Natural Law Background of the Due Process of Law," *Columbia Law Review* 31 (1931), p. 56.
[8]Haines, *The Role of the Supreme Court,* op. cit., pp. 159–165.

TABLE 11

Dominant Constitutional Norms Invoked in Supreme Court Decision Making, 1790–1973

Norms	Federalist/ Marshall 1790–1835	Taney/ Miller 1836–1890	Modern Conservatism 1890–1937	Modern Liberalism 1937–1969	Contemporary Conservatism 1970–
Vested (natural) rights	●				
Contract clause	●	●	●		
Commerce clause	●	●	●	●	
Diversity clause		●	●		
10th Amendment			●		
14th Amendment (due process and equal protection)			●	●	●
5th Amendment			●	●	●
1st Amendment			●	●	●
6th Amendment				●	●
4th Amendment				●	●
8th Amendment				●	●

politically of the pre-Marshall Court was *Chisholm* v. *Georgia,* which would have had the effect of extending considerably the scope of judicial review in the federal courts over state action; but this decision was overruled explicitly in less than two years by the adoption of the Eleventh Amendment to the Constitution. Under Marshall the Court wrote its natural-law theory of vested rights into the contract clause in such decisions as *Fletcher* v. *Peck,* upholding the Yazoo Land fraud and denying to the states the power to control the disposition of public lands, and *Dartmouth College* v. *Woodward,* upholding the right of a former king of

England to give a private American corporation rights in perpetuity and denying to the states the authority to substitute public control over higher education for such closed corporations. State authority to regulate business enterprise was denied by the Marshall Court, on the new basis of the commerce clause, in decisions such as *Gibbons* v. *Ogden* and *Brown* v. *Maryland.* There were no important decisions upholding claims of civil liberty during this period, and criminal trials in the federal courts—except for political crimes, during the Adams and Jefferson administrations—were relatively rare. The Marshall Court did decide *Barron* v. *Baltimore,* a case involving a claim of *property* right under the eminent domain clause of the Fifth Amendment and holding that the states were not bound by the Bill of Rights; the effect of this decision was clearly anti-civil libertarian.

THE TANEY/MILLER ERA

During the second period, the Court continued to rely upon the contract and commerce clauses as the primary constitutional norms to buttress the rationalization of decisions, but these were now redefined to support quite different outcomes than had been their function in the hands of Marshall. State authority to encourage economic development was upheld by the Taney Court, in preference to a monopolistic claim of vested rights, in *Charles River Bridge* v. *Warren Bridge;* and in *Cooley* v. *Board of Wardens of Port of Philadelphia* the Taney Court upheld state authority to regulate selective aspects of foreign and interstate commerce, subject to the approval of the Court itself. The Court also undertook to encourage an expansion of the diversity jurisdiction of the federal courts, with the ostensible objective of aiding economic development through the establishment of a uniform system of judge-made commercial law. In *Swift* v. *Tyson* the Court ruled that a section of the Judiciary Act of 1789, requiring that the federal courts follow state law in diversity cases, applied only to state statutory law—not to judge-made or common law. Of course, *Swift* v. *Tyson* is an exception that contradicts our general characterization of this period as one of economic liberalism, for the enlargement of the authority of federal courts to make policy independent of both Congress and the state legislatures was good Federalist doctrine.

Nor was the Taney Court any less conservative than the Marshall Court in questions of civil liberties. *Luther* v. *Borden* involved what we might call today a reapportionment controversy: the Dorr Rebellion attempted to extend the suffrage beyond the extremely narrow and aristocratic base authorized by the pre-

Revolutionary colonial charter that still functioned as Rhode Island's state constitution in 1841. The Taney Court denied a judicial remedy to Luther, who had supported Dorr, and thus in effect upheld the status quo and the conservative state government with the minority-rule electoral base that supported it. In the *Dred Scott* case, the Taney Court not only upheld the constitutionality of slavery but went out of its way to declare that the national government had no authority to prevent the extension of slavery to the national territories; Negroes were declared to be incapable of enjoying the status of citizenship under the Constitution of the United States because they were inferior beings who had no rights that the white man was bound to respect. Negroes had no civil rights or liberties under the Constitution, although the "dominant race" who owned them could, of course, claim constitutional rights to property in slaves.

Chief Justice Taney died during the Civil War; we have selected Associate Justice Samuel F. Miller to symbolize the latter half of the second period because he was the outstanding member of the Court at that time. The Court continued to rely upon the same constitutional norms (the contract, commerce, and diversity clauses), although the Fourteenth Amendment—which was adopted soon after the Civil War—became the principal repository for the higher-law theories of natural law and natural rights, particularly near the end of the period. What distinguishes the Miller Court from the succeeding period of Modern Conservatism is that it *resisted* the widespread and continuing attempts of the legal-business community to induce it to convert the new amendment into a check upon state regulatory power over the rapidly developing industrial system. Typical decisions were those in the Slaughterhouse Cases, in which the Court upheld the authority of a state to regulate butchering and the movement and storage of animals within a large city, and the Granger Cases, in which the Court sided with farmers by upholding state authority to regulate the rates to be charged by grain elevators and by railroads. Both of these decisions thus were economically liberal. The Miller Court's civil liberties decisions, however, were just as conservative as had been those of earlier periods of the Supreme Court.

The Court had explained in great detail, in Justice Miller's opinion in the Slaughterhouse Cases, that the Thirteenth, Fourteenth, and Fifteenth Amendments all had been adopted—in effect, as the terms of the victors upon the vanquished—for the sole and exclusive purpose of safeguarding the civil rights and liberties of the recently emancipated Negro slaves; therefore, such new constitutional norms as the privileges and immunities, equal protection, and due process clauses of the Fourteenth Amendment had no bearing upon the property rights of businessmen and their claims to be constitutionally exempt from governmental regulation. That was in 1873, during the middle of the Reconstruction period. Ten years later, however, six of the nine justices were different men, and the Court announced in the Civil Rights Cases that discrimination against Negroes by hotels, theaters, and railroads was not prohibited by the amendment and that, therefore, the congressional legislation which *did* prohibit such discrimination was unconstitutional; only public discrimination by the state itself would be illegal. But the Miller Court already had ruled in *Hall* v. *DeCuir* that a Louisiana statute *prohibiting* racial segregation on common carriers within the state was an unconstitutional burden upon interstate commerce; thus the upshot seemed to be that, in the view of the Supreme Court, neither the national nor the state governments could prevent segregation and discrimination against Negroes. The Miller Court also decided that the Fourteenth Amendment had not changed the policy announced by the Taney Court in *Barron* v. *Baltimore:* the Bill of Rights applied only to the national government. The criminal defendant in *Hurtado* v. *California* had no right to a due process of law that included indictment by a grand jury; only Mr. Justice Harlan (Sr.), the former slaveowner from Kentucky who had also dissented alone in the Civil Rights Cases, agreed with Hurtado. Patently, the above decisions were anti-civil libertarian in effect. The general consequence of the policies adopted by the Miller Court was that, some twenty years after its adoption and at the close of the second period, the Court had refused to use the Fourteenth Amendment to restrain the states in regulating either business or Negroes or the conduct of criminal trials.

THE ERA OF MODERN CONSERVATISM

The third period begins at the end of the first century of the Supreme Court's existence. It is characterized by a complete reversal of the Court's policies in regard to economic issues, with both state and national authority to regulate the economy restrained by a bewildering array of constitutional norms that now commended themselves to the Court's majorities. In addition to the commerce and diversity clauses—and the contract clause, which was increasingly displaced by the due process clause of the Fourteenth Amendment—the Court invoked and manipulated the First, Fifth, and Tenth Amendments, and both the due process and equal protection clauses of the Fourteenth. Prior to 1890 the Court had had little occasion to concern itself with national regulation of business enterprise, because there was very little statutory or administrative basis for such regulation by the national government until the impact of Populism in the late 1880s resulted in the establishment of the Interstate Commerce Commission (1887) and the adoption of the Sherman Antitrust Act (1890). But the legislative and executive systems of the national government began for the first time to define a continuing general set of liberal socioeconomic programs, and there was a vast increase in counterpart activity by the states at about the same time that the transition was completed from an essentially agricultural to an essentially industrial economy. Of course, the new legislative and executive policies of both the national and state systems were direct responses to the changed social and economic conditions brought about by industrialization; and the conservative interests that had lost control over the legislative and executive systems shifted their major attention—successfully—to the control of the judiciary in general and of the United States Supreme Court in particular. The turning point came in 1890 in the Minnesota Rate Case *(Chicago, Milwaukee & St. Paul Ry.* v. *Minnesota),* in which the Court announced that state administrative regulation of railroad rates was unconstitutional unless subject to judicial approval. Thus railroad lawyers would no longer be directed, as in the Granger Cases, to take their cases to the electorate if they considered state rates to be too low; under the Minnesota Rate Case, they were now invited to take their cases to the courts, which would decide (under the due process rubric) what during the preceding decade had been a political question, meet only for the determination of the voters and their legislative representatives. By 1895 the floodgates were opened, and in that year the Supreme Court announced a whole series of probusiness decisions. The following are the better-known harbingers of the new conservatism on the Court: the Sugar Trust Case, *United States* v. *E. C. Knight Co.,* emasculating the Sherman Antitrust Act by removing (albeit temporarily) manufacturing from its scope; *In re Debs,* affirming the criminal conviction of a union leader for the offense of leading what had been a peaceful strike against the Pullman Company in Chicago, until President Cleveland ordered the regular army into action against the workers and against the wishes of the governor of Illinois, who protested the need for and the use of troops in order to maintain order; and *Pollock* v. *Farmers' Loan and Trust Co.,* in which the first peacetime national income tax was declared unconstitutional. There was a continuing output of similar decisions during the next forty years.

The Court's policies remained conservative, so that the pattern of conservatism in both civil liberties and economic issues was indeed the same as that for the Federalist/Marshall period, thus supporting Arnold Paul's characterization of the Modern Conservative period as one of "neo-Federalism."[9] Typical of the Court's civil liberties decisions during this period were *Plessy* v. *Ferguson,* upholding a Louisiana statute *requiring* segregation on common carriers within the state (cf. *Hall* v. *DeCuir,* above) against constitutional claims based on the Thirteenth and Fourteenth Amendments and establishing for the next half century the doctrine of "separate but equal rights" for Negroes; *Schenck* v. *United States,* denying the constitutional right of freedom of the press to a socialist protester against universal military suffrage; and *Gitlow* v. *New York,* approving the criminal conviction by a state court of a leading communist writer for having published a communist "Manifesto." There was, however, one significant difference between the civil liberties decisions during the third and the earlier two periods. It was not a qualitative difference in the direction of the outcome of such decisions but was rather a quantitative difference: the sheer volume of cases raising claims of civil liberty, against both national and state action, was much greater and was accelerating as the period drew to a close. There was also a difference in that Harlan (Sr.) alone dissented in behalf of civil liberties claims during the second period, while both Holmes and Brandeis (and during the last few terms of the period, Stone and Cardozo [succeeding Holmes]) frequently argued the civil libertarian cause during the third period. In this sense, the half century of dissents by Harlan (Sr.), Holmes, and Brandeis was one factor that helped to pave the way for the Court's conversion to a policy of civil libertarianism, just as Field's dissent for a quarter of a century in behalf of free enterprise, initially alone but subsequently in the company of Bradley and others, had helped to make possible the Court's reversion to a policy of economic conservatism during the third period.[10]

THE ERA OF MODERN LIBERALISM

The fourth period marks a reversion to the policy of judicial restraint with regard to economic issues that the Court had followed throughout the middle decades of the nineteenth century. But even more importantly, perhaps, it denotes the first time in our constitutional history that the Supreme Court followed a policy

[9]Arnold M. Paul, *Conservative Crisis and the Rule of Law: Attitudes of Bar and Bench, 1887–1895* (Ithaca: Cornell University Press, 1960), pp. 229, 231, 233, 237.
[10]See Walton H. Hamilton, "The Path of Due Process of Law," in *The Constitution Reconsidered,* ed. Conyers Read (New York: Columbia University Press, 1938), pp. 168–190.

of judicial activism in support of civil rights and liberties. The contract clause was forgotten, and the policy upon which federal diversity jurisdiction had been based for a hundred years was sharply reversed—the decision in *Swift* v. *Tyson* was labeled by the Court itself as "unconstitutional" in *Erie Railroad Co.* v. *Tompkins*. The commerce clause was reconsidered and found to contain the major basis of constitutional support for a vast increase in national regulatory programs; at the same time, the commerce clause was also capable of accommodating many of the programs of state regulation of business that would have been declared burdens upon interstate commerce at any time during the four decades prior to 1937.

But the most impressive changes occurred in the content of the Fourteenth Amendment. During the third period, the due process and equal protection clauses of this amendment had only one function: to protect private property against "meddlesome" and "arbitrary" public interference. These same constitutional clauses were emptied of their economic content by overruling decisions of the Roosevelt Court during the decade subsequent to 1937,[11] and they became instead the repositories for many of the civil liberties enumerated in the Bill of Rights. Due process initially came to mean the First Amendment rights—freedom of speech, press, assembly, and religion; later, it subsumed the right to a fair criminal trial (with cognate clauses in the Fifth, Sixth, and Eighth Amendments); and subsequently it was extended to include the right to privacy analogized to the Fourth Amendment. Similarly, the equal protection clause of the Fourteenth Amendment (which is *prima facie* applicable only to the states and not to the national government) has been found to contain guarantees of racial equality and fair electoral representation that have been fed back into the due process clause of the Fifth Amendment, so that the process of federalization of civil liberties has developed on a broad front, with the states and national government alike bound by constitutional clauses that heretofore had been thought to apply only to the one or to the other, but not to both.

We shall not undertake at this point to suggest decisions typical of the fourth period, as we have done for earlier periods, because in Chapter Five we already have exemplified in considerable detail the policy content of the Supreme Court's contemporary output.

---

[11]C. Herman Pritchett, *The Roosevelt Court: A Study in Judicial Politics and Values, 1937–1947* (Chicago: Quadrangle Books, Inc., paperback edition, 1969), pp. 71–81, 270–273, 300–301; and Schubert, *The Constitutional Polity,* op. cit.

CONTEMPORARY CONSERVATISM

Similarly, we have discussed in Chapter Five a variety of policy outputs typical of the early years of the Burger Court. Clearly the freewheeling libertarianism of the Warren Court during the 1960s began to decelerate conspicuously by the end of the decade. A clear majority of the Warren Court liberals were gone by 1969: Goldberg had quit in favor of a more overtly political career at the U.N.; Fortas was forced to quit because of his moonlighting activities as counsel to one of the Court's litigants; Chief Justice Warren had retired; and Hugo Black had become one of the Court's leading conservatives in regard to many of the burning issues of the decade—black and peace power, and the liberation of youth and females. Consequently, the appointments of Warren Burger as chief justice, and of Harry Blackmun to fill the long-standing Fortas vacancy, came as something of an anticlimax. When Powell and Rehnquist replaced Black and Harlan in the fall of 1971, the effect upon the Burger Court's ideological balance was not very great: Rehnquist for Harlan was a trade-off; and Powell was probably somewhat less conservative politically, but more conservative economically, than the very sick and very old man whose place he took. Probably nothing less than the infusion of some young and fresh radical blood—persons like the Black and Douglas of the late 1930s—could have maintained the crusading drive to catalyze social change that had characterized the Warren Court. Instead Nixon did his best to put at least one southern conservative on the Court, but he ultimately had to settle for Powell. Nixon did succeed in appointing two elderly midwestern Republicans, both with substantial experience on the federal bench; but only in the youthful Rehnquist, and to a lesser extent in the chief justice, did he manage to bring to the Court really sophisticated hard-line conservatives. The Burger Court could not, of course, expect to accomplish an immediate repeal of all of the judicial "legislation" of the Warren Court. But on the other hand, the Burger Court clearly was not going to coddle criminals, peaceniks, and radicals whose forte is physical violence. The era of modern liberalism had come to an abrupt end, and in its place the prospects seemed inescapable for the predominance of a strongly conservative mood in both the Supreme Court and the rest of the federal judiciary, at least throughout the seventies and probably beyond that.

A FUNCTIONAL THEORY OF SUPREME COURT POLICY MAKING

An understanding of the reason for the Court's infrequent but dramatic reversals on both major policy issues requires an examination of the relationship of political lag to the Court's decision making. We may begin with the Dooley dictum that "no matther whether th' constitution follows th' flag or not, th' supreme coort follows th' iliction returns."[12] It is inevitable that in the *long* run the Supreme Court will follow the election returns; but it takes a very special set of circumstances for this to take place in the *short* run. This is because (as we explored in detail in Chapter Five) a major input for the Court's decision making consists of the belief systems of the justices themselves, and the content of judicial values is largely determined by the choices that Presidents make in their appointments to the Court. A major swing in public opinion (such as that which resulted in the elections of Jackson and Franklin Roosevelt, and the absence of which resulted in the defeat of William Jennings Bryan) produces Presidents who are relatively extreme (in position on the liberalism-conservatism continuum); and such men try to appoint justices who also represent the values of the new majority. If the new political majority can hang together for at least a decade, it is virtually certain that the value orientation of a majority of the justices of the Supreme Court will be transformed. But there may also be a lag of several years before the normal attrition in Court membership (through death and retirement) creates enough vacancies for a reversal in the control of the Court to take place. Thus President Jackson appointed five Democratic associate justices, in addition to Taney, during his eight years in office; and with the exception of one Whig, only Democrats were appointed to the Court during the next quarter of a century. Conversely, beginning with Lincoln's appointments in 1862, and with the exception of Field (a "Peace Democrat" whom Lincoln appointed in 1863), only Republicans were appointed to the Court during the next quarter of a century. It was not until the 1880s, however, that the issues of slavery, the war (and its advent and aftermath), and territorial expansion were displaced by a rising concern for the economic and social problems brought about by the Industrial Revolution.

Radical students born in the middle of the twentieth century, accustomed to misperceiving the Democratic party as generally no more liberal than the Republican, should not (but probably do) need to be reminded that Populism was a revolt against *both* major

[12]Finley Peter Dunne, "The Supreme Court's Decisions," in his *Mr. Dooley's Opinions* (New York: Russell Publishing Co., 1901); and Earl Latham, "The Supreme Court and the Supreme People," *Journal of Politics* 16 (1954), pp. 207–235; and Robert A. Dahl, "Decision-Making in a Democracy: The Role of the Supreme Court as a National Policy-Maker," *Journal of Public Law* 6 (1957), pp. 279–295.

parties and that Grover Cleveland, although he was the only Democrat to be elected to the presidency during the fifty-two years spanned by the Lincoln and Wilson inaugurations, was no liberal. Cleveland appointed four Democrats to the Court during his two separated terms of office. These included Chief Justice Fuller, a corporation lawyer from Chicago who displaced Field as the leader of the Court's conservatives; L. Q. C. Lamar and White, both conservative southerners; and Peckham, an upstate New Yorker who wrote the majority opinion in *Lochner* v. *New York*—the case that frequently is considered to symbolize the extremity of the Court's economic conservatism. President Harrison's four appointments, during the Cleveland interregnum (1889–1893), were just as conservative as Cleveland's, as exemplified by his choice of David Brewer, a Republican from Kansas who happened to be Field's nephew. These men, plus Field himself, comprised a majority of the Court during the critical years 1888–1896; it was they (and the Cleveland-Harrison administrations that put them in office) who were responsible for the Court's conversion from a general policy of economic liberalism to one of economic conservatism during the early 1890s. Indeed, it was in part in reaction to the decisions of 1895 that William Jennings Bryan emerged as the Democratic-Populist presidential candidate in 1896; and it was Bryan's defeat by McKinley that assured the continuation of the Court's newly embraced economic policies: "The judicial triumph of conservatism in the spring of 1895 had been confirmed by the political triumph of 1896."[13]

In the transition from the second to the third periods, the Supreme Court changed first and anticipated the election returns that signified the defeat of Populism, because the two major parties had closed ranks during the middle 1880s and for the next dozen years offered the electorate a choice between conservative candidates only. The inevitable result was that the Court itself was packed with conservatives. As a regional party, the Populists were strong enough to force the enactment of liberal legislation, but they did so at the cost of pushing the Supreme Court to a much more conservative position, because of the failure of the People's party to control the presidency—and therefore the Supreme Court.

Woodrow Wilson was the only Democratic President, other than the conservative Cleveland, to serve between Lincoln and Franklin Roosevelt. One might ask why Wilson's election did not foreclose the third period and change the Court. There are several reasons why it did not. First, he did *not* come to office as the result of a major change in public opinion, such as supported Jackson

---

[13]Paul, *Conservative Crisis,* op. cit., p. 226.

and Franklin Roosevelt. Wilson was a minority President whose first term was made possible only because of the third-party candidacy of Theodore Roosevelt. The progressive legislative reforms to which Wilson was committed were limited to his initial two years, in part because of the advent of the First World War. Furthermore, Wilson made too few appointments to effect a major change in the Court. His predecessor, Taft, had taken great care to pack the Court with men who shared his own conservative views; Taft had made six appointments during the three years preceding Wilson's inauguration. During his eight years in the presidency, Wilson himself had only three vacancies to fill, one of which materialized only because Associate Justice Charles Evans Hughes resigned in 1916 to become the Republican presidential candidate in opposition to Wilson. Moreover, Wilson's selections were not such as to maximize his influence upon the Court: the first, McReynolds, was an arch-conservative who was paired for the next two decades in opposition to the liberal Brandeis, who was second, while his third selection, Clarke, was so liberal that he resigned from the Court after half a dozen years in order to campaign more actively for world peace. Thus the net impact of Woodrow Wilson's appointments was a complete stand-off, with no ideological residue sufficient to change the Court's policy making in *either* direction.

POLITICAL LAG AND COURT PACKING

A century before the New Deal, Andrew Jackson had packed the Court as a matter of course, appointing a majority of five justices as vacancies materialized and then inducing Congress to expand the size of the Court (during his closing months in office) from seven to nine in order "to insure a majority in that tribunal favorable to State Banks and negro slavery."[14] The "gold Democrat" Cleveland, in his first term, and Harrison (a "gold Republican") had between them appointed a new majority to the Court before the second Cleveland inaugural and the Panic of 1893, with which it coincided. In the first of these instances, there was no lag between the electoral and judicial changes; in the second, the judicial change actually preceded its electoral ratification—a case of the election returns following the Supreme Court! But with Franklin Roosevelt and the transition from the third to the fourth period, it was different. Here the question of lag was critical; it was

[14]W. A. Sutherland, "Politics and the Supreme Court," *American Law Review* 48 (1914), p. 395.

the *failure* of the Supreme Court to follow the election returns that resulted in the constitutional revolution of 1937.

Although Roosevelt had won decisively in 1932 and had been reelected in 1936 by what was then the most overwhelming plurality in history, a majority of the Supreme Court pursued a recklessly activist policy in declaring unconstitutional several of the key statutory provisions of the New Deal program. Three months after his reelection to a second term, not a single vacancy had occurred in the Court's membership, and the four justices of the core conservative bloc (two Republicans and two Democrats) had served for an average tenure of over nineteen years. It appeared to Roosevelt that all of them were following the example of the late Chief Justice Taft, who had written to his brother the year before his own death: "I am older and slower and less acute and more confused. However, as long as things continue as they are, and I am able to answer in my place, I must stay on the court in order to prevent the Bolsheviki from getting control."[15] (The letter was written in 1929, and the apparent reference is to justices who might be appointed by Hoover, whom Taft considered to be a dangerous radical.) With a number of cases further challenging the New Deal already docketed for decision during the next five months, Roosevelt chose to launch a public attack upon the Court in a message to the Congress on February 5, 1937, accompanying his proposal to reform the Court.

The President made two tactical errors: (1) he chose to be devious and attacked the justices for being old and inefficient instead of for the real reason, which was that they were too conservative; (2) consequently, he did not distinguish among them but attacked the whole Court, thus including Chief Justice Hughes and such liberal justices as Brandeis and Cardozo. Roosevelt's request for authority to appoint a bevy of "assistant justices" to help the "Nine Old Men" with their work was turned down by Congress, as public opinion rallied to the defense of the Court as an institution and as the justices themselves lobbied very effectively with the congressional opposition to the administration in both parties.[16] Hughes and Roberts, during the preceding six years—and also up to this point in the then-current term—had voted

---

[15]Henry F. Pringle, *The Life and Times of William Howard Taft* (New York: Farrar and Rinehart, 1939), II, p. 967.
[16]Joseph Alsop and Turner Catledge, *The 168 Days* (New York: Doubleday & Company, Inc., 1938); and Leonard Baker, *Back to Back: The Duel Between FDR and the Supreme Court* (New York: The Macmillan Company, 1967).

consistently with the conservative bloc of four; but the threat was now sufficiently great that, weeks before the Congress had reached a decision on the President's "court-packing" proposals, "Hughberts" began, on March 1, 1937, to form a new majority with the liberal bloc of three, voting to sustain the constitutionality of the New Deal legislation at issue.[17] One effect of this stratagem was to help defeat Roosevelt's plan by demonstrating that no external reform of the Supreme Court was necessary—because the Court already had reformed itself. The same new majority of the Court hung together (over the vociferous protests of the now dissenting conservatives) until the end of the term in June, when the senior conservative justice—Van Devanter, who had been appointed to the Court by Taft in 1911—resigned. Before the end of his second term, Roosevelt had appointed a new majority to the Court.

A second and probably a more important effect of the Hughes-Roberts "switch in time that saved nine" is that there proved to be no turning, either back or away, from a complete reversal in the Court's policies toward both economic issues and civil liberties. The Supreme Court had indeed followed the election returns, but only under extreme duress; yet it was only another twenty years until the Court was again anticipating election returns, this time by formulating more liberal policies than either the presidency or Congress were prepared to support, except in part and then with reluctance.[18] The reasons for this, the dilemma of the Warren Court, will now be discussed.

PROCRASTINATION

Although it is by no means an activity unique to judicial policy making, procrastination is both a characteristic and an indispensable aspect of the decision-making process in the federal judicial system. From the point of view from which lawyers typically discuss

---

[17]Glendon Schubert, "The Hughberts Game," in *Quantitative Analysis of Judicial Behavior* (New York: The Free Press of Glencoe, 1959), pp. 192–210.

[18]G. Theodore Mitau, *Decade of Decision: The Supreme Court and the Constitutional Revolution, 1954–1964* (New York: Charles Scribner's Sons, 1967); Schubert, *The Constitutional Polity,* op. cit., Chapter 3; and Harry J. Hogan, "The Supreme Court and the Crisis in Liberalism," *Journal of Politics* 33 (1971), pp. 257–292. Cf. Stuart S. Nagel, "Court-Curbing Periods in American History," *Vanderbilt Law Review* 18 (1965), pp. 925–944, and also his "Causes and Effects of Constitutional Compliance," in *Political and Legal Obligation: NOMOS, Vol. XII,* ed. J. Roland Pennock (New York: Atherton, 1969).

what Hamlet referred to as "the Law's delay," judicial procrastination is an undesirable and dysfunctional characteristic of judicial systems.[19] This is thought to be so because procrastination is evidence of inefficiency, laziness, incompetence, or (more likely) of all three in combination; in terms of the interests of litigants, one of the best-known maxims of Anglo-American culture is that "justice delayed is justice denied," particularly in trial courts. There are, however, other relevant perspectives than efficiency and justice to individuals that ought to be considered in discussing judicial procrastination—at least when we are dealing with appeals courts like the U.S. Supreme Court.

Some theorists of the American political party system have emphasized that the essential task of the politician is not to *raise* issues but, rather, to reduce the level of political tensions by *sublimating* issues as much as possible. This is, of course, a conservative point of view, and one that is now under heavy attack by radicals.[20] Throughout the third period of Modern Conservatism the federal courts in general and the Supreme Court in particular were very successful in keeping sublimated both of the major issues of equalitarianism—racial and voting equality—that ultimately became of central importance in the Warren Court's policy making.[21] But just as soon as the Roosevelt Court had a marginal liberal majority, the Court began to champion a series of equalitarian causes, none of which had any substantial support either elsewhere in the national political system or in the state political systems. First came a series of decisions, which were to extend throughout the decade of the 1940s, upholding the right to proselytize of the radical right-wing religious movement known as Jehovah's Witnesses.[22] Half a dozen years later, during the middle of World War II, came the first of the liberal "white primary" decisions,[23] that were of particular importance to subsequent policy development in regard to both racial equality and fair representation. Also during the 1940s, there were several decisions invalidating racial discrimination in commercial accommodations for interstate and

[19]Hans Zeisel, Harry Kalven, Jr., and Bernard Buchholz, *Delay in the Court* (Boston: Little, Brown and Company, 1959).
[20]Cf. Kenneth M. Dolbeare and Phillip E. Hammond, *The School Prayer Decisions: From Court Policy to Local Practice* (Chicago: University of Chicago Press, 1971).
[21]Schubert, *The Constitutional Polity,* op cit.
[22]*Lovell* v. *Griffin,* 303 U.S. 444 (1938); see C. Herman Pritchett, *The Roosevelt Court,* op. cit., pp. 93–100 and 293n.7.
[23]*Smith* v. *Allwright,* 321 U.S. 649 (1944).

international travel, in restrictive racial covenants, and in the graduate admission policies of state universities. And at the close of World War II, in June 1946, the Court came within one vote of announcing the policy on reapportionment which, lacking that single vote, became delayed for sixteen years.[24]

The reasons for the sixteen-year delay may be briefly summarized as follows: in *Colegrove* v. *Green* Rutledge (one of the four liberal justices) wrote an opinion in which he stated his agreement with the other three liberals, who dissented in favor of reapportionment; but Rutledge nevertheless voted with the three conservatives to form a four-to-three majority in favor of the status quo. Both Rutledge and Murphy died two years later, but in any event it would have taken five favorable votes to have established a pro-reapportionment policy, with a full Court of nine justices participating. *Colegrove* v. *Green* was decided under quite exceptional circumstances, with only seven justices participating due to a vacancy in the chief justiceship which occurred more than six weeks *after* the case was argued and about seven weeks before the decision was announced, and due also to the absence of Jackson who had been prosecuting Nazi war criminals in Nuremburg throughout the 1945 Term of the Court. It was not until Brennan's appointment in 1956 that the critical majority necessary to the decision of *Baker* v. *Carr* was available, and by then the Court was too preoccupied with the enforcement and expansion of its racial integration policies for the time to be ripe for the opening of a second front in what we might call its war with the "Old Deal"—the reactionary and antidemocratic forces that still remained dominant at the close of World War II in so many sectors of American political life.

It is precisely here, in the timing of the relationship between the Court's racial equality and fair representation policies, that judicial procrastination appears to have had instrumental value for the realization of greater social justice. The School Segregation Cases were initially argued in December 1952, immediately after Eisenhower's election; they were reargued again a year later, and the basic decision on the merits came in May 1954. But the Court withheld its mandate and restored the cases to the docket for additional argument, which was to be focused upon the question of how the Court's substantive policy decision was to be enforced. A year later, in May 1955, the Supreme Court announced its "man-

---

[24] *Colegrove* v. *Green,* 328 U.S. 549 (1946); *Baker* v. *Carr,* 369 U.S. 186 (1962); and Glendon Schubert, *Reapportionment* (New York: Charles Scribner's Sons, 1965).

date" decision:[25] the United States district courts were told, in effect, that it was up to them to try to figure out how to persuade or to force local communities to desegregate their public schools, and they were told to proceed with this task "with all deliberate speed." The Supreme Court itself proceeded to avoid reviewing any of the "enforcing" decisions of the lower courts[26] during the next three years, until the events of 1957 in Little Rock had raised the question of enforcement as a policy issue upon which the attention of the entire nation was focused. When the showdown came in September 1957, it was visiting United States District Judge Ronald N. Davies from North Dakota who acted to enforce the 1954 policy of the School Segregation Cases; and it was not until a year later that the Supreme Court finally intervened in an enforcement question[27] by backing up the court of appeals for the eighth circuit, which had reversed the anti-integration slowdown authorized by John E. Miller, the regular district judge for the Western Arkansas District. Even then, almost six years after the issue initially was argued before the Court, there were no integrated schools in two of the school districts (in Virginia and in South Carolina) that had been formal parties to the initial litigation; and more than a decade and a half after the "mandate" decision, there were many counties in Southern states, and many urban districts elsewhere in the country, in which all public schools remained segregated.[28] A literal reading of the record, as we have described it, suggests that the Supreme Court procrastinated in reaching a firm decision on

[25]For a discussion, based in part upon material from the diary of one of the participant justices (Burton), of Warren's prolonged and ultimately successful efforts to achieve unanimity in the decision, see S. Sidney Ulmer, "Earl Warren and the *Brown* Decision," *Journal of Politics* 33 (1971), pp. 689–702; and for a thoughtful reappraisal of the implications, for both research policy and public policy, of scholarly use of such judicial diaries and related memoranda, see Ulmer's "Bricolage and Assorted Thoughts on Working in the Papers of Supreme Court Justices," *Journal of Politics* 35 (1973), pp. 286–310.

[26]For analyses of the work of the district judges, see Jack W. Peltason, *Fifty-Eight Lonely Men* (New York: Harcourt Brace Jovanovich, Inc., 1961); and Kenneth N. Vines, "Federal District Judges and Race Relations Cases in the South," *Journal of Politics* 26 (1964), pp. 337–357, and cf. his "Southern State Supreme Courts and Race Relations," *Western Political Quarterly* 28 (1965), pp. 5–18.

[27]*Cooper* v. *Aaron*, 358 U.S. 1 (1958).

[28]See the *Southern School News and Race Relations Law Reporter* for details; and see the Symposium "Affirmative Integration: Studies of Efforts to Overcome *De Facto* Segregation in the Public Schools," *Law and Society Review* 2 (1967), pp. 11—165.

the school segregation issue and that its mandate to the lower courts—to act "with all deliberate speed"—was an open invitation for them to procrastinate. However, the Supreme Court had no assurance that it would receive any support from the Eisenhower administration or from a Congress in which the coalition of conservative Republicans and southern Democrats was relatively more powerful than it had been for over a quarter of a century; only minimal help could be expected from state judges in the very parts of the country where segregation was most entrenched; and the national district judges upon whom the Court was going to have to rely were themselves mostly southern Democrats. We can assume that the justices who decided the School Segregation Cases were convinced that they had—or could obtain—the long-range support of a national majority; but there was no short-run way in which such a national majority could help the Court in getting public schools desegregated. Acting, as it did, under such limitations, a quick decision with a demand for rigid implementation would have forestalled the possibility of political support being mustered to back up the Supreme Court, so procrastination was perhaps the only way to make possible pragmatic solutions to the problem of means of implementation.

The issue of racially segregated schools, however, was as old as the nation. Why had it taken the Supreme Court almost a century to find out that "separate educational facilities are inherently unequal" and therefore unconstitutional? Why had it taken until 1964 for the Supreme Court to discover the nascent principle of fair representation—one person, one vote—in a clause of the Constitution that had lain dormant since the year before the establishment of the Supreme Court? It was not until the Democratic party mobilized the black vote in the big cities of the Northeast and the Midwest, not until the demographic changes that accompanied and followed World War II (including the migration of millions of blacks from the South to the big cities elsewhere in the country), not until the general educational upgrading of the populace that accompanied the affluence of the war and postwar periods, and not until many other basic changes had occurred in the structure of American political society (mainly within the past three decades) that there was anything like—and then only fleetingly—a national political majority in favor of racially integrated public schools.

Thus there are two reasons why the Court did not act sooner. First, the Supreme Court began to define a broad policy of racial integration, initially in areas less politically sensitive (because less fundamentally important) than the public schools, *just as soon as* Roosevelt had replaced a majority of the justices. Second, not only was it of some importance that the Court begin to build its general policy of racial integration first (as it had been doing) in less sensitive areas than public education, but it is also probably true that there was no supporting national majority even by the early 1950s. If these assumptions are correct, then it was not so much the Supreme Court that procrastinated on the issue of public school integration; it was more the American people who procrastinated, awaiting a more enlightened day when not merely an elite but a mass of citizens would reject the intolerance, the bigotry, and the economic irrationality that underlay the structuring of two systems of public schools. By the early 1970s, however, it seemed apparent that such a day of public enlightenment was not yet at hand, nor even wholly visible in any proximate future.

With the incumbency of the Kennedy administration in 1961, the Supreme Court could count upon the support of the Department of Justice to aid and to augment the activities of the district courts in the enforcement of the Court's various (and still expanding) policies of racial equality. And the announcement, at about the same time, of the returns of the 1960 census, in relation to the malapportionment of state legislatures and the districting of the national House of Representatives, resulted in a number of lawsuits throughout the country, several of which were pressed upon the Court. By 1961 it was politically feasible for the Court to consider raising another major issue of national policy: there was majority support among the justices to support a policy of fair representation, and such a policy might conceivably attract the acquiescence of a national plurality—after all, the object of the policy was to deemphasize the political influence of small minorities and to expand the influence of larger ones.

Although we might say that the Supreme Court had procrastinated on the issue of fair representation throughout the first six decades of the twentieth century, a broader perspective would suggest that procrastination, with regard to most policy issues most of the time, is the normal posture of the Supreme Court, just as it is also the normal posture of the presidency and of the Congress. From this point of view, entropy is to be assumed, unless and until special conditions arise to overcome it. Our analysis has suggested that three of the functional prerequisites to major policy innovation by the Supreme Court are (1) that the Court be "packed" with a majority of justices favorable to the proposed policy change; (2) that a national "majority" be willing to accept the change; and (3) that the general political context be such that the Court's making the policy will not seriously jeopardize the Court's capacity to assure the realization of other major policies to which it remains committed.

JUDICIAL ACTIVISM AND RESTRAINT

We are now in a position to suggest a functional theory of judicial activism and restraint. The Court's basic policies remain stable over long periods of time, and changes that do occur reflect very fundamental changes in the general political system, of which the Court is a component part. The justices themselves are goal oriented, and their basic goals are the same as those that motivate other political actors. Majority rule among the justices determines the policy goals that the Court supports, and it is the underlying stability in the general political system that accounts for the continuity in the Court's policy making, by assuring that the judicial majority will reflect the dominant majority in the larger political system. If Supreme Court justices were appointed for four-year terms in phase with the presidential electoral cycle, then it could be anticipated that there would be considerably less stability in the Court's policy making, because Court majorities would be more responsive to the short-run waves than to the long-run currents of political change. Under our constitutional system, it is precisely at the times of major realignment in the political party system that the Supreme Court is most likely to become involved in conspicuous and dramatic conflict with the presidency and Congress, because the majority of the justices then represent the minority in the new political realignment.

One possible definition of judicial activism is that it consists of any attempts of justices to change the policies of the Court. Thus, when a majority of the justices agree upon the direction of change that they deem desirable in regard to a particular policy, the position of the Court is activist. But if the effect of such changes is to bring the Court's policies into correspondence with preceding changes in congressional and presidential policies, the Court is not usually *perceived* as being activist, since observers of the Court's action tend to focus upon conflict between the Court and either the President and Congress or spokesmen for the states. Rather, the Court is perceived as being most activist when it changes its policies so as to conflict with the policies established by other major decision makers of the national or the state governments. Conversely, a majority of justices who agree with previously established Court policies could be considered to have exercised judicial restraint; that is, when other major decision makers change their policies and the Court does not change, conflict occurs because the justices refuse to accept the policy change, which constitutes judicial restraint. This concept of judicial activism, however, though perfectly consistent and logical, must be rejected because it results in a definition of judicial restraint that contradicts common sense, ordinary usage of the words, and the usual understanding.

An alternative functional theory of judicial activism and restraint defines activism in terms of disharmony, and restraint in terms of harmony, between the policy of the Court and that of other decision makers. We define "other decision makers" quite broadly, to include (1) Congress, the President and administrative agencies, and lower national courts, and (2) the analogous officials of state governments. Table 12 specifies the types of possible relationships. According to this theory, the Court is activist whenever its policies are in *conflict* with those of other major decision makers. If we consider the first cell of Table 12, it is clear that when there is no change in the policy of either the Court or another decision maker, there will be no conflict between them, and we have defined restraint to mean the absence of conflict.[29] In the second cell, the Court adheres to an established policy (i.e., it "follows *stare decisis*") in spite of the fact that another decision maker has made a policy change; and in the third cell, the Court changes its policy but the other decision maker does not. In either of these situations, the Court has taken an activist position because

TABLE 12

Activism and Restraint in Supreme Court
Policy Making

| | | Other Decision Makers | |
		Dynamic	Static
Supreme Court	Static	(2) Activism	(1) Restraint
	Dynamic	(4) Restraint or Activism	(3) Activism

[29]It should be understood that this analysis is completely relativistic. We assume that whatever may be the existing state of consensus between the Court and other decision makers, it is appropriate to speak of greater or the same or a lesser degree of policy agreement than presently obtains, irrespective of the direction of change when either actor assumes a dynamic role. Hence, "absence of conflict" means no further *increase* in conflict between the Court's policies and those of other decision makers.

its policy is in conflict with that of another major decision maker. In the fourth cell, the Court's position may be one of either activism or restraint, depending upon whether the *direction* and *rate* of the change in the Court's policy are different from or the same as those of the other decision maker: when the policy changes are in opposite directions or unequal in rate, the Court is activist, and when the policy changes coincide, the Court exercises restraint. It should be clear both that this analysis applies irrespective of the substantive content of the policy at issue and that it applies equally to instances in which the Court's position is liberal and those in which it is conservative.

The most typical example of the restraint that results from static agreement is found in the Court's many decisions denying jurisdiction to review the decisions of lower courts, when the lower court has followed the Supreme Court's policy and that policy is in agreement with that of, say, Congress. In such an instance there is rarely any reason for the Supreme Court to make a decision on the merits, unless the Court wishes to publicize the fact that it has *not* changed its position on the issue. An example of such a decision on the merits is *United States* v. *Midwest Oil Co.,*[30] in which the Court followed the unbroken judicial and presidential and congressional precedents of a century in upholding the authority of the President to make temporary withdrawals of public lands.

The second type of situation, in which the Court remains static in the face of an outside policy change, is one that typically occurs because of the frequent lag between change in the Court's personnel and the more rapid change that occurs in other political decision-making systems. The conflict between the Hughes Court and the New Deal provides an obvious example, as exemplified by the Sick Chicken Case *(Schechter Poultry Corp.* v. *United States).*[31] The administration had established a national program for price fixing in retail sales, labor regulation, and production control *(inter alia)* that went far beyond anything similar that had been attempted in peacetime; and the Court stuck to its more recent commerce clause precedents, declaring the statute to be unconstitutional.

The third situation, and the second type of activism, is that in which the Court becomes the protagonist in policy making, while other political decision makers stand pat. The School Segregation Case *(Brown* v. *Board of Education)*[32] is one of many possible examples. In that decision, the Court announced a national policy of public school integration which neither the President nor

[30]236 U.S. 459 (1915).
[31]295 U.S. 495 (1935).
[32]347 U.S. 384 (1954).

Congress was immediately prepared to support, let alone to make; the fact that this policy was to a greater or lesser extent in conflict with the practices of every state in the Union requires no demonstration.

Of the two possibilities that can arise in the fourth situation, dynamic agreement between the Court and other policy makers is the more common. For example, the Court exercised restraint in *National Labor Relations Board* v. *Jones & Laughlin Steel Corp.*,[33] one of the first major decisions to follow the Court's policy reversal after Roosevelt's assault, by agreeing to the same kind of expanded interpretation of the commerce clause that it had refused to accept less than two years earlier in the Sick Chicken Case. The other possibility is for the Court to change in the opposite direction from a policy change by another decision maker, as exemplified by the decision in *Pollock* v. *Farmers' Loan and Trust Co.*,[34] the case in which the first peacetime national income tax was declared unconstitutional. In 1881, the Court had upheld a temporary national income tax that had been adopted during the Civil War. But the statute enacted in 1894 was generally (and correctly) recognized as constituting a major policy change in the direction of economic liberalism; the Court's decision, under the circumstances, was an equally major policy change in the direction of economic conservatism.

Judicial review, in the narrow sense of declarations by the Court that national or state legislation is unconstitutional, is simply one of the technical forms that judicial activism can assume when the Court finds itself in conflict with legislative policy makers.[35] When the Court majority takes one of the positions that we have classified as constituting restraint, it is possible, of course, for an individual justice or a minority of justices to behave as activists, in which event he or they will dissent from the decision of the majority. It follows that when a majority of the Court is activist, dissenters will argue in their opinions the virtues of judicial restraint, just as a majority will preach restraint to activist dissenters.[36] Both of these types of behavior are readily observable in

[33]301 U.S. 1 (1937).

[34]157 U.S. 429 (1895).

[35]For a discussion of judicial activism through statutory interpretation, see Martin Shapiro, *Law and Politics in the Supreme Court: New Approaches to Political Jurisprudence* (New York: The Free Press of Glencoe, 1963); and also his *The Supreme Court and Administrative Agencies* (New York: The Free Press, 1968).

[36]See Glendon Schubert, "Jackson's Judicial Philosophy: An Exploration in Value Analysis," *American Political Science Review* 59 (1965), pp. 940–963; and also *Dispassionate Justice,* ed. Schubert (Indianapolis: The Bobbs-Merrill Company, Inc., 1969), pp. 20–21.

the opinions of the justices throughout the history of the Court. As a relatively liberal justice, in regard to both civil liberties and economic issues, on an activist conservative Court, Holmes' frequently employed strategy of arguing judicial restraint (rather than the substantive merits of issues) was quite rational, and it probably impaired the position of his more conservative colleagues much more effectively than a direct attack might have done. Holmes' famous dissent in *Lochner* v. *New York*,[37] for example, did not quarrel (as Harlan Sr. did) with the majority on the question of whether a ten-hour day would be more healthful for employees in bakery sweatshops than a sixteen-hour day; Holmes argued instead the proposition that, right or wrong, the state legislature rather than the United States Supreme Court had the constitutional right to establish policy on the question. On the other hand, a justice who utilizes the same argument in behalf of judicial restraint, at a time when the Court frequently is dominated by a majority of activist liberals, has no alternative but to dissent consistently in what functionally is a defense of conservative values. This is precisely the posture that was assumed during his last two decades as a Supreme Court justice by Frankfurter, an avowed proponent of both civil liberties and economic liberalism *before* he joined the Court but also an acknowledged student and avowed disciple of Holmes.[38]

From a functional point of view, therefore, the Court is activist when its decisions conflict with those of other political policy makers, and the Court exercises restraint when it accepts the policies of other decision makers. We can reasonably anticipate the continuation of substantially more restraint on the part of the Burger Court, vis-à-vis the Nixon Administration during the 1970s, than the Warren Court manifested toward *either* Republican or Democratic administrations during the 1950s and 1960s.

[37]198 U.S. 45 (1905).
[38]For a thoughtful reappraisal of Holmes, see Yosal Rogat, "Mr. Justice Holmes: Some Modern Views—The Judge as Spectator," *University of Chicago Law Review* 31 (1964), pp. 213–256.

The Study of Judicial Policy Making

In this concluding chapter we shall consider the research that bears most directly upon the matters discussed in the preceding text. A few of the references cited in the footnotes are of sufficient general importance to be listed here also; but most of the works discussed in this chapter are new references because my intent is to complement, not to duplicate, the footnote citations. Reports of social science studies of courts, judges, and law increased considerably during the 1960s and early 1970s, particularly in the cross-disciplinary fields of judicial process and behavior, sociology of law, and legal ethnography. The most extensive essay and bibliography (almost 1100 items) is apparently my "Judicial Process and Behavior, 1963–1971" in James A. Robinson, ed., *Political Science Annual: An International Review*, Vol. 3, 1972 (Indianapolis: The Bobbs-Merrill Co., Inc., 1972), pp. 73–280, the principal findings of which are summarized in my "Judicial Process and Behavior during the Sixties: A Subfield, Interdisciplinary, and Crosscultural Overview," *PS* 5 (1972): 6–15. I intended this bibliographical essay to supplement a much briefer and earlier essay of mine, "Behavioral Research in Public Law," *American Political Science Review* 57 (1963): 433–445. Also written to articulate with the same earlier article is Gerald Rigby and James Witt, "Bibliographical Essay: Behavioral Essay in Public Law, 1964–1967," *Western Political Quarterly* 22 (1969): 622–636. Other useful surveys, focusing upon research during the sixties, include: David J. Danelski, "Public Law: The Field," *International Encyclopedia of the Social Sciences* (New York: The Macmillan Company, 1968), pp. 175–183; C. Herman Pritchett, "Public Law and Judicial Behavior," *Journal of Politics* 30 (1968): 480–509, and "The Development of Judicial Research," Chapter 2 in Joel Grossman and Joseph Tanenhaus, eds., *Frontiers of Judicial Research* (New York: John Wiley & Sons, Inc., 1969), pp. 27–42; Glendon Schubert, "Judicial Behavior," *International Encyclopedia of the Social Sciences* 8 (New York: The Macmillan Company, 1968), pp. 307–315, and "Behavioral Jurisprudence," *Law and Society Review* 2 (1968): 407–428. For a listing of traditional works in the field of public law, see Henry J. Abraham, *The Judicial Process,* 2nd ed., (New York: Oxford University Press, Inc., 1968), pp. 381–472. For a bibliography from the anthropological point of view, see Laura Nader, Klaus-Friedrich Koch, and Bruce Cox, "The Ethnography of Law: A Bibliographic Survey," *Current Anthropology* 7 (1966): 267–294. There are no good corresponding essays from the sociological or legal points of view, but see the bibliographies now published semiannually in *Law and Society Review.*

Several relevant symposia include: "Jurimetrics," *Law and Contemporary Problems* 28, No. 1 (Winter 1963); "Frontiers of Legal Research," *American Behavioral Scientist* 7, No. 4 (December 1963); "Law and Society," *Social Problems* 13, No. 1 (Supplement, 1965); and "Social Science Approaches to the Judicial Process," *Harvard Law Review* 79 (1966): 1551—1628. Three readers have been published: Glendon Schubert, ed., *Judicial Behavior: A Reader in Theory and Research* (Chicago: Rand McNally & Co., 1964); Herbert Jacob, ed., *Law, Politics and the Federal Courts* (Boston: Little, Brown and Company, 1967); and Thomas P. Jahnige and Sheldon Goldman, eds., *The Federal Judicial System: Readings in Process and Behavior* (New York: Holt, Rinehart & Winston, Inc., 1968). In addition to these books of readings, there are three volumes that collect previously unpublished original research studies, including: Glendon Schubert, ed., *Judicial Decision-Making* (New York: The Free Press of Glencoe, 1963); Joel Grossman and Joseph Tanenhaus, eds., *Frontiers of Judicial Research* (New York: John Wiley & Sons, Inc., 1969); and Glendon Schubert and David J. Danelski, eds., *Comparative Judicial Behavior: Cross-Cultural Studies of Political Decision-Making in the East and West* (New York: Oxford University Press, Inc., 1969). The behaviorally oriented text-casebooks in constitutional law include my *Constitutional Politics: The Political*

Behavior of Supreme Court Justices and the Constitutional Policies That They Make (New York: Holt, Rinehart & Winston, Inc., 1960); Harold J. Spaeth, *The Warren Court: Cases and Commentary* (San Francisco: Chandler Publishing Co., 1966); Joel B. Grossman and Richard S. Wells, eds., *Constitutional Law and Judicial Policy Making* (New York: John Wiley & Sons, Inc., 1972); and Walter F. Murphy and Joseph Tanenhaus, *The Study of Public Law* (New York: Random House, Inc., 1972).

THE JUDICIARY IN THE AMERICAN POLITY

How systems theory relates to political analysis is the subject of William C. Mitchell, *The American Polity: A Social and Cultural Interpretation* (New York: The Free Press, 1962), and H. V. Wiseman, *Political Systems: Some Sociological Approaches* (New York: Praeger Publishers, Inc., 1966). Jay A. Sigler is explicitly concerned with systems theory as a frame of reference for the study of judiciaries in his *An Introduction to the Legal System* (Homewood, Illinois: Dorsey Press, 1968); so also are Sheldon Goldman and Thomas P. Jahnige, "Eastonian Systems Analysis and Legal Research," *Rutgers-Camden Law Journal* 2 (1970): 285—300, and Ovid C. Lewis, "Systems Theory and Judicial Behavioralism," *Case Western Reserve Law Review* 21 (1970): 361—465. Theodore L. Becker advocates what he calls "functional structuralism" in his *Comparative Judicial Politics: The Political Functioning of Courts* (Chicago: Rand McNally & Co., 1970).

In the American constitutional polity, the major relationships at the boundaries of the federal judicial system involve the Congress, the presidency, administrative agencies, and the states. These boundary relationships are best discussed in John R. Schmidhauser and Larry L. Berg, *The Supreme Court and Congress: Conflict and Inter-Action, 1945–1968* (New York: The Free Press, 1972); Walter F. Murphy, *Congress and the Court* (Chicago: University of Chicago Press, 1962); Robert Scigliano, *The Supreme Court and the Presidency* (New York: The Free Press, 1971); Glendon Schubert, *The Presidency in the Courts* (Minneapolis: University of Minnesota Press, 1957); Martin Shapiro, *The Supreme Court and Administrative Agencies* (New York: The Free Press, 1968); and John D. Sprague, *Voting Patterns of the United States Supreme Court: Cases in Federalism, 1899–1959* (Indianapolis: The Bobbs-Merrill Co., Inc., 1968). Gerald Garvey, in his *Constitutional Bricolage* (Princeton: Princeton University Press, 1971), uses anthropological and exchange theory as the basis for suggesting a new interpretation of American constitutional development, employing concepts that better reflect the fundamental social changes taking place than do the legal concepts relied upon by judges in their opinions.

The selection of Supreme Court justices, especially in relation to their age, education, and prior experience in public office, is the subject of Cortez A. M. Ewing, *The Judges of the Supreme Court, 1789–1937* (Minneapolis: University of Minnesota Press, 1938). Somewhat broader in scope, analyzing social and economic attributes and discussing developments through 1957, is John R. Schmidhauser, "The Justices of the Supreme Court: A Collective Portrait," *Midwest Journal of Political Science* 3 (1959): 1–59. Subsequent empirical discussions include Sheldon Goldman, "Characteristics of Eisenhower and Kennedy Appointees to the Lower Federal Courts," *Western Political Quarterly* 18 (1965): 755–763; Harold W. Chase, "The Johnson Administration: Judicial Appointments, 1963–1966," *Minnesota Law Review* 52 (1968): 965–999; and Barry C. Wukasch, "The Abe Fortas Controversy: A Research Note on the Senate's Role in Judicial Selection," *Western Political Quarterly* 24 (1971): 24–26. John Schmidhauser has discussed how age is related to the selection and vacation of office by American appellate judges in a pair of articles: "Age and Judicial Behavior: American Higher Appellate Judges," and "When and Why Justices Leave the Supreme Court," Chapters 9 and 10 in Wilma Donahue and Clark Tibbits, eds., *Politics of Age* (Ann Arbor: Division of Gerontology, University of Michigan, 1962). The only instance in which a Supreme Court justice was forced to resign (to avoid impeachment) is discussed by Robert Shogan, *A Question of Judgment: the Fortas Case and the Struggle for the Supreme Court* (New York: The Bobbs-Merrill Co., Inc., 1972).

The selection of federal judges, as a process which involves boundary relationships between the federal judicial system and the American political system, is discussed in Harold W. Chase, *Federal Judges: The Appointing Process* (Minneapolis: University of Minnesota Press, 1972), and Sheldon Goldman, "Judicial Appointments to the United States Courts of Appeal," *Wisconsin Law Review* 1967: 186–214. The role of the American Bar Association, as the major interest group concerned with the selection of federal judges, is analyzed by Joel Grossman, *Lawyers and Judges: The ABA and the Politics of Judicial Selection* (New York: John Wiley & Sons, Inc., 1965); and Sheldon Goldman, "Views of a Political Scientist: Political Selection of Federal Judges and the Proposal for a Judicial Service Commission," *Journal of the American Judicature Society* 53 (1968): 94–98.

Two books that stress the public opinion leadership function of the organized legal profession, especially during the formative years of the ABA, are Benjamin R. Twiss, *Lawyers and the Constitution: How Laissez Faire Came to the Supreme Court* (Princeton:

Princeton University Press, 1942) and Arnold M. Paul, *Conservative Crisis and the Rule of Law: Attitudes of Bar and Bench, 1887–1895* (Ithaca, N.Y.: Cornell University Press, 1960). An analysis of the contemporary movement to establish, through state legislation, what amounts to a "closed shop" for legal practice, is Dayton D. McKean, *The Integrated Bar* (Boston: Houghton Mifflin, 1963). Both the political life of the ABA and factors based upon custom in the institutional environment for policy making by the Supreme Court are dealt with by John R. Schmidhauser in Chapter 4 of his *The Supreme Court: Its Politics, Personalities, and Procedures* (New York: Holt, Rinehart & Winston, Inc., 1960).

There are several excellent studies of various aspects of the sociology of the legal profession. Law school selection and training are analyzed, on the basis of survey data, by Seymour Warkov (with Joseph Zelan) in *Lawyers in the Making* (Chicago: Aldine Publishing Company, 1965). Among the many studies of legal practice now available, one of the earliest and best is Jerome Carlin's case study of the Chicago bar, *Lawyers on Their Own* (New Brunswick, N.J.: Rutgers University Press, 1962); a very different kind of legal practice is described by Lee Loevinger, in his "A Washington Lawyer Tells What It's Like," *George Washington Law Review* 38(1970): 531–545. Judge Loevinger, who graciously introduced the first edition of the present book, was for five years a member of the Federal Communications Commission; since 1968 he has been associated in private practice with a major Washington law firm. Heinz Eulau and John D. Sprague, *Lawyers in Politics: A Study in Professional Convergence* (Indianapolis: The Bobbs-Merrill Co., Inc., 1964), is a comparative study of lawyer roles in state legislative systems; Andrew C. Mayer, "The Lawyer in the Executive Branch of Government," *Law and Society Review* 4 (1970): 425–444, focuses upon lawyers in administrative roles; and Michael Cohen, "Lawyers and Political Careers," *Law and Society Review* 3 (1969): 563–574, gives a broad synthesis, based on an appraisal of the primary research studies on the subject of the political career patterns of lawyers in both national and state systems. Even broader in scope is Martin Mayer's portrait of the law as a profession: *The Lawyers* (New York: Harper & Row, Publishers, 1966). One of the few examples of comparative role analysis involving the study of judges is David J. Danelski, "Legislative and Judicial Decision-Making: The Case of Harold H. Burton," in S. Sidney Ulmer, ed., *Political Decision-Making* (New York: Van Nostrand Reinhold Company, 1970), pp. 121–146; another is C. Thomas Dienes, "Judges, Legislators, and Social Change," *American Behavioral Scientist* 13 (1970): 511–522. Judith Shklar has written a discerning analysis of law as an ideology, in her *Legalism*

(Cambridge: Harvard University Press, 1964); and my *Dispassionate Justice: A Synthesis of the Judicial Opinions of Robert H. Jackson* (Indianapolis: The Bobbs-Merrill Co., Inc., 1969) also focuses upon various components of legalism as the ideology of the "practical" American lawyer.

FEDERAL JUDICIAL STRUCTURES

The most general studies of judicial systems in the United States are Lewis Mayers, *The American Legal System,* rev. ed. (New York: Harper & Row, Publishers, 1964); Herbert Jacob, *Justice in America: Courts, Lawyers, and the Judicial Process,* 2nd ed. (Boston: Little, Brown and Company, 1972); and Henry Abraham, *The Judicial Process,* 2nd ed. (New York: Oxford University Press, Inc., 1968). The best and most recent general discussions of the federal court system, from points of view quite similar to that presented in the present text, are Richard J. Richardson and Kenneth N. Vines, *The Politics of Federal Courts* (Boston: Little, Brown and Company, 1970); and Sheldon Goldman and Thomas P. Jahnige, *The Federal Courts as a Political System* (New York: Harper & Row, Publishers, 1971). Jack W. Peltason's *Federal Courts in the Political Process* (New York: Random House, Inc., 1955) is a concise political analysis of the national judicial system, from the point of view of interest-group theory.

Marvin Schick has written the first full-length study of a lower federal court, in his *Learned Hand's Court* (Baltimore: The Johns Hopkins Press, 1970); and with particular regard to the United States Court of Appeals for the District of Columbia, see Burton M. Atkins, "Decision-Making Rules and Judicial Strategy on the United States Courts of Appeals," *Western Political Quarterly* 25 (1972): pp. 626–642. Studies are also available of one of the federal courts of special jurisdiction, in Marion T. Bennett, "The United States Court of Claims, A 50-Year Perspective," *Federal Bar Journal* 29 (1970): 284–304; and of the court system in one of the smaller and more remote United States territories, in Charles Timothy Morgan, "The Judiciary in American Samoa," *UCLA Law Review* 18 (1971): 581–591. One major aspect of military justice is discussed by Luther C. West in "A History of Command Influence on the Military Judicial System," *UCLA Law Review* 18 (1970): 1–156.

There are several fairly recent books dealing with the Department of Justice, including Luther A. Huston, *The Department of Justice* (New York: Praeger Publishers, Inc., 1967); and Luther A. Huston, Arthur S. Miller, Samuel Krislov, and Robert G. Dixon, Jr., *Roles of the Attorney General of the United States* (Washington: American Enterprise Institute, 1968). A somewhat more critical viewpoint is expressed in John T. Elliff, *Crime, Dissent, and the Attorney General: The Justice Department in the 1960s* (Los Angeles: Sage Publications, Inc., 1971). Federal judicial administration is discussed by Peter G. Fish, in a series of articles and a forthcoming book: "Crises, Politics, and Federal Judicial Reform: The Administrative Office Act of 1939," *Journal of Politics* 32 (1970): 599–627; "The Circuit Councils: Rusty Hinges of Federal Judicial Administration," *University of Chicago Law Review* 37 (1970): 203–241; "The Politics of Judicial Administration: Transfer of the Federal Probational System," *Western Political Quarterly* 23 (1970): 769–784; and *The Politics of Federal Judicial Administration* (Princeton: Princeton University Press, forthcoming).

FEDERAL JUDICIAL FUNCTIONS

In the past there has been a dearth of quantitative analyses of the functions and outputs of the national judicial system, although by the end of the sixties there were indications that this state of affairs was beginning to change. Nevertheless, the periodic and systematic surveys of judicial work were few in number and limited in value primarily to lawyers rather than to social scientists. The editors of the *Harvard Law Review* publish annually (November issue) some summary statistics on the Supreme Court's disposition of its workload for the term ending in the previous June. There are also, of course, the official reports, such as the *Annual Report of the Director of the Administrative Office of the United States Courts* and the *Annual Report of the Attorney General of the United States,* published by the Superintendent of Documents and by the Department of Justice respectively; unfortunately, the data they present are in a form designed for lawyers and budget officers, rather than social scientists. The only good study concerned with Supreme Court supervision of lower courts, both national and state, from a political and administrative rather than a legal point of view, is Felix Frankfurter and James M. Landis, *The Business of the Supreme Court* (New York: The Macmillan Company, 1928). Although it is a valuable historical analysis, the Frankfurter and Landis book is now out of date with regard to such matters as the Court's dockets, jurisdictional decision making, and formal and informal rule making as means of supervising lower courts. A more recent discussion of the Court's workload and summary (including jurisdictional) decision making is in Glendon Schubert, *Quantitative Analysis of Judicial Behavior* (Glencoe, Ill.: The Free Press, 1959), Chapter 2.

Turning to qualitative analyses of the national judicial system, we are confronted with a superfluity of commentary. The overwhelming tendency among law professors has been to justify the policy-making function of the national courts. Two particularly articulate statements of this sort are Arthur Selwyn Miller and Alan W. Scheflin, "The Power of the Supreme Court in the Age of the Positive State," *Duke Law Journal,* 1967: 265–320, 522–551; and Arthur Selwyn Miller, "Toward a Concept of Constitutional Duty," *The Supreme Court Review: 1968* (Chicago: University of Chicago Press, 1968), pp. 199–246. Political scientists, on the other hand, have tended to view judicial policy making as a brake upon the wheel of progress, and their skepticism has been reflected in such studies as Alpheus T. Mason, *The Supreme Court: Instrument of Power or of Revealed Truth, 1930–1937* (Boston: Boston University Press, 1953), and also his *The Supreme Court from Taft to Warren,* rev. ed. (Baton Rouge: Louisiana State University Press, 1968). A qualitative review of the Supreme Court's decisions, written from the point of view of the traditional constitutional law categories but by political scientist Paul Bartholomew, is published annually in the December issue of *Western Political Quarterly.*

DECISION-MAKING PROCEDURES

A general discussion of adjudication procedures, written for undergraduate social science majors rather than for law students, is political scientist C. Gordon Post's *An Introduction to the Law* (Englewood Cliffs, N.J.: Prentice-Hall, Inc., 1963). Also intended for a lay audience is lawyer Delmar Karlen's *The Citizen in Court: Litigant, Witness, Juror, Judge* (New York: Holt, Rinehart & Winston, Inc., 1964). Four law professors have edited a collection of articles and court opinions that exemplify the legal approach to judicial decision-making procedures: Carl A. Auerbach, Willard Hurst, Lloyd K. Garrison, and Samuel Mermin, *The Legal Process: An Introduction to Decision-Making by Judicial, Legislative, Executive, and Administrative Agencies* (San Francisco: Chandler Publishing Co., 1961). For a sociopsychological approach to the same subject, see Hans Toch, ed., *Legal and Criminal Psychology* (New York: Holt, Rinehart & Winston, Inc., 1961), Chapters 1–7.

The emergence among American sociologists during the sixties of an interest in law, the legal profession, and even in some aspects of the judicial system, was a significant phenomenon that produced a growing body of research to supplement and complement the political science work in judicial process and behavior. The most general recent compilations are a law school text casebook edited by two law professors, Lawrence M. Friedman and Stuart Macaulay, *Law and the Behavioral Sciences* (Indianapolis: The Bobbs-Merrill Co., Inc., 1969), and a text by sociologist Edwin M.

Schur, *Law and Society: A Sociological View* (New York: Random House, Inc., 1968); and a reader by sociologist Rita James Simon, ed., *The Sociology of Law: Interdisciplinary Readings* (San Francisco: Chandler Publishing Co., 1968). Two essays that offer somewhat different perspectives of the subject are Leon Mayhew, "The Sociology of Law," in Talcott Parsons, ed., *American Sociology: Perspectives, Problems, Methods* (New York: Basic Books, Inc., Publishers, 1968), pp. 171–183; and Jerome H. Skolnick, "The Sociology of Law in America: Overview and Trends," *Social Problems* 13, No. 4 Supplement (Summer 1965): 4–39. A comparative perspective is provided by Renato Trèves and J. F. Glastra van Loon, *Norms and Actions: National Reports on Sociology of Law* (The Hague: Martinus Nijhoff, 1968); and in two books by Australian law professors, Geoffrey Sawer, *Law in Society* (New York: Oxford University Press, Inc., 1965), and Julius Stone, *Law and the Social Sciences in the Second Half Century* (Minneapolis: University of Minnesota Press, 1966).

The process of decision making in the Supreme Court is described in Part One of my *Constitutional Politics* (New York: Holt, Rinehart & Winston, Inc., 1960), pp. 1–171; John R. Schmidhauser, *The Supreme Court: Its Politics, Personalities, and Procedures* (New York: Holt, Rinehart & Winston, Inc., 1960); and Samuel Krislov, *The Supreme Court in the Political Process* (New York: The Macmillan Company, 1965). Decision making by the federal courts of appeals has been analyzed by Kenneth N. Vines, "The Role of the Circuit Courts of Appeal in the Federal Judicial Process: A Case Study," *Midwest Journal of Political Science* 7 (1963): 305–319; Richard J. Richardson and Kenneth N. Vines, "Review, Dissent and the Appellate Process: A Political Interpretation," *Journal of Politics* 29 (1967): 597–616; Sheldon Goldman, "Voting Behavior on the United States Courts of Appeals, 1961–1964," *American Political Science Review* 60 (1966): 374–383, and also his "Conflict and Consensus in the United States Courts of Appeals," *Wisconsin Law Review* 1968: 461–482. Little work yet has been done on the decision-making process in federal district courts, but see Kenneth M. Dolbeare, "The Federal District Courts and Urban Public Policy: An Exploratory Study (1960–1967)," Chapter 12 in Joel Grossman and Joseph Tanenhaus, eds., *Frontiers of Judicial Research* (New York: John Wiley & Sons, Inc., 1969), pp. 373–404.

Trial courts are also the particular focus of Jerome Frank's *Courts on Trial: Myth and Reality in American Justice* (Princeton: Princeton University Press, 1950). Frank, who was a leading "legal realist" during the 1920s and 1930s, was an appellate judge but never a trial judge; Karl N. Llewellyn, another leading realist who was a law professor but never an appellate judge, has provided a treatise on appellate courts, *The Common Law Tradition: Deciding Appeals* (Boston: Little, Brown and Company, 1960). A standard work on adjudication procedure in criminal cases is Lester B. Orfield, *Criminal Procedure from Arrest to Appeal* (New York: New York University Press, 1947); other recent books which empathize with criminal defendants include Arnold S. Trebach, *The Rationing of Justice: Constitutional Rights and the Criminal Process* (New Brunswick, N.J.: Rutgers University Press, 1964); Abraham S. Blumberg, *Criminal Justice* (Chicago: Quadrangle Books, Inc., 1967), and also a reader edited by Blumberg, *Law and Order: The Scales of Justice* (Chicago: Aldine Publishing Company, 1970); James R. Klonoski and Robert I. Mendelsohn, eds., *The Politics of Local Justice* (Boston: Little, Brown and Company, 1970); and Stuart S. Nagel, ed., *The Rights of the Accused: In Law and Action* (Beverly Hills, California: Sage Publications, Inc., 1972). A similar book, written from an "insider" point of view by a sociologist who acted as participant-observer in an urban police force and prosecutor's office, is Jerome H. Skolnick, *Justice Without Trial: Law Enforcement in Democratic Society* (New York: John Wiley & Sons, Inc., 1966). A more general (and comparative) study of criminal trial procedure is Delmar Karlen (in collaboration with Geoffrey Sawer and Edward M. Wise), *Anglo-American Criminal Justice* (New York: Oxford University Press, Inc., 1967).

A comprehensive law school-type casebook reader, intended for use in undergraduate classes, is *Criminal Justice: Introductory Cases and Materials* (Mineola, New York: The Foundation Press, Inc., 1973), by Stanford University law professor John Kaplan; an alternative reader, edited by political scientist George F. Cole, is *Criminal Justice: Law and Politics* (Belmont, California: Wadsworth Publishing Co., Inc., 1972). Two research papers, both of which were presented before panels at annual meetings of the American Political Science Association, are Malcolm M. Feeley, "Two Models of the Criminal Justice System: An Organizational Perspective" (1971), and Alan M. Sager, "The Law and Order Phenomenon: An Overview and a Critique" (1972). William M. Landes, "An Economic Analysis of the Courts," *Journal of Law and Economics* 14 (1971): 61–107, is a study of decision making in criminal trials, from the point of view of economic theory and utilizing statistical methods.

Interest in jury research, from a behavioral science point of view, was relatively high during the late sixties and early seventies. An excellent survey of social science research on petit juries, for a period of almost half a century beginning in 1925, is Howard S. Erlanger, "Jury Research in America: Its Past and Future," *Law and Society Review* 4 (1970): 345–370. Michael H. Walsh, "The

American Jury: A Reassessment," *Yale Law Journal* 79 (1969): 142–158, is a negative critique of Harry Kalven, Jr., and Hans Zeisel, *The American Jury* (Boston: Little, Brown and Company, 1966), a work that reports the results of a questionnaire survey of a highly biased sample of judges, concerning their observations and recollections of jury behavior; equally negative is A. E. Bottoms and Monica A. Walker, "The American Jury: A Critique," *Journal of the American Statistical Association* 67 (1972): 773–779. Examples of more recent and better designed research include Fredric Merrill and Linus Schrage, "Efficient Use of Jurors: A Field Study and Simulation Model of a Court System," *Washington University Law Quarterly* (1969): 151–183, an analysis of efficiency in the use of jurors' time in a federal district court; and Rita James Simon and Linda Mahan, "Quantifying Burdens of Proof: A View from the Bench, the Jury, and the Classroom," *Law and Society Review* 5 (1971): 319–330, which compares probability estimates and verdict decisions for groups of simulated juries, students, and judges.

Examples of the considerable body of recent research that has focused upon the question of bias (of various kinds) in jury selection and behavior include David Rotman, "Jury Selection and the Death Penalty: *Witherspoon* in the Lower Courts," *University of Chicago Law Review* 37 (1970): 759–777; Rita James Simon and Thomas Eimermann, "The Jury Finds Not Guilty: Another Look at Media Influence on the Jury," *Journalism Quarterly* 48 (1971): 343–344; and three articles which discuss sexual bias, Hans Zeisel, "Dr. Spock and the Case of the Vanishing Jurors," *University of Chicago Law Record* 37 (1969): 1–18, Eloise C. Snyder, "Sex Role Differential and Juror Decisions," *Sociology and Social Research* 55 (1971): 442–448, and Stuart Nagel and Lenore Weitzman, "Sex and the Unbiased Jury," *Judicature* 56 (1972): 108–111.

POLICY-MAKING ANALYSIS

There are several excellent case studies of the political sources and consequences enveloping a particular litigation. One such study, by a political scientist, emphasizes the political aspects of group activity in the sponsorship and management of a series of litigations involving the enforceability of restrictive racial covenants in real estate sales: see Clement E. Vose, *Caucasians Only: The Supreme Court, the N.A.A.C.P., and the Restrictive Covenant Cases* (Berkeley: University of California Press, 1959). Subsequent studies of interest group access to the judiciary include Robert H. Birkby and Walter F. Murphy, "Interest Group Conflict in the Judicial Arena: The First Amendment and Group Access to the

Courts," *Texas Law Review* 42 (1964): 1018–1048; and Nathan Hakman, "Lobbying the Supreme Court—An Appraisal of 'Political Science Folklore,'" *Fordham Law Review* 35 (1966): 15–50. A book written by a journalist whose beat for *The New York Times* used to be the Supreme Court narrates the tale of how an individual outcast influenced the constitutional policy governing indigent appeals from criminal convictions in the state court systems: Anthony Lewis, *Gideon's Trumpet* (New York: Random House, Inc., 1964).

Although they do not classify and report the relevant information systematically, the numerous judicial biographies are an excellent source of data on judicial attributes. Among the best of the earlier works are Albert J. Beveridge, *The Life of John Marshall* (New York: Houghton Mifflin Company, 1916); and Charles Fairman, *Mr. Justice Miller and the Supreme Court, 1862–1890* (Cambridge: Harvard University Press, 1939). The best of the more recent biographies include David J. Danelski, *A Supreme Court Justice Is Appointed* (New York: Random House, Inc., 1964); John P. Frank, *Justice Daniel Dissenting* (Cambridge: Harvard University Press, 1964); Alpheus Thomas Mason, *William Howard Taft* (New York: Simon & Schuster, Inc., 1965); Fowler V. Harper, *Justice Rutledge and the Bright Constellation* (New York: The Bobbs-Merrill Co., Inc., 1965); and J. Woodford Howard, Jr., *Mr. Justice Murphy: A Political Biography* (Princeton: Princeton University Press, 1968). Not all great justices (if we accept as our criterion of "greatness" the consensual judgment of constitutional historians) have been the subject of great biographies, nor are the best biographies necessarily about the most famous justices; for an empirical analysis of the modal attributes associated with preeminence on the Supreme Court, see Stuart S. Nagel, "Characteristics of Supreme Court Greatness," *American Bar Association Journal* 56 (1970): 957–959. Among the works on incumbent justices is Lewis Fenderson's *Thurgood Marshall* (New York: McGraw-Hill Book Company, 1969), which is intended primarily to instill pride in young blacks.

A series of article-length biographies of a dozen justices appears in each of three symposia: "Studies in Judicial Biography," *Vanderbilt Law Review* 10 (1957): 167–413, and 18 (1965): 367–716; and Allison Dunham and Philip B. Kurland, eds., *Mr. Justice,* rev. ed. (Chicago: University of Chicago Press, 1964). Another series, thirty-eight much briefer sketches of Supreme Court justices, can be found in Rocco J. Tresolini, *American Constitutional Law* (New York: The Macmillan Company, 1959), pp. 633–659. Special bibliographies on judicial biography have been published in Abraham, *The Judicial Process,* op. cit., pp. 341–344; Arthur N.

Holcombe, *Securing the Blessings of Liberty* (Glenview: Scott, Foresman and Company, 1964), p. 178; and John R. Schmidhauser, "The Justices of the Supreme Court: A Collective Portrait," *Midwest Journal of Political Science* 3 (1959): 50–57. Methodological articles on this subject include Jack Peltason, "Supreme Court Biography and the Study of Public Law," Chapter 11 in Gottfried Dietze, ed., *Essays on the American Constitution: A Commemorative Volume in Honor of Alpheus T. Mason* (Englewood Cliffs, N.J.: Prentice-Hall, Inc., 1964), pp. 215–227; and Robert M. Spector, "Judicial Biography and the United States Supreme Court: A Bibliographical Appraisal," *American Journal of Legal History* 11 (1967): 1–24.

There is an increasing literature on the subject of policy conversion as a process, as the attention of behavioral research scholars has focused upon the human factors in judicial decision making. Especially influential upon research and teaching by political scientists have been two books by C. Herman Pritchett, *The Roosevelt Court: A Study in Judicial Politics and Values, 1937–1947* (Chicago: Quadrangle Books, Inc., paperback edition, 1969), and *Civil Liberties and the Vinson Court* (Chicago: University of Chicago Press, 1954), which are about the attitudes of Supreme Court justices. The tactics of personal influence, in the interrelationships among Supreme Court justices as a small group, are analyzed in Walter F. Murphy, *Elements of Judicial Strategy* (Chicago: University of Chicago Press, 1964). Sociologist Edward Green has surveyed a much larger group of trial judges of the Philadelphia criminal courts, in relation to differences in their sentencing behavior: *Judicial Attitudes in Sentencing* (New York: St. Martin's Press, Inc., 1961). My own book *The Judicial Mind: The Attitudes and Ideologies of Supreme Court Justices, 1946–1963* (Evanston, Ill.: Northwestern University Press, 1965) is a study of the relationships among judicial attitudes, voting behavior, social and political and economic ideologies. The prediction of judicial decisions (votes, opinions, and policy outcome) is discussed in Chapter 5 of my *Judicial Behavior,* op. cit.

Policy norms are the subject of an immense literature, since this is the subject to which traditional legal scholarship long has largely been confined. That type of analysis is well represented by C. Herman Pritchett, *The American Constitutional System* (New York: McGraw-Hill Book Company, 1963). Similar but more specialized studies include Martin Shapiro, *Freedom of Speech: The Supreme Court and Judicial Review* (Englewood Cliffs: Prentice-Hall, Inc., 1966); Samuel Krislov, *The Supreme Court and Political Freedom* (New York: The Free Press, 1968); and Arthur Selwyn Miller, *The Supreme Court and American Capitalism* (New York: The Free Press,

1968). Two books that analyze criticism of the Warren Court during the fifties and sixties are Clifford M. Lytle, *The Warren Court and Its Critics* (Tucson: University of Arizona Press, 1968); and G. Theodore Mitau, *Decade of Decision: The Supreme Court and the Constitutional Revolution, 1954–1964* (New York: Charles Scribner's Sons, 1967).

Several case studies (or collections of case studies) of the empirical context of particular Supreme Court decisions are now available, including C. Herman Pritchett and Alan F. Westin, eds., *The Third Branch of Government: 8 Cases in Constitutional Politics* (New York: Harcourt Brace Jovanovich, Inc., 1963), Lucius J. Barker and Twiley W. Barker, Jr., *Freedoms, Courts, Politics: Studies in Civil Liberties* (Englewood Cliffs, N.J.: Prentice-Hall, Inc., 1965); and Walter F. Murphy, *Wiretapping on Trial: A Case Study in the Judicial Process* (New York: Random House, Inc., 1965).

Two of the leading survey studies of mass attitudes toward, and information concerning, the Supreme Court, are Kenneth M. Dolbeare and Phillip E. Hammond, "The Political Party Basis of Attitudes Toward the United States Supreme Court," *Public Opinion Quarterly* 32 (1968): 16–30; and Walter F. Murphy and Joseph Tanenhaus, "Public Opinion and the United States Supreme Court: A Preliminary Mapping of Some Prerequisites for Court Legitimation of Regime Changes," *Law and Society Review* 2 (1968): 357–384. Richard M. Johnson's *The Dynamics of Compliance: Supreme Court Decision-Making from a New Perspective* (Evanston: Northwestern University Press, 1967) is a case study of compliance with the Supreme Court's school prayer and Bible-reading decisions, in a rural midwestern school district; William K. Muir, Jr., *Prayer in the Public Schools: Law and Attitude Change* (Chicago: University of Chicago Press, 1967) is a similar study (but using different methods) in an urban midwestern school district. Also a case study of freedom of religion, but in relation to the enforcement of compulsory state school attendance laws, is Harrell R. Rodgers, Jr., *Community Conflict: Public Opinion and the Law: The Amish Dispute in Iowa* (Columbus: Charles E. Merrill Publishing Co., 1969). Several other case studies of compliance with Supreme Court policies have been collected in David H. Everson, ed., *The Supreme Court as Policy-Maker: Three Studies on the Impact of Judicial Decisions* (Carbondale, Illinois: Southern Illinois University, Public Affairs Research Bureau, 1968); and Theodore L. Becker and Malcolm Feeley, eds., *The Impact of Supreme Court Decisions: Empirical Studies* (New York: Oxford University Press, 1973). See also Stuart S. Nagel, "Causes and Effects of Constitutional Compliance," in J. Roland Pennock, ed., *Political and Legal Obligation, NOMOS Vol. 12* (New York: Atherton Press, Inc., 1969).

More recent studies include a book which suggests a theoretical framework for impact analysis, in addition to discussing the empirical research: Stephen L. Wasby, *The Impact of the United States Supreme Court: Some Perspectives* (Homewood, Illinois: Dorsey Press, 1970). Neal A. Milner, *The Court and Local Law Enforcement: The Political Impact of Miranda* (Beverly Hills: Sage Publications, Inc., 1971), reports a comparative analysis of police practices in four Wisconsin cities. Martin Shapiro's "The Impact of the Supreme Court," *Journal of Legal Education* 23 (1971): 77–89, introduces a symposium on the subject, which includes several reports of empirical research such as Kenneth M. Dolbeare and Phillip M. Hammond, "Inertia in Midway: Supreme Court Decisions and Local Responses," *Journal of Legal Education* 23 (1971): 106–122, a comparative study of five cities in a midwestern state; and Donald R. Reich, "Schoolhouse Religion and the Supreme Court: A Report on Attitudes of Teachers and Principals and on School Practices in Wisconsin and Ohio," *Journal of Legal Education* 23 (1971): 123–143, based upon a survey comparing responses for two midwestern states. Harrell R. Rodgers and George Taylor, "Pre-Adult Attitudes Toward Legal Compliance: Notes Toward a Theory," *Social Science Quarterly* 51 (1970): 539–551, is a study of political socialization and the attitudes of children toward the policy decisions of courts. Two studies of congressional response to Supreme Court policy changes include John R. Schmidhauser, Larry L. Berg, and Albert Melone, "The Impact of Judicial Decisions: New Dimensions in Supreme Court–Congressional Relations, 1945–1968," *Washington University Law Quarterly* 1971: 209–251; and John H. Laubach, *School Prayers: Congress, the Courts, and the Public* (Washington: Public Affairs Press, 1969).

POLITICAL IDEOLOGY AND JUDICIAL ACTIVISM

Discussion of political ideology presumes knowledge about the political culture of a country. A facet of American political culture that has long been of particular interest to students of constitutional law is that of the American political community during the latter third of the eighteenth century, when the structure of the present constitutional system was constructed. Behaviorally oriented studies of the early stages of development of the American polity began to appear during the 1960s, and a few relevant examples can be suggested. Richard L. Merritt's *Symbols of American Community, 1736–1775* (New Haven: Yale University Press, 1966) is a content analysis of the output of the communications media for the period studied. S. Sidney Ulmer, "Sub-group Formation in the Constitutional Convention," *Midwest Journal of Political Science* 10 (1966): 288–303, is a pioneering application of some of the methods developed for the study of judicial behavior to the analysis of the expression and sources of state interests, in voting by the delegates to the Philadelphia Convention of 1787. Lee Benson, *Turner and Beard: American Historical Writing Reconsidered* (Glencoe, Illinois: The Free Press, 1960), includes a leading political historian's appraisal of the effect of political culture and political ideology upon political behavior in and at the time of the convention, and during subsequent developmental changes during the nineteenth century. Even broader in scope is the sweeping historical and comparative developmental analysis by Seymour Martin Lipset, a leading political sociologist, in his *The First New Nation* (New York: Basic Books, 1963), which contrasts the budding American polity of two centuries ago with those of the new nations of Africa and Asia today, and also traces changes in the development of the (putatively schizophrenic) American polity through those two hundred years. Geoffrey Gorer's *The American People: A Study in National Character,* rev. ed. (New York: W. W. Norton & Company, Inc., 1964), provides the perspective of an English cultural anthropologist, writing, however, almost a generation ago. The standard history of the Supreme Court was written by a lawyer with a conservative orientation: Charles Warren, *The Supreme Court in United States History,* 3 vols. (Boston: Little, Brown and Company, 1922–1923). An alternative interpretation, written from the point of view of the denouement of American progressivism, is provided by James Allen Smith in his now classic work, *The Growth and Decadence of Constitutional Government* (New York: Holt, Rinehart & Winston, Inc., 1930). A reappraisal from a contemporary point of view is provided in Stephen B. Wood, *Constitutional Politics in the Progressive Era: Child Labor and the Law* (Chicago: University of Chicago Press, 1968). More radical views are expressed by Gustavus Myers in his *History of the Supreme Court of the United States* (Chicago: Charles H. Kerr, 1925), which employs a crude version of Marxism to reinterpret the Court's decisions as having been made with a view to the justices' personal profit. Equally radical is William W. Crosskey's *Politics and the Constitution in the History of the United States* (Chicago: University of Chicago Press, 1953), which purports to demonstrate semantically how the vast majority of Presidents, congressmen, and Supreme Court justices have misunderstood the "true" meaning of the Constitution. Fred Rodell's *Nine Men: A Political History of the Supreme Court from 1790 to 1955* (New York: Random House, Inc., 1955) is a liberal critique of what has been most of the time a rather conservative group of lawyer-politicians.

There are also many historical studies of the periods in terms of which Chapter Five analyzed changes in the development of constitutional policy by the Supreme Court; indeed, Robert G. McCloskey's *The American Supreme Court* (Chicago: University of Chicago Press, 1960) corresponds, in its chapter organization, to that classification, and his Chapters 5 and 6 are particularly valuable for the period of conservatism. Charles Grove Haines, *The Role of the Supreme Court in American Government and Politics, 1789–1835* (Berkeley: University of California Press, 1944) is the leading work on the Marshall Court. For the Taney Court, see Charles Grove Haines and Foster Sherwood, *The Role of the Supreme Court in American Government and Politics, 1835–1864* (Berkeley: University of California Press, 1957). The best modern work on constitutional history is a two-volume tome by William F. Swindler, *Court and Constitution in the 20th Century* (Indianapolis: The Bobbs-Merrill Co., Inc.), Volume 1: *The Old Legality, 1889–1932* (1969) and Volume 2: *The New Legality, 1932–1968* (1970). Alpheus T. Mason's *The Supreme Court from Taft to Warren* (Baton Rouge: Louisiana State University Press, 1958) focuses upon the transition from modern conservatism to modern liberalism, as does also my *The Constitutional Polity* (Boston: Boston University Press, 1970).

There is an extensive literature on judicial review, activism, and restraint. Charles A. Beard thought that he had settled once and for all, more than half a century ago, the controversy over the intent of the framers regarding the Supreme Court's power of judicial review, when he published *The Supreme Court and the Constitution* (Englewood Cliffs, N.J.: Prentice-Hall, Inc., 1962 ed.); this edition also contains an extensive bibliography on judicial review. Charles Grove Haines' *The American Doctrine of Judicial Supremacy,* rev. ed. (Berkeley: University of California Press, 1932) is a historical analysis of the developmental use of judicial review by American courts. The continental divide between modern conservatism and liberalism in the Court's use of judicial review is the Court-packing episode of 1937, a detailed journalistic account of which is provided in Joseph Alsop and Turner Catledge, *The 168 Days* (New York: Doubleday & Company, Inc., 1938). Robert H. Jackson's *The Struggle for Judicial Supremacy* (New York: Alfred A. Knopf, Inc., 1941) is a briefer and less scholarly but well-written account that focuses upon the Supreme Court and especially upon his own battles—as Roosevelt's Solicitor General during the height of the legal attack upon the New Deal—with the Hughes Court. Two general contemporary studies, both by political scientists, are Charles Allen Miller, *The Supreme Court and the Uses of History* (Cambridge: Harvard University Press, 1969); and Robert J. Steamer, *The Supreme Court in Crisis: A History of Conflict* (Amherst,

Massachusetts: University of Massachusetts Press, 1961).
Contemporary controversy over judicial activism and restraint in general, and in the use of judicial review in particular, is reflected in a bifurcation of professional opinion between law professors and political scientists. Most law professors have identified with the courts and justified the good (i.e., liberal) works produced by (for example) early Warren Court policy making. See, for example, Eugene V. Rostow, *The Sovereign Prerogative: The Supreme Court and the Quest for Law* (New Haven: Yale University Press, 1962) and Charles L. Black, Jr., *The People and the Court: Judicial Review in a Democracy* (New York: The Macmillan Company, 1960). Most political scientists, on the other hand, identified with legislatures and tended to view judicial policy making as a perversion of the democratic process, even when it might be used—temporarily, no doubt—to accomplish such desirable goals as racial equality and legislative reapportionment. This point of view is well expressed by Wallace Mendelson in *Justices Black and Frankfurter: Conflict on the Court* (Chicago: University of Chicago Press, 1961) and by Charles S. Hyneman in *The Supreme Court on Trial* (New York: Atherton Press, Inc., 1963). However, the extension during the late sixties, to law and political science faculties alike, of radical orientations toward legal and political (including judicial) behavior, indicates that we can anticipate considerably more support to be mobilized during the seventies, on behalf of judicial activism. Examples of the instrumentally focused radical jurisprudence include, from the law side, Joel F. Handler, "The Role of Legal Research and Legal Education in Social Welfare," *Stanford Law Review* 20 (1968): 669–683, Richard C. Wasserstrom, "Lawyers and Revolution," *University of Pittsburgh Law Review* 30 (1968): 125–133, and Lawrence Friedman, "Legal Culture and Social Development," *Law and Society Review* 4 (1969): 29–44; and from political scientists, Stuart S. Nagel, "Some New Concerns of Legal Process Research within Political Science," *Law and Society Review* 6 (1971): 9–16, Harry P. Stumpf, "Law and Poverty: A Political Perspective," *Wisconsin Law Review* 1968: 694–733, and Louis Masotti and Michael A. Weinstein, "Theory and Application of Roscoe Pound's Sociological Jurisprudence: Crime Prevention or Control?" *Prospectus* 2 (1969): 431–449. On the responses of judges to the efforts of social scientists to educate and influence courts, see Abraham L. Davis, *The United States Supreme Court and the Uses of Social Science Data* (New York: MSS Information Corporation, 1973); and Herbert Garfinkel, "Social Science Evidence and the School Segregation Cases," *Journal of Politics* 21 (1959): 37–59.

INDEX OF CASES

INDEX

82 81 80 79 78 77 76 75 74

1 2 3 4 5 6 7 8 9 10 11 12 13 14 15 16 17 18 19 20 21 22 23 24 25